Aesthetic Justice

Intersecting Artistic and Moral Perspectives

Pascal Gielen &
Niels Van Tomme (eds.)

Antennae
Valiz, Amsterdam

Aesthetic Justice
Intersecting Artistic and Moral Perspectives

Pascal Gielen & Niels Van Tomme (eds.)

With contributions by
Zoe Beloff
Arne De Boever
Mark Fisher
Mat Fraser
Pascal Gielen
Kerry James Marshall
Viktor Misiano
Carlos Motta
Nat Muller
Julie Atlas Muz
Tessa Overbeek
Gerald Raunig
Dieter Roelstraete
Hito Steyerl
Julia Svetlichnaja
Hakan Topal
Niels Van Tomme
Samuel Vriezen
Christian Wolff

Contents

Introduction
Opening the Quest for Justice

Pascal Gielen

Niels Van Tomme

When morality is at issue, science loses its objectivity and art its autonomy. There is a taboo on speaking from a moral point of view. That holds true to this very day for the scientific enterprise, where for instance people are still struggling with the statute of critical theory. Is that in fact science? Phenomenologists, sociologists and psychologists preferably suppress their opinions and ideological positions through an obligatory and comprehensive exhibition of methodology. Philosophers and other social scientists do better not to focus on the good and the utopian, but to stick to the pragmatics of the attainable. Whereas politics and the mass media are brimming with moralism, the majority of academics hope to maintain their legitimacy through a dry exposition that almost seems indifferent. Or, to put it more correctly, in today's political rhetoric, a nearly sterile technocratic administrator's jargon – the likes of 'the budget must be balanced' – is alternated with the most deprecatory pronouncements – the likes of 'scum from the suburbs'. In the mass media, attention is diverted from systemic faults, structural macro politics, and economic mechanisms by its focus on a particular politician's perversion of power or an individual banker's hand in the till. Self-respecting scholars prefer to stay on the sidelines of all this squabbling. If they do concern themselves with concrete problems, they go to work like an engineer, searching for faults in the system, possible managerial innovations, increases in efficiency, and practical technical administrative advice. Neutral researchers prefer to do this without questioning the purpose of such an administration or what power relations the systemic faults are occurring within.

In contrast to such detached, scientific tendencies with regard to moral issues, let us examine the debut of the Greek sceptical philosopher Carneades of Cyrene in the city of Rome in 155 BC. One has to take into account that this was a major—intellectual event for which people had gathered in huge numbers. And, as it turns out, the audience was shocked by Carneades' speeches, which were delivered with much aplomb and a calculated sense of ethical confrontation, speaking with great rigor in favour of justice on the first day, and then with equal persuasion against it on the next. Carneades' infamous argument against justice is exemplified by his well-known thought experiment about the plank over which two shipwrecked sailors fight, the piece of wood being the only means by which one of them can survive. Asking us to imagine ourselves afloat on the sea after being shipwrecked with but a single plank in sight, Carneades' confrontation lies in the problem that the plank can only hold one person and that it is already occupied. Are we justified in pushing the other person off, thereby intentionally killing them, if we can secure our own survival this way? In other words: is it justifiable to pursue our own preservation by killing another person, knowing that otherwise the other person will be responsible for our own death? Taking this radical thought experiment to its extreme without offering any straightforward answer or solution, the Greek philosopher not only perverts widely accepted classical notions of justice, but also the role of the philosopher in society. Carneades importantly removes himself from the pragmatism of the feasible, as it is outlined above, while positioning philosophical thinking at the foreground of ethical discourse. Leaving aside the moral implications of his thought-provoking dilemma, Carneades' argument clearly points to conflicts of justice that arise when confronted with one's own survivability. In staging this well-conceived thought experiment, whose problematic moral questioning remains unresolved, Carneades brought on a crisis, or at least an anomaly in thinking about justice.

Confronted with a world in which conflicts of justice are met with neutral, scientific reasoning, is there a position similar to the one of Carneades — confrontational yet inspiring — to take in for artists and critical thinkers working today? While the majority of artists in the nineteen-eighties and early nineties mainly concentrated, under the guise of autonomy, on problems of form, the idiosyncratic elaboration of concepts or highly personal ideas, and the development of a personal style, since the mid-nineties there seems to have been a countermovement going on. In contrast to the scientific enterprise, artists are avoiding moral issues less and less often and are also more expressly entering ideological discourses, or are already focusing on the questions around them. Meanwhile, questions about justice, about what is good and bad, about 'the right' course of action are being presented more explicitly in artistic work. Both 9/11 — especially the United States' reaction to it — and the winding up of the global financial crisis merely primed the pump of this artistic engagement in the West. The events of 2001 and late 2007, 'first a tragedy, then a farce,' as Slavoj Žižek said of them with a nod to Karl Marx, have inspired many an artist to question the complexity of the contemporary status quo. Broadening their focus beyond the terrorist attack in

New York and the stock market crisis, more and more artists have made the issue of justice central to their work. Some have come up with rather direct, at times naïve proposals and short sighted interpretations that avoid the complexity of a claim for justice. Others have fallen into the same moralism of populist politicians or the mass media.

Many of the artistic examples and interviews with artists in this book, however, demonstrate that it is possible to conduct intelligent research on claims for justice and pronouncements of justice from an artistic point of view. But they also show that this is often an extremely complex quest that regularly is only a small step away from the noted pitfalls. Political correctness and moralism continually lurk around the corner. Moreover, the question of justice is extremely complex and contextual, as is demonstrated by the contributions in the third section of this book. The conceptualization and understanding of justice depends on the specific geopolitical context; the ways in which one can effectively formulate an answer from an artistic point of view depend on local political, economic, social and ethical histories. What is striking is that the artists and (art) theorists who have contributed to this book are extremely aware of this. Their reflections on works at the intersection of art and morality, of artistic autonomy and social conscience, of self-preservation and sacrifice, are perhaps the most instructive part of this book. Artistic strategies as well as ethical considerations and personal assessments are discussed quite openly in *Aesthetic Justice*.

In the first section of the book, 'The Problem of Justice and Its Aesthetic Possibilities', theorists as well as artists provisionally attempt to interpret the specificity of *aesthetic* justice. In what respect can this form of justice give this loaded concept a different colour and interpretation? Justice, and especially the manner in which fair verdicts and pronouncements are reached, seems to be in some sort of crisis nowadays. Neoliberal capitalism's relentless destruction of social institutions, and consequently any familiar sense of solidarity and security, threatens our collective outlook on justice as well. This far-reaching constellation seems to make our sense of justice devoid of any meaning, perhaps just an empty signifier from a recent past when the social welfare state at least tentatively provided security and care. In a sense, the current neoliberal realm wants us to believe that there is no other governing regime or ideology imaginable than the one that is currently in place. To counteract this sense of socio-political malaise, this first section turns its gaze to artistic practices and aesthetic strategies to explore ways in which we, through thinking along with aesthetics, can forge a new conceptualization of justice, one that is freed from the current stifling sense of social and political determination. Using the device of imagination, and its powerful potential to imagine a 'what if,' a different reality than the one we see currently unfolding, the texts in this first chapter investigate ways in which our sense of justice can, albeit temporarily, be restored. How do the arts differ in their signification of these issues? And do they ultimately also offer answers to the above-mentioned crisis of justice — or is this sooner about opening up a specific potentiality?

Sociologist Pascal Gielen, in the opening essay of the book, states that 'sequentially, justice comes after ethics and before utopia'. He thus provides a theoretical framework for understanding why ideas of justice always need to be grounded in a future vision of society, the very thing that is presently being withheld from us. By using the coordinates of time and space, his essay offers a critical mapping of the condition of justice in broader society, and suggests breaking open the prevailing neoliberal matrix by means of aesthetics. At the same time, however, he remains sceptical about the pragmatic implications of such artistic gestures.

Further building upon this questioning attitude, theorist Mark Fischer proposes abandoning the figure of the villain from today's culture. He believes that our prevalent belief in the moralizing regime of good and evil, and its corresponding pathological call-out culture, doesn't correspond to the actual lack of justice in the real world. The condition for a new emergence of justice, Fischer suggests, lies in in the act of taking collective responsibility to reveal broader means, individual as well as collective, by which the system keeps perpetually reproducing itself.

Whereas Fischer considers this act a foremost philosophical and aesthetic task, artist and writer Hito Steyerl takes a more paradoxical position. Questioning the very possibility to overcome a juridical and metaphysical state of limbo, Steyerl looks at the state of indeterminacy between life and death through Schrödinger's cat. In this thought experiment in which a feline may be both dead and alive, the observer who opens the box will finally decide the cat's fate. For Steyerl, the box becomes a means

of communication between the dead and the living, between that which speaks and that which lies mute forever.

More affirming but equally reluctant to draw easy conclusions, Samuel Vriezen, in his conversation with Christian Wolff, looks at how the American composer has used the vernacular of avant-garde and experimental music to express, or mediate, an increasingly political and social agenda. Wolff suggests that the question of achieving justice through music should be found in the intentional act of creating it, of bringing justice into the context in which one operates, even though it doesn't exist as a given thing or can never be achieved as such.

Concluding the first part of the book, philosopher Gerald Raunig provides an insightful philosophical inquiry on justice, aesthetics, and 'the good life', of what he considers 'the art of living beautifully'. Positioning Alexander Gottlieb Baumgarten as the founding father of modern aesthetics, he offers a far more radical reading of the eighteenth-century philosopher than is usually given. For Raunig, Baumgarten conceptualizes the idea of beauty first and foremost as a dark and confusing horizon, an idea he takes as a starting point to elaborate on the actualization of the possibility of an aesthetic sphere of law.

After 'The Problem of Justice and Its Artistic Possibilities' has presented a conceptual discussion of the current crisis of justice and the specificity of *aesthetic* justice, the second part of the book chiefly presents the work of artists. A selection of interviews and critical dissertations introduces possible practical approaches to aesthetic justice. The title of this section, 'Justice on Stage, Justice Reframed', refers to the various ways in which justice and pronouncements of justice are translated and/or further problematized in artistic contexts. Taken together, these texts render more complex straightforward artistic approaches to the problem of justice, making the case that its aesthetic variety has to be situated within the regime of representation. For the artists under consideration, the creation of work is not so much an act against current political and social injustices but rather despite them. Making visible the systems of representation and power structures that allow these injustices to flourish, they offer alternative means to intervene in the spectacle of representation. Considering these aesthetic strategies, what further questions do these artists raise? Why did they become fascinated with the theme of justice? What strategies are they developing? What are the pitfalls of their approaches? And what are their successes and failures, their triumphs but also their fears?

In his text about the French choreographer Jérôme Bel and the Palestinian artist Larissa Sansour, curator Niels Van Tomme looks at how these artists bypass, and potentially offset, dominant modes of representation. Addressing significantly varying subjects such as disability and Palestinian self-determination, Bel and Sansour nevertheless share an opposition to strictly delineated and restrictive modes of representation, either as victims or as threats, which are rarely produced from within. Aesthetic justice, suggests Van Tomme, can be found in these artists' attempts toward a more just representation, but should always be considered a temporal projection rather than a clearly defined goal, and is therefore a justice 'always yet-to-come'.

Finding a correspondence with such modes of critique, Kerry James Marshall has found, in the experience of a certain lack — the lack of African American subjects — within the art historical canon, the impetus to start producing work. In his conversation with curator Dieter Roelstraete, Marshall talks about the issue of under-representation; which, he states, is a very different crisis than the one of exhaustion from which the Western European tradition is suffering. Marshall's work, argues Roelstraete, mainly functions as a critique of dominant visual culture, constantly reminding us how social, economic, and political conditions determine how art and art history are being produced.

As a counterpoint to these strategies of visibility and agency, political theorist Julia Svetlichnaja, in her essay about Chilean artist Alfredo Jaar, warns of obvious convergences of art and justice. According to her, the imminent danger of such convergences is that the arts are being turned into a quasi social service based upon an uncomplicated identification with the Other. Instead, Svetlichnaja argues, Alfredo Jaar's socially and politically motivated work, in which the image's inability to represent reality is often the subject, makes the very power structures visible that create the divide between 'us' and 'them', without ever dissolving it. In Jaar's work, she claims, the viewer is made aware of his/her responsibility to, and multiple accommodations of, these power structures, which creates a sense of inner conflict that questions the very desire for closure and justice.

Similarly questioning the attainability of the idea of justice, theorist Arne De Boever forcefully juxtaposes two recent films that deal in drastically different ways with France's colonial past: Rachid Bouchareb's *Indigènes* (2006) and Michael Haneke's *Caché* (2005). Whereas Bouchareb's film, quite bluntly, provides a seemingly concrete solution with regard to justice for the Algerian people, this ultimately turns out to be false and corrupted within the representational realm. Haneke's radical aesthetics of showing less, and of ultimately refraining from any sense of closure for France's unresolved colonial past, captures, according to de Boever, the horrific spirit of France's individual and collective psyche. Haneke's aesthetic strategy ultimately turns out to be far more elaborate and confrontational within the political realm, providing a conceptualization of justice that remains interminable.

To conclude, artists and theatre makers Mat Fraser and Julia Atlas Muz, in their conversation with critic Tessa Overbeek, explain how they use the language of freak shows, cabaret, experimental dance, and socially engaged theatre to stage confrontational but always vulnerable representations of the physically disabled body and female sexuality. For them, these humorous and performative acts become exercises in visibility that are opposed to continuing, widespread forms of exploitation. Justice, they claim, is in the first place a freeing of judgment in which one confronts and re-evaluates one's own prejudices and shortcomings.

Finally, in the third and last section of the book, 'Justice and Its Geopolitics', theorists, artists and other professionals show how justice not only depends on the geopolitical context, but also how the significance and interpretation of artistic activities depend on the environment in which they arise, and ultimately also where they are produced and exhibited. Russia or the Middle East obviously are not Western Europe or the United States, but what actually makes these contexts so specific and different? By introducing a number of reflections on justice from within highly specific geopolitical frameworks, we highlight the myriad ways in which art works produced within these milieus interact with some geo-specific conceptualizations of justice. In presenting these texts, we establish an open dialogue between seemingly detached global contexts — Russia, Turkey, Columbia, the US, and the Middle East — and underscore how a continuing, never-ending quest for justice is made tangible, notwithstanding the fact that it often seems impossible to achieve. As these varying authors and artists make clear, it is possible to propose alternative positions with regard to justice in such a way that they can provide new models and fresh perspectives, or occasionally counteract such easy solutions altogether.

In his thorough analysis of the post-Soviet condition, curator and writer Viktor Misiano states that the dismantlement of Soviet communism removed the utopian perspective from Russian society, posing a problem for the possibility of justice. Instead of realizing a better, not yet existent future, the Russian post-communist condition is one in which the past has to be realized within the present, the very thing that was already realized in the West and in pre-communist Russia. Reflecting on the periods of transition and stabilization following this post-utopian break, Misiano points to the societal difficulties and gaps that arise with the disappearance of the common. Stating that there is currently no alternative to the neoliberal consensus, he ultimately finds hope in the troubling aesthetics of trauma.

Shifting the focus to contemporary Turkey, artist and sociologist Hakan Topal writes about the Uludere Massacre, one of the most controversial incidents of the last decade in Turkey. During this official airstrike, thirty-four mostly innocent teenagers were killed on charges of 'suspected terrorism' while crossing the border with Iraq. In his text, Topal elaborates on the specifics of artistic research based upon encounters during his trip to the region and the questions it poses with regard to representation. Considering collateral damage, condolence payments, and the (im)possibility of official forms of justice and retribution within the context of global war, Topal makes a case for aesthetics as a producer of intimate knowledge.

Similarly devoted to a questioning of justice within an extremely violent political context, Columbian artist Carlos Motta, in a conversation with curator Niels Van Tomme, proposes forms of narrative justice as a way to come to terms with various assassinations of moderate liberal and left wing political leaders throughout Columbia's modern history. For Motta, the concept of narrative justice refers to a notion of justice detached from the judicial field, which instead focuses on narrative and communication as pillars of a possible reconciliation. During this conversation, however, it becomes clear that such processes are far from straightforward and often clash with the political context in which the work is situated. Motta, despite the unresolved tensions in his work, transforms such conflicts into encounters through which he can question forms of representation and critically engage the arts.

Visual artist Zoe Beloff's participation on a non-organizational level with Occupy Wall Street in New York City provided an occasion to mount a staging of Bertold Brecht's *The Days of the Commune* in public space. In her text, Beloff investigates how this contextual staging of Brecht's play about the Paris Commune doesn't offer a nostalgic escape from the present, but instead helps us think through ways in which we can reimagine past historical events as an inspiration and call to action for the future. Aesthetic justice, in her view, is the responsibility for artists to lay bare and acknowledge power relations within society, thereby creating new forms of radical, popular art.

In the closing essay of the book, curator Nat Muller focuses her attention on the Middle East, looking at strategies of refusal as a foremost political and aesthetic position. The artists she discusses, ranging from Syrian photographer Hrair Sarkissian to the Lebanese artist duo Joana Hadjithomas and Khalil Joreige, often use refusal as a gesture against interpretation. At the same time, however, it is also a way to escape specific hegemonic imaginaries projected on the region, such as war, devastation, destruction, and loss. These gestures of refusal, Muller argues, are not only to be found within the representational realm but could also be interpreted as a refusal to be forgotten or erased. They become, for her, a reminder of the essence of aesthetic justice: to take in a position, or to refuse consciously and willingly to do so.

By presenting artistic practices related to justice, as well as reflections on them, *Aesthetic Justice* not only shines a light on the specificity of these artistic practices but also makes it clear that they differ from the political and activist art of the nineteen sixties and seventies. Although many of the positions under consideration seek to accommodate a shift in thinking about modes of representation and forms of renewed artistic engagement, there is also a specific focus on questions of civil society and a continuing attempt to oppose, or redirect, injustices from within the current global neoliberal realm. Perhaps the strongest asset of the arts within such processes is not so much their ability to facilitate concrete political and social change, but their potential to increase an understanding and awareness of the *possibility* of change. Not unlike Carneadas in his confrontational thought experiment at the beginning of this introduction, the artists and theorists in this book call upon imagination as a foremost strategic device, something that often further problematizes rather than solves the complexity of the question of justice.

Moreover, the difference between these practices and other forms of engaged art, such as the recent interpretations of community art or activist political work discussed in the *Art in Society* series of books, comes to the fore. Unlike the ubiquitous moralizing and politically correct babbling, today's artist seems to judge without passing sentence. In other words, she or he comes up with sharp judgments but leaves the verdict open for the public of the artistic work. In that respect, works of art differ from moralizing opinions in politics and the media, or from the juridical verdict of a judge. Although the artist's view is often extremely sharp, (s)he rarely offers concrete closure or straightforward solutions. With aesthetic justice, the verdict is often left up to the viewer. In this way, the artist's quest also open up alternative ways of dealing with justice in real life — allowing, to use Slavoj Žižek's prophetic words, 'the intervention of a mysterious agency that we can call, in a Platonic way, the eternal idea of freedom and justice'.[1]

Aesthetic Justice: Intersecting Artistic and Moral Perspectives could not have come about without the committed effort of theorists and the openhearted talks with artists, for which we sincerely thank them. We also wish to express our gratitude for the support of the Mondriaan Fund and the Research Centre Arts in Society. The stimulating collaboration with our publisher Valiz was again something we could count on for this project. It made us love to make this book.

August 2014, Antwerp/New York

Bibliography

—   Slavoj Žižek, 'Why fear the Arab
    revolutionary spirit?', in *The Guardian*,
    February 1, 2011, www.theguardian.com/
    commentisfree/2011/feb/01/egypt-tunisia-
    revolt, last accessed August 14, 2014.

Part 1

The Problem of Justice, and its Aesthetic Possibilities

Walking Straight from the Imaginary into the Common Here and Now

The Matter of Aesthetic Justice

Pascal Gielen

The Moment of Justice

Sequentially, justice comes after ethics and before utopia. The ethical consideration of what is good and what is evil must be made prior to any pronunciation about the justice of a given situation. It is only after we have defined such conditions as child labour, paedophilia, the prosperity gap between North and South or, say, the free-market process in medicine, the repression of women and migrants or denying civil rights to illegal aliens as 'unjust' that an act of justice can be initiated. In turn, ethical guidelines are supported by a future vision of a society. The distinction between good and bad actions is based, among other things, on the effects these actions may have in the future. Certain persistent behaviour may, for instance, lead to an ecological disaster or steer us in the direction of a corrupt society. Ethics are based in part on predictions and speculations that are difficult to substantiate.

Since we cannot know the future with complete certainty, and as futurology is not yet a science based on empirical proof, moral science will have to rely partly on artists, philosophers and other speculative minds who hold up a convincing image of the future to us, as has been argued before (see Gielen, 2014). For instance, in order to formulate an ethics concerning privacy, we took some of our cues from George Orwell's dystopian *1984*. Artists in particular are quite good at designing such utopian and dystopian visions. Their sojourn in the world of fiction also affords them the time and some social credit to engage in a bit of Messianic behaviour. Whether their representations are in any sense real is a different matter. Or, to put it differently and more abstractly: the more feasible the fictions or conjectures of artists become, the greater the chance that ethics come into play. Only when a sizeable group of people start to believe in the possible world or worlds created and described by artists, prophets or philosophers does moral science step in to set the guidelines for leading a 'good life'. Because of their empathetic power, aesthetic representations are often more convincing and more influential than a scientifically founded calculation or a rationally argued scenario of the future. The rules for the game of life are drawn up by projecting them onto a possibly different (either utopian or dystopian) world — a world that may sometimes seem to lie far ahead in time.

An act of justice intervenes at the exact moment between a formulated set of ethics on the one hand and a generally accepted vision of the future on the other. A claim for justice can only be made when the distinction between good and evil has already been made, when moral science has already crystallized into rules, either explicitly articulated or not. Only then can a sense of justice arise and only then does it become possible to draw the line between justice and injustice at all. An act of justice, for instance the exposure of a wrong by a journalist, the verdict of a judge or a work by an artist that causes outrage, not only comes after ethics, it also confirms a specific ethics, and in doing so confirms faith in the possibility of a particular future at the same time.

In other words, an act of justice is a performative act. It activates and confirms ethical rules through pronouncements and actual behaviour. Based on guidelines for living provided by moral science, an act of justice hopes to pave the way to a 'good world' far removed from dystopia. In other words, justice shapes that teleological path between now and later, between here and a better yonder. Judges do not pronounce verdicts only to rectify a wrong, but also with an eye toward a better, more just future. Without such a horizon, justice would be 'pointless' in both meanings of the word: it would have neither meaning nor direction. Or one could say, justice would have no meaning because it would have no direction. Taking a view of the future into account is essential; without it, an act of justice could not exist at all. Whereas ethics point to a certain direction, acts of justice actually go in a certain direction and thus 'realize' the way to a desired outcome and future.

Bearing the above in mind, one could also say that justice navigates the border zone between, on the one hand, the assumed reality or the real present and, on the other hand, an imagined horizon. Or, more concisely, justice mediates on the curious path between non-fiction and fiction. It does so in the hope that dystopian aspects of the fiction will not materialize, while the utopian aspects will become non-fiction.

A person who in good conscience and faith acts according to the ethical guidelines of justice tries, in other words, to transform certain fictions into realities. He or she attempts to create or recreate reality in the image of the ideal. In that sense we might say the act of justice is an attempt to convert an imagined better world into an actual reality. Those who are concerned with justice may therefore be called 'do-gooders' without a trace of irony.

The moment in time discussed above and the performative character of justice have special consequences for those artists who introduce aspects of justice into their work. They are leaving the familiar territory of fiction to actually influence contemporary reality. They return from the fiction of a possible future to intervene in the here and now. Artists, prophets, philosophers or other speculative minds who concern themselves with pronouncements about justice and calls for justice not only travel from fiction to non-fiction, but are also time travellers who move from an either desired or to-be-avoided imaginary prospect back to reality in order to intervene in the here and now. In short, these travellers display an idiosyncratic form of diachronous behaviour, for they travel against the flow of time. They leave an imagined future world and measure it against the actual situation, upon which an act of justice follows. After all, the call for greater justice embedded in such an act requires an image of a future when this justice has been realized. And, as already stated, at the same time this act of justice hopes to pave the way to a better world that is now still only part of an imagined future. Therefore, this is not an act of romantics, otherworldly dreamers or other utopians who flee from the present, but rather one of realistic pragmatists who have travelled back from an imagined future in order to intervene in reality. Those who call for justice from an artistic point of view also engage in a gesture that is the opposite of an exodus. Aesthetic justice, by contrast, is a gesture *within the world or within society* and does not evade empirical reality but rather confronts it.

As we know, in the late 1960s and in the 1970s, many artists undertook quite a few adventurous imaginary journeys to the future and, once returned to their present, proclaimed and tried to bring about justice. So aesthetic justice is certainly not a novelty. One of these travellers was Danish artist Palle Nielsen, who attempted to turn the tide and forge a different future with an exhibition. In 1968, he organized an event in the Moderna Museet in Stockholm — *The Model. A Model for a Qualitative Society* — in which he demonstrated this travelling nature. Said Nielsen:

> My final goal is to find the ultimate form in which people can communicate with each other. If that form could have worked within existing society, I would have accepted that society, but I soon discovered it to be impossible. Society

is built on other premises, other circumstances, and that is why I have to try to change society so that it gains a different economic structure, because there are greater possibilities — but we are still far, far away from an ideal way for people to communicate with each other. (Nielsen in an interview with Louise Rydén, held in 1968, in: Larsen, 2010)

The use of the word 'far' not only points to this artist's travelling nature. The above citation also reveals the artist's conviction, based on his experience with a possible future, that it is necessary to intervene in the actual present. Nielsen's intention was to actually change society through his art, and his act of justice consisted of this practical experiment with an alternative model of society. The title of Nielsen's 'exhibition' also clarifies the central theme of this publication. The word 'model' refers to modelling or designing something. With Nielsen, aesthetic justice is not confined to designing a fictitious world, as in a play, choreography, painting, installation or composition. In this case, the aesthetics are attempting to cross the borders of the unreal in order to intervene in real life. With *The Model...*, Nielsen indeed wished to re-model society, and in doing so, he automatically entered the realm of politics. And, as we and Jacques Rancière know by now, the meaning of the word 'politics' is to shape society. Like Rancière's aesthetic thinking, aesthetic justice is a way of shaping our living together (Rancière, 2007). And doing so from a strong sense of what is just.

The Site of Justice

While justice as a performative act can be situated on the timeline between now and later, the 'site' of justice is located between two social domains, that of the private and that of the public domain. It is exactly there that judgement is passed. In a pronouncement of justice, injustice inflicted upon private individuals or legal entities takes on a public character. Personal suffering, poverty, abuse or repression are lifted out of the private domain and made public. With matters of justice, such a transformation can only take place if the public domain is open to it, which in turn is only possible when there are collectively accepted rules, values and standards with which to construct a 'narrative' around a claim for justice. Only when, for instance, it is commonly agreed that men and women should be treated as equals can a specific case

of physical or mental domestic violence become the subject of an appeal for justice. The private case only becomes public because it is acknowledged by the collective. Appeals for justice forge such connections. Therefore, justice is not only situated in the liminal area between the private and public domain but also between the individual or particular incident and the communal incident.

Judgements that remain personal are not pronouncements of justice but belong to the domain of personal morality or even sometimes to that of psychotherapy. By contrast, judgements that only concern the domain of the collective are exclusively part of the public domain. Justice intermediates between these two domains and is therefore part of the commons, the collective. According to philosophers Michael Hardt and Antonio Negri (2009) this is where private and public meet. Or, rather, the commons is neither private nor public and is therefore capable of mediating between the two domains. An act of justice reveals what has lain hidden in the private domain but is worthy of becoming a public item. It pulls individual problems into the public domain and at the same time puts an issue that is also of private interest on the public agenda. In other words, an act of justice makes visible what had been invisible until then.

This process of revealing also gives a public and political dimension to a private issue. In a call for justice, issues such as child abuse in the Church, euthanasia for the terminally ill or homosexual love shift from being private to being public, from being an individual item to a collective one. This is why an act of justice is a crucial political act. It reveals what until then had been regarded as an intimate, psychological, individual and private problem. Once made public, the problem immediately acquires the weight of a judgement by a social community.

From that perspective, it also becomes plausible that a legal verdict does not exclusively follow a course opposite to that of exodus, as stated earlier. Justification also presents itself as a ghost-driver in the hegemonial lane of the currently prevailing neoliberalism, or, rather, repressive liberalism. After all, this ideology tends to push everything into the private domain and places what used to be collective responsibilities upon the shoulders of the individual. With study loans, private insurance and pension plans, neoliberalism attempts to both privatize and individualize all claims to justice. This undermines both the commons and the possibility of collective guarantees such as solidarity between regions or generations, which also restricts individual freedom, including that of choice. Hence the somewhat paradoxical notion of 'repressive liberalism'. The individual is not made free but is in fact declared an 'out-law', which leads to an increasingly restrictive egocentric predicament (see also Gielen, 2013). It becomes more and more difficult for justice to row against this stream.

Having said that, it may be stated that appeals for justice are situated at the intersection of everyday reality and utopia on the one hand, and between the individualized private domain and the collectively shared public domain on the other hand. The chilly winds of repressive liberalism make it increasingly difficult to remain standing in this open place. This is the contemporary fate of justice in general, but what about the specific form of justice that is the subject of this book?

Aesthetic Justice

At the least, the use of the adjective 'aesthetic' suggests that there are also other forms of justice. One can, for instance, proclaim and enforce justice on rational-scientific, religious or legal-technical grounds. Someone who predicts the disastrous effects of, let's say, climate change on the basis of rational calculations, however, will arrive at appeals for justice in an entirely different manner than someone who does so on the basis of aesthetics. Starting from rational reasons, one predicts the future based on empirical measurements in the present. That future may look the same as the fictitious world of artists. Scientists, however, take an entirely different path than artists. Whereas researchers calculate a path to the future starting from facts established in the present, artists return to the present from an imagined vista.

Believers in the Judaic, Christian or Islamic tradition of a Messiah, on the other hand, are guided in their sense of justice by transcendental excursions to a world beyond and outside our reality in time. The Messiah certainly comes flying in from a completely different universe than the artist. From there, he or she may well point to a better path for this world, but the real paradise is de facto out of reach of our worldly existence. Believers can only partly realize heaven on Earth, as the real ideal world is only attainable in the hereafter. While they are still on Earth, believers must be content with the shadow of a transcendental life that can only be led in paradise, beyond this world and time. Although artists are certainly capable of fervently believing in transcendental

fictions, their own fictions have been of a more secular nature since the Age of Enlightenment. This means that their utopian fictions can only be realized on Earth. In that sense, the arty type differs fundamentally from the religious Messiah.

Finally, greater justice can also be proclaimed on lawful, legal-technical or procedural grounds, but here too, the argumentation starts from what is written in the here and now and not, like with that of the artist, fictitious laws that perhaps could be written. In short, scientists, believers, judges and artists can all arrive at similar claims for justice, but the path they take is of a completely different nature.

As said, artists who concern themselves with justice travel from their own imagined (and secular) world to an actual present, with the goal of bringing presently experienced non-fiction closer to the ideal fiction of their own imagination. One of history's lessons, however, is that designing a society on the basis of such fictions does not necessarily lead to actually living together in a more just way. In the past, artists in positions of power may well have led us onto some of the darkest pages in history. The chance to save the world from this perhaps lies down a different path. Whereas totalitarian regimes based on an aesthetic design subordinate the public interest and common good to individual, private ambitions, aesthetic justice takes the opposite route. The latter transforms private problems into public issues and individual matters into collective claims. This is perhaps one of the differences in design of totalitarian and democratic regimes.

The important thing here is that aesthetic justice presupposes the idea of travel, even a quite specific and most peculiar form of travel: a journey through time from a fictitious — because it is imagined — future to a real present. This type of imaginary travel is becoming increasingly difficult at the present juncture. More precisely. it is not so much the journey to the imaginary that is blocked, but rather the return trip. The impact that the experiences of such a journey might have on reality is nowadays met with trepidation.

Within the desire economy of consumerism, one may escape in daydreaming but preferably not return laden with ideals. When an artistic person attempts such pragmatism, he or she is quickly dismissed as a naive idealist or is simply declared insane. At the least, attempts will be made to exile this justice-seeking artist to the harmless world of fiction again. As long as artists stay within the white walls or black box of the art world, they are allowed to meddle with social and political commitment. This is precisely where art that is concerned with justice is on the rise, perhaps because all subversive potential is neutralized within the customary domain of fiction. This is not the case, however, when artists move beyond the institutional boundaries of the imaginary. This fear of designers who attempt to actually control society is not altogether unjustified, by the way, as pointed out earlier. The point is that the eschatology of a better future is subjugated to quite repressive bureaucratic demands nowadays. Travelling from too distant of a future, from too big of a Utopia to the present is therefore made nigh impossible. It is becoming harder and harder to defend a state of happiness that cannot be obtained in the relatively short term. Within the realism cult of currently prevailing repressive liberalism, such prospects demonstrate little sense of reality.

The Iron Cage at the End of History
This ban on migration from all too distant futures was probably best underpinned intellectually by the post-Communist proclamation by Francis Fukuyama. Although in the last chapter of his *The End of History and the Last Man* (1992) this American philosopher does admit that liberal democracy will always be full of tensions and contradictions, we can't help getting the impression that we have reached our final destination. There may be a few slight imperfections in the neoliberal paradise, but as far as maximum attainable happiness is concerned, we are definitely at the top. So anyone who comes knocking at the door with claims and promises from a very distant future is met with mounting disbelief.

Whereas Fukuyama, being a good intellectual, adds some nuance to his assertions, a generation of professional pragmatics in the decade following his credo were much more categorical. As with any good Thomas theorem, their belief that we had reached the maximum attainable utopia began to turn into reality because of how they actually behaved. Since the beginning of the 1990s, an army of neo-managers, network managers, accreditors, auditors, bureaucrats and digicrats has emerged that effectively has ruled out any too distant perspective. From then on, what is real is what is considered attainable and calculable and is therefore measurable.

Within capitalistic realism (Fisher, 2009), an unreal belief in makeability is reconciled with a suffocating short-term perspective. Everyone's dream can become true and realized in the reasonably short term, since we have in fact already reached the best possible utopia. If personal happiness is still found to fall short of perfection, all it certainly takes to reach that perfection is a few calculable steps. All the rest is obstinacy; and personal coaches, social workers, and therapists are available to ease the pain and steer all recalcitrant behaviour back to the straight and narrow path of realism. In this manner, dreams and wishes that are too exuberant are brought back within the measure of calculability.

And since we have reached the end of history, our horizon does not expand beyond our personal interest. At the end of history, it is impossible to have grand dreams that stretch beyond our individual lifespan. Transgenerational ambitions are met with reservations at best. At the end of history, one's perspective is shrunk to whether one can afford a student loan, a travel insurance policy or a personal life insurance plan. Those who still focus their gaze on infinity are perhaps allowed to wander about for a while, but are soon encouraged to show more sense of reality. We are already living in paradise. This is as good as it gets, and only wild speculative minds and lottery winners think otherwise. For all the others, slack is measured in millimetres and even that can only be obtained under the highest personal guarantees and on individual credit. The liberal dream has been fulfilled, the capitalist utopia has been realized. No more collective responsibility beyond this point. Those who wish to go further do so at their own risk and on their own account. Those who wish to make claims for justice within this limited horizon don't get much further than a fiscal year.

The end of history may not be today, but it is not far beyond a measurable time span. Rationally measurable justice is completely different from aesthetic justice. Justice claims that are based on what is feasible and manageable have a much more limited depth perspective than the imaginary spaces that are based on the possibilities of the impossible. That is perhaps the essence of the post-Communist, post-ideological and therefore post-political age: the ideal must not go beyond the measurable horizon. Within the post-political climate, such an ideal can at best reach the level of being average. Also, it is no longer a collectively attainable common good, but only one that can be reached by individual effort on one's own behalf. Within such a context, what is just is what is attainable for the ego here and now. Injustice can only occur when this individual path is blocked.

It is only this personal sense of injustice that will remain after the demolition of the welfare state has been completed. After that, only a violation of personal interest will be regarded as an injustice, for instance in the case of an individual breach of contract by an insurance broker, an employer, a teacher, a physician or a politician. In short, the new citizens in the neoliberal 'state of justice' are reduced to individual consumers. Their rights are reduced to property rights and politicians are reduced to ombudsmen and guardians of consumer interests. Any perceived injustice can only be defined and regarded as such if the individual has insured his or her own rights in all sorts of contracts.

At the end of history, by the way, it is also that individual's personal responsibility to determine his or her ethical boundaries. The welfare state's structural mechanisms of solidarity are after all being replaced now by an appeal to individual sentiments in media-directed aid efforts, from *Live Aid* to *Solidarity for Syria*. Collective welfare is increasingly being made dependent on the individual's goodwill to contribute to a good cause. As sociologist Zygmunt Bauman says:

> the task of cutting down the suprahuman boundlessness
> of ethical responsibility to the capacity of an ordinary
> human's sensitivity, an ordinary human's power
> of judgment and ability to act, tends now... to be
> 'subsidiarized' to individual men and women. In the
> absence of an authoritative translation of the 'unspoken
> demand' into a finite inventory of prescriptions and
> proscriptions, it is now up to each individual to set the
> limits of her or his responsibility for other humans and to
> draw the line between the plausible and the implausible
> among moral interventions – as well as to decide how
> far she or he is ready to go in sacrificing personal welfare
> for the sake of fulfilling moral responsibility to others.
> (Bauman, 2008: 51).

And so, we are denied two things at the end of history: collective insurance or solidarity as well as long-term or transgenerational vision or planning. The individual as the maximum unit

and the productive years of a person's life as the longest possible time span make up the coordinates of the contemporary neoliberal matrix. That matrix is the iron cage into which humankind has quite happily stepped for the fourth time in a row since the advent of capitalism — to dust off Max Weber's metaphor once again (Boltanski and Chiapello, 2005).

The first time that (Western) mankind did this was when it lost its faith (in Protestantism, in Weber's case) and subsequently engaged itself only with a secular predestination doctrine of personal gain. From that moment on, mankind would be constantly torn between the pursuit of freedom and a longing for security. Perhaps it is this oscillating motion that defines the most important tensions within capitalism.

With the Industrial Revolution, freedom (read: liberalism), that decoy and life force of capitalism, was once again offered on a golden platter. Lured by greater personal prosperity, people were torn away from their local community and family ties in order to work in factories in the cities. A growing bureaucracy, indispensable to the central management of big industry, relieved organizations from the necessity of appointing family members and other forms of nepotism. Cutting family ties in professional appointments generated a new liberty. In compensation, the system also offered new securities through rules and procedures. After all, within a bureaucracy there are objective rules for obtaining certain positions, and individual skills and diplomas prevail over favouritism. A well-oiled bureaucracy guided a society in a pendicular motion between newly offered freedoms and securities from an 'ascribed' to an 'achieved' career path, as is the common terminology among sociologists. It was one of the models Henry Ford offered to the workers who built his cars, and it earned him a reputation as a trustworthy manager.

Ideally, within Fordism everyone was rewarded according to their own skills, effort and capacity. As we know, however, by the end of the 1950s and early 1960s this bureaucracy was carried too far, leading to a new iron cage. The capitalist promise of freedom went under in strict hierarchies, rigid organograms and other obsolete and restrictive constructs. In short, the longing for security prevailed over the pursuit of freedom. Massive strikes and student uprisings had to break open that new iron cage again. Stressing authenticity, creativity, flexibility, and individual self-fulfilment was post-Fordism's answer to this revitalized dream of freedom. At the same time, the new labour model demolished, and still does so today, the perceived overregulation by the welfare state so that creative entrepreneurs could develop their activities in full freedom.

As a result, we now find ourselves at a point in history where individuals are confronted with their own boundaries, and the accompanying short-term perspective is busily forging yet another new iron cage. Freedom is now restricted by instruments that are designed by neo-managers and auditors. The buyers of this new, now digital, cage make up the repressive liberal matrix alluded to earlier.

In the professional art world, however, the coordinates of this matrix were not that unknown. As source of inspiration for the post-Fordist labour model (see Gielen, 2009), the art world had embraced individual freedom and creativity since the beginning of the modern era. But ever since art has been paired with the adjective 'contemporary', history too does not reach much further than what is being produced today. After all, contemporaneity is not a historical category. It has no past and therefore no future, either. After the label 'modern art' had been replaced by 'contemporary art' — at a juncture that ran conspicuously parallel to the advent of neoliberalism and post-Fordism, by the way (see also Gielen, 2009 and 2013) — the collective artistic schools or 'isms' also evaporated. By the end of the nineteenth century, art had already become a highly individualistic matter and since the 1980s artists have kept losing more and more artistic brothers and intellectual soul mates.

When collective categorizations become increasingly inconceivable, marking social time in terms of generations becomes less useful. Manifold and visible changes occur at an infernal pace, being the rule rather than the exception. Collective experiences are so short-lived and appear in such rapid succession that multiple generations simultaneously experience them as their own. Drawing lines between generations is therefore a rather arbitrary gesture within this post-Fordist condition. Any attempt to draw such a line is nowadays more likely to lead to confusion than produce a clear cartography of a society. The nanoseconds it takes for novelties to intrude into our lives not only prevent the crystallization and solidification of attitudes and behavioural

patterns, but also value patterns and even collectively shared worldviews. In other words, the foundations of the spirit of the times that are needed to construct a generational identity have melted away.

This also has consequences for artistic generations. In the 1990s, the artistic movements were definitely laid to rest and with them all feelings of solidarity between soul mates. Success in the art world is achieved amongst sharp competition, in which it is everyone for themselves. So, in other words, at the end of history the world of contemporary art dances to the coordinates of the neoliberal matrix too. What's more artists are by now very skilled in deploying this hyper-individualism. Perhaps this is why Bauman, quoted earlier, regards them as a prototype:

> Our lives, whether we know it or not and whether we relish the fact or bewail it, are works of art. To live our lives as the art of living demands, we must — just as artists must — set ourselves challenges that are difficult to confront up close, targets that are well beyond our reach, and standards of excellence that seem far above our ability to match. We need to attempt the impossible. And we can only hope, without benefit of a trustworthy prognosis, let alone of certainty, that with long, grinding, and often exhausting effort we may still manage to meet those standards and reach those targets and so rise to the challenge. Uncertainty is the natural habit of human life — although it is the hope of escaping uncertainty that is the engine of human pursuits. (Bauman, 2008: 18)

In the Common Here and Now

Perhaps today's hyper-competitive and hyper-individual circumstances are the reason why a growing number of artists are leaving the world of professional art or turning to other fields such as community art or political activism. After the artistic cynicism of post-modernism, it looks like social, political, and ecological engagement are booming again. So too with expressions of aesthetic justice, as can be found in the works of artists such as Alfredo Jaar, Michelangelo Pistoletto, Hito Steyerl or Carlos Motta, which, however fundamentally different they may be, are endeavours to leave the present-day conditions of the contemporary art world. One of their strategies is to again propose the possibility of travelling afar and investigating the potential of utopian visions. The Italian artist Pistoletto, by the way, makes quite literal references to that with his notion of The Third Paradise.

Besides these artists' efforts to once again stretch time and broaden the horizon, we also see attempts to transcend individuality. Pistoletto, for instance, does so with his organization 'Cittadellarte'. At the very least, the claims for justice that these artists make in their work transcend their own issues of form in order to again make pronouncements about society itself and about what befalls a collectivity that they feel associated with. If the artist is to be a protagonist, as Bauman suggests, these implementers of aesthetic justice feel that it should first of all be de-individualized. The belief in the power of individuals to shape or change themselves must be destroyed in order to acknowledge the necessity of collective solidarities again and to re-institute them.

It may be clear by now that aesthetic justice attempts to break open the prevailing neoliberal matrix. It can only achieve this, however, by escaping from the actual art world itself. Attempts to escape from the contemporaneity of the contemporary art world are fervent endeavours to once again intervene in history and write history again, thereby putting an end to 'the end of history'. This is perhaps why the artistic works that are described here as expressions of aesthetic justice may sometimes appear to be rather 'uncontemporary'. For instance, some critics accuse this tendency of being an aesthetic relapse to the 1960s. Others doubt whether these demands for justice still belong to the domain of art. Indeed, the quest for a new place and a new time is a very heterogeneous affair in which the boundaries between art and politics, between aesthetics and ethics, and between individuality and collectivity become blurred. Aesthetic justice is the result of an act in which subjectivity is shaped without solidifying into a specific identity. It is not an act of being but of becoming: between reality and utopia, between reality and imagination.

This means that the adjective 'aesthetic' introduces another important distinction in comparison to rational or procedural forms of justice. For, since the modern era, works of art are open to receiving meaning. Multiple interpretations of aesthetic forms are possible and the same goes for imaginary worldviews or utopian projections. These tend to evoke 'open endings' that allow for interpretation time and again, enabling them to escape rational calculability and procedural (objective) testability as well

as the dogmatism of a religious view of the future. In a performative act of religious, rational-scientific or legal-procedural justice, the object (a person or situation) of this act is condemned to a fixed identity and forced to take an established course. The person or situation is labelled as either 'good' or 'bad', after which a precisely defined course of correction is imposed. That is, after all, what judges, auditors — or priests in the confessional box — do.

In the case of an art work, however, for the sake of openness the course to take is not yet established. The object of aesthetic justice (for instance, the beholder) is not pinned down or confirmed in an identity. On the contrary, aesthetic justice irritates its object, challenges it to discard its identity without offering a well-defined path to take. An act of aesthetic justice does not address identity, but existence. It questions the acts or existence of its object without offering a clear answer to the question of 'the right path'. Whereas the object of other forms of justice is told what it has done and therefore what it is, and is then told what it should do to return to 'the right path', aesthetic justice questions the beholder without pointing him or her in a clear and obvious direction. This leaves the beholder in an existential quest of deep uncertainty. The only thing that remains, as Bauman already implied, is the hope of escaping from this uncertainty. The beholder is not brought to despair by a fixed belief system, a rational calculation or a legal deduction but by a sensitive (aesthetics as aisthesis) opening up of many possible roads. He or she is incited to go on a quest, the outcome of which is uncertain for the beholder and the artist alike.

In that sense, aesthetic justice is different from political-activist art and also from community art, in which the beholder or participant is pointed in the 'right' direction. With aesthetic justice, artists do point out that everything that is can also always be different, but without knowing whether the alternative roads are better. They put issues up for debate without any of the demystifying criticism that pretends to unveil the truth and therefore to know the true path. In that respect also, this form of making art may be different from the emancipatory art of the 1960s. Artists who engage in aesthetic justice do not know the right path, all the more so because they question their own identity as well. By jumping from the imaginary into the real present, they place themselves outside the familiar situation that society has assigned them. By pointing out a possible utopian future again – however vague it may be – they also make an attempt to free themselves from the contemporaneity of the contemporary art world. Those who wish to escape from the new iron cage of individual calculability must dare to undertake un-contemporary practices. Making claims for justice with aesthetic means from an artistic position is one such strategy. Those who also, while having an eye for utopia, aim for something that transcends individuality, are at least making an attempt to emancipate themselves from the end of history.

These artists subject themselves to their own aesthetic justice, putting their own contemporary identity at stake to immerse themselves in an uncertain world, which is yet to come or not. By throwing themselves in the world outside of the familiar artistic space, artists discard their immunity. They are not outside of society in some safe, distant place from which to comment on the world, as critical artists have done before. On the contrary, they are right in the middle of the common here and now. By including calls for justice in their work, they make themselves extremely vulnerable to much more than what lies within the reach of traditional art criticism. These artists expose themselves to the world, which then inevitably poses them existential questions. How should they relate again to this world? Who are they? What are they doing here? And why are they doing what they do? Who are they to claim justice? In short, what is their *raison d'être?*

Bibliography

- Bauman, Zygmunt, *The Art of Life* (London:Wiley-Blackwell, 2008).
- Boltanski, Luc and Eve Chiapello,, *The New Spirit of Capitalism* (London and New York: Verso Books, 2005).
- Fisher, Mark, *Capitalist Realism: Is There No Alternative?* (Winchester UK: Zero Books, 2009).
- Fukuyama, Francis, *The End of History and the Last Man* (New York: Free Press, 1992).
- Gielen, Pascal, *The Murmuring of the Artistic Multitude. Global Art, Memory and Post-Fordism* (Amsterdam: Valiz, 2009).
- Gielen, Pascal, 'Art and Repressive Liberalism.' In K. Van den Berg and U. Pasero, (eds.) *Art Production Beyond the Market* (Berlin: Sternberg Press, 2013), pp. 215-238.
- Gielen, Pascal, 'Situational Ethics: an Artistic Ecology', In G. Cools, and P. Gielen, *The Ethics of Art* (Amsterdam: Valiz, 2014), pp. 8-22.
- Hardt, Michael and Antonio Negri, *Commonwealth* (Cambridge MA: Harvard University Press 2009).
- Larsen, Lars Bang, *The Model. A Model for a Qualitative Society* (Barcelona: Macba, 2010).
- Rancière, Jacques, *Het esthetische denken* (Amsterdam: Valiz, 2007).

The New Problem of Evil

Mark Fisher

The New Problem of Evil

One of the most disappointing moments in twenty-first century mass media came when Rupert Murdoch was brought before the British House of Commons Select Committee for Culture, Media and Sport in 2011. The hearing had been convened to determine Murdoch's level of involvement in the practice of phone hacking, which had been used by Murdoch's most notorious newspaper, the *News of the World*. (The scandal would quickly lead to the newspaper's closing down.) No doubt, the television audience that gathered to see Murdoch questioned had secretly hoped for something like the climactic scene of Rob Reiner's 1992 film *A Few Good Men*. This unexceptional legal thriller is remembered now only for the witness-box outburst by Jack Nicholson's Colonel Jessup: 'You can't handle the truth!' Jessup is successfully goaded by Tom Cruise's lawyer into admitting his role in an informal disciplinary regime which has led to the death of at least one man. The speech is remembered because Jessup obligingly plays — or overplays — the role of stage villain. (Overplaying might be said to be constitutive of the art of playing the stage villain — excess comes as standard here.)

Perhaps this scene is also remembered because it delivers narrative and libidinal satisfactions we cannot find when faced with the actuality of late twentieth-and early twenty-first- century capitalist power. For what we enjoy in Jessup's tirade is his full identification with the 'evil' of which he is accused. This is no mealy-mouthed apology, no carefully worded press statement. Instead, we see Jessup fully *embody* the obscene underside of power. The hubris and the excess are not merely admitted to; they are actively performed. Jessup cannot control himself. The 'truth' to which he famously refers no longer skulks in shadowy corridors, in gloomy dungeons, in small print; it erupts out of him, he cannot help but expose it to the public gaze.

Needless to say, Murdoch provided his audience with none of this. There was to be no moment where he outed himself as a ruthless tyrant. Some argued that his appearance at the hearing (a slightly bewildered old man, hard of hearing, testy, but not exactly aggressive) was another kind of performance altogether. They maintained that the persona Murdoch assumed was both a deception designed to court sympathy and an exercise in bathos, which aimed to deprive the proceedings of all drama. In any case, Murdoch's appearance at the hearings was more like a vignette from the HBO television series *The Wire* than the famous scene from *A Few Good Men*.

Much of the power of *The Wire* – and also many of its claims to 'realism' – came from its refusal to offer its audience the pleasure of seeing it done. If there was a source of malignancy in *The Wire*, it could barely be represented, still less personified or embodied. For this source was the system itself, a vast interlocking network involving drug crime, policing, politics and education, which it took all of the series' five seasons to lay out. The system not only supplants the role of the villain, it is also, in effect, the main protagonist of the series. The system appears as an anti-agency which absorbs and neutralises practically all of the struggles aimed at changing it. This protean capacity of the system to reproduce itself sets the fatalistic rhythm of the series. We look in vain for 'villains' here. Instead of an evil figure whom we can blame, *The Wire* presents us with someone like William Rawls (John Doman), a manager who repeatedly acts in his own interests and in the interests of the police's managerialist bureaucracy. What defines Rawls' – and the reason that he infuriates and frustrates us – is his 'realistic' accommodation to the system. Yet Rawls compliance with its bureaucratic protocol is evidently not the source of the system's malignancy; it is just one means by which the system achieves its own self-reproduction. Rawls' cynical conformism shows that not only has he has adapted to this world without heroes and villains, he thrives in it; whereas the various efforts of the mavericks and misfits in the Major Crimes Unit indicate that they cannot similarly adjust.

Part of *The Wire*'s 'reality effect' is rooted in the way it continually frustrates – but not completely – the efforts of these mavericks and misfits. Other police dramas have taught us to expect such figures inevitably to triumph, to win out against the system that has disdained and rejected them. It is clear from very early on that there is to be no such triumph in *The Wire*. There is to be no justice, aesthetic or otherwise (and the fact that Bill Rawls shares a surname with one of the best-known philosophers of justice is surely no accident). In much television, especially crime drama, culture delivers what the social and political world cannot. The villain is identified, caught and punished; justice is done, and seen to be done. The aesthetic representation of justice serves to make good a deficit of justice in the actual world. But much of the value of *The Wire* comes from the way it uses a new aesthetic form – the extended television series – to pose political and ethical questions. If there is no easily delimited source of malignancy, then how are we to even conceive of justice now? And this problem of conceptualization becomes in part an aesthetic one, both because our existing thinking about justice is inevitably coloured by the aesthetic models we have inherited, and also because any attempt to re-imagine justice must involve dispensing with those outmoded and/or inadequate aesthetic modes, and inventing new ones.

Returning now to the (muted) spectacle of Murdoch at the hearings, it is clear that our disappointed hopes there were testament to the persistent pull of melodrama on the contemporary imagination. For what we wanted was Murdoch to take on the role of that staple of melodrama, the stage villain. Melodrama and the stage villain feature in Fredric Jameson's recent book *The Antinomies of Realism*, which was ostensibly about the nineteenth century realist novel. Yet Jameson's theorizations have implications far beyond this particular aesthetic form; they also bear upon the fictional structuration of social reality itself. In realism, Jameson argues, the structures of melodrama don't entirely disappear – rather, they are subject to an (always incomplete) process of erasure. The mark of 'realism', according to Jameson, is the absence of meaning. Taking his cue from Barthes' concept of the 'reality effect' in *Writing Degree Zero*, Jameson argues in *The Antinomies of Realism* that 'If it means something, it can't be real'.[1] The signature of realism becomes for Jameson nothing less than the eruption into the narrative of *affect*. Affects are understood – in the terms established by post-Deleuzean 'affect theory' – as those sensations which must be opposed to 'named emotions', intensities which cannot be owned by individual subjects. Affect is crucial for Jameson's purposes because of its very 'meaning' and theatricality. As Jameson establishes – nowhere better than in his bravura discussion of Zola – affect in the realist novel seethes beyond the narrative structure, threatening to overwhelm it entirely. He writes of 'a tremendous fermenting and bubbling pullulation in which the simplicity of words and names is unsettled to the point of an ecstatic dizziness by the visual multiplicity of the things themselves and the sensations that they press on the unforewarned observer'.[2] Such intensities become the markers of the 'realistic' for the very reason that they have neither allegorical meaning nor narrative function. They cannot be contained

by melodrama, whose 'very essence' is 'theatricality', the staging
for an audience.[3] Theatricality in this sense presupposes a certain
structuring; events don't just happen, they are narrated only inso-
far as they are supposed to have meaning for an audience.

As melodrama dissolves, one of its central defining elements — the villain — disappears with it. 'The mission of affect,'
as Jameson programmatically puts it, lies 'in the very weakening
of the melodramatic structure, the gradual effacement of the villain.'[4] But this effacement produces a crisis; or, rather, it points to
and intensifies a philosophical and aesthetic crisis of which it is
a symptom. Without a villain who self-consciously understands
himself as evil, what are we to do with the very concept of evil?
'The stage villain is all exterior, and can declare his essential villainy as largely as he likes, in spoken language and gesture. Even
the villains of epic must declare themselves in soliloquy: "Which
way I fly is Hell; myself am Hell"; "Evil, be thou my Good!" But
that is, indeed, the philosophical conundrum par excellence,
namely how my "good" could ever be evil. For philosophy, indeed,
all evil must be "radical evil", in Kant's sense, evil done for evil's
sake; we do it because we like it...'[5] Yet this figuration of 'evil'
has been difficult to pull off. As Jameson argues, it quickly slid
into a clinical diagnosis of sadism. If this is offered and accepted
as a *genuine* diagnosis — rather than a moralizing condemnation
dressed up in pseudo-clinical garb — it deprives us of the capacity
to attribute blame, thereby stripping the very concept of evil of
any coherence. One audacious implication of Jameson's line of
reasoning here is that the whole binary opposition between good
and evil must now be understood as a melodramatic structure.

Typically, the mass-mediated figuration of 'evil' since the
1960s has incorporated sadism — but this has been understood
more as a libidinal proclivity than as a pathological compulsion.
The prototype here is the master villain of the James Bond movies
— which, despite its being mocked by the Doctor Evil character
in the *Austin Powers* films, remains the dominant model for evil in
contemporary Hollywood. The defining feature of this character
is the combination of an insouciant detachment with a sensual-
ist's delight in cruelty. These villains are refined, they absolutely
will not be ruffled. Their power consists in the exaggerated display of composure and civility; when they conspicuously consume
expensive cuisine while the hero is being tortured, they never fail
to offer something to the hero. But, in the Bond villain case, there

is always some ostensibly pragmatic motivation for the elaborate schemes; they don't just want to cause suffering, they want wealth, and/or power. It was perhaps inevitable that this kind of villain should evolve into the Hannibal Lecter figure, where the pretext of instrumental motivation gives way to pure sadism — the enjoyment of suffering for its own sake — and the act of cruelty is conflated *with* the civilized meal. But, even as Lecter has clearly stepped into the shoes of the stage villain, he is no longer a figure of 'evil' — either because we must classify him as mad, or because he belongs to some space in which the binary opposition between good and evil no longer operates. Lecter, you might say, is the stage villain for an age that no longer believes in evil. And here we confront what I am calling 'the new problem of evil'.

In Christian theology, the problem of evil arose from the seeming incompatibility between God's properties — omniscience, omnipotence, benevolence — and the existence of suffering. How could an all-powerful, all-knowing, benevolent being countenance the existence of suffering? Philosophers of religion distinguished 'moral' evil (caused by human agency) from 'natural' evil (suffering caused by natural disasters, illnesses, death and, indeed, birth).The concept of natural evil makes it clear that the real problem concerns suffering, rather than evil as we now understand it. Moral evil can be attributed to free will, but this explanation cannot be straightforwardly deployed when it comes to suffering caused without human agency (although the concept of original sin was one attempt ultimately to root all suffering in humanity's rebellion against God).

The rather different problem of evil I am referring to here is the challenge which the concept of evil poses to atheists. The problem now is that we no longer believe in evil. Or, to be more accurate, we know that there are no grounds any more for belief in evil, yet we find ourselves unable to give up acting *as if* we believe in it. None of this — not least the formulation 'as if'— would be in the least surprising to Kant. Many of Kant's most intricate arguments operated as explanations for the persistence of theological and voluntaristic forms of thinking after Enlightenment science ought to have debunked them. Kant's claims here concerned not what was really the case — since we were constitutively incapable of being able to establish this — but only what our cognitive apparatus predisposed us to think. On the one hand, Kant decoupled morality from religion — his categorical imperative produced a formula for the Good that had no need for divine decree – but, on the other hand, he maintained that morality depends on belief in freedom, immortality and God.

So it's no accident that, in his discussion of the effacement of the villain, Jameson turns to Spinoza and his concept of 'sad passions'. If Kant's philosophy was a compromise with theology, then Spinoza's was a decisive break with residual theological thinking. (And Kant's work can be seen as part of a retrospective attempt to contain the dangerous implications of Spinoza's philosophy for ethics.) Long before Nietzsche, it was Spinoza who was the great thinker operating 'beyond good and evil'. His contribution in this respect essentially consisted of two moves, both of which (at one level) have become commonplaces of contemporary thought, but which (at the level of our everyday thinking and reflexive assumptions) remain impasses in which we are still trapped. Firstly, Spinoza rejected any absolute conception of good or evil. 'Good' and 'evil' could only be defined in relation to the interests of particular creatures. Secondly – and by contrast with Kant, who would famously posit a noumenal space in which human beings could still be thought of as causing their own actions – Spinoza inserts human behaviour into an exceptionless sequence of causation. All actions are caused, and so-called human will or volition is not by any means the first cause; it is itself the product of very long chains of causation. The fact that we might only ever understand these chains of causation inadequately does not mean that they are not there.

Spinoza, then, is a philosopher whose work demands that we leave melodrama and its dramaturgy behind. And we can say that the persistence of the melodramatic is a sign of contemporary culture's resistance to Spinozism. The good/evil binary keeps returning – not only in capitalist entertainment (look at how a new version of the stage villain became central to the appeal of reality TV), but also in the pathological compulsions of an ostensibly left-wing 'call-out culture', which urges us to blame systemic tendencies such as racism and patriarchy on the proclivities of an ever-shifting, constantly renewing cast of individuals. But Marx as much as Spinoza tried to cure us of our moralizing desire to blame individuals. Part of the problem is that villainy seems to be a necessarily individual concept, which blocks us from thinking about collective agency. The figure of the 'conspiracy' is a flawed attempt to figure a malign collective agency; flawed, precisely because it tends to think of collective agency on the model of individual villainy. The task — and it is an aesthetic as much as it is a purely philosophical endeavour — is to make visible the impersonal and collective chains of cause and effect by which the system reproduces itself. How are we to achieve justice without relying on the obsolete figure of the villain? How, that is to say, are we to move beyond the aesthetic paradigms of moralizing melodrama? For all the libidinal satisfactions that some no doubt derive from causing suffering, there is no villain stroking a white cat behind the scenes running things, and we must cure ourselves of our desire to find one.

Notes

1   Fredric Jameson, *The Antinomies of Realism* (Brooklyn and London: Verso Books , 2013), p. 37.
2   Ibid., p. 54.
3   Ibid., p. 140.
4   Ibid., p. 139.
5   Ibid., p. 116.

Missing People
Entanglement, Superposition, and Exhumation as Sites of Indeterminacy

Hito Steyerl

X.

In 1935, Erwin Schrödinger devised an insidious thought experiment. He imagined a box containing a cat, which could be killed at any moment by a deadly mixture of radiation and poison. Or it might not be killed at all. Both outcomes were equally probable. The consequences of thinking through this situation were much more shocking than the initial setup, however. According to quantum theory, there wasn't just one cat inside the box, dead or alive. There were actually two cats: one dead, one alive—both locked into a state of so-called 'superposition'; that is, co-present and materially entangled with one another. This peculiar state lasted as long as the box remained closed.

Macrophysical reality is defined by either/or situations. Someone is either dead or alive. Schrödinger's thought experiment boldly replaced mutual exclusivity with an impossible coexistence—a so-called state of indeterminacy.

But that's not all. The experiment becomes even more disorienting when the box is opened and the entanglement (*Verschränkung*) of the dead and the live cat abruptly ends. At this point, either a dead or a live cat decisively emerges, not because the cat then actually dies or comes to life, but *because we look at it*. The act of observation breaks the state of indeterminacy. In quantum physics, observation is an active procedure. By taking measure and identifying, it interferes and engages with its object. By looking at the cat, we fix it in one of two possible but mutually exclusive states. We end its existence as an indeterminate interlocking waveform and freeze it as an individual chunk of matter.

To acknowledge the role of the observer in actively shaping reality is one of the main achievements of quantum theory. It's not radiation or poison gas that ultimately decides the fate of the cat, but the fact that it is identified, seen, described, and assessed. Being subject to observation provokes the second death of the cat: the one that ends its state of limbo.

X.

According to common logic, a missing person is either dead or alive. But is she really? Doesn't this only apply at the moment when we find out what happened to her? When she turns up or when her remains are identified?

But what, then, is the state of 'missing' itself? Does it take place inside Schrödinger's box, so to speak? Is it being both dead and alive? How can we understand its conflicting desires, to want and to dread the truth at the same time? The urge to both move on and keep hope alive? Perhaps the state of missing speaks of a paradoxical superposition that cannot be understood with the conceptual tools of Euclidian physics, human biology, or Aristotelian logic. Perhaps it reaches out to an impossible coexistence of life and death. Both are materially interlaced in limbo — as long as no observer opens the 'box' of indeterminacy. Which is, in many cases, a grave.

X.

In 2010, Spanish prosecutor Baltasar Garzon brushed up against the state of superposition.[1] Two years prior, he had brought charges against leading officials of the Franco regime, including General Franco himself, for crimes against humanity. He opened investigations into the disappearance and suspected murder of around 113,000 people — mostly Republicans from the Civil War period — as well as the forceful appropriation of 30,000 children. Many of the disappeared ended up in mass graves around the country, which at that time were being patiently dug up by relatives of the disappeared and volunteers. None of the thousands of kidnappings, disappearances, summary executions and killings by starvation or exhaustion had ever been prosecuted legally in Spain. And total impunity had been made legal by a so-called 'amnesty law' in 1977.

Garzon's case was the first to challenge this situation. Predictably, it ran into immediate controversy. One of the many points on which he was challenged was that many of the accused, including Franco himself, were dead. And according to the law, if they were dead then Garzon had no jurisdiction. He found himself in a legal deadlock: he had to assert that the dead were still alive in order to investigate whether they were dead in the first place, and guilty in the second.

This is where superposition comes into play, since a potential legal argument in this case can be derived from Schrödinger's paradigm. Garzon could have argued that one had to get to the point of being able to open Schrödinger's box. Only then could one determine whether the defendants were dead or alive, and until this happened, a state of superposition between life and death had to be assumed. Franco, for instance, had to be proven dead. If not, it had to be assumed that he was in a state of superposition,

until proper observation and measurement could take place. As long as Franco was at least potentially alive, investigations into the crimes of the Franco period could continue.

But the state of superposition not only affected the accused perpetrators. It also determined the legal status of many of the disappeared. As lawyer Carlos Slepoy argued, any disappeared person, regardless of the date of disappearance, had to be assumed to be alive. As long as he or she was in a state of having been kidnapped and not yet found, the crime was ongoing. It could not fall under any statute of limitations. As long the victims weren't proven dead — as long as they were still missing — they were in a state of superposition and indeterminacy. While the crime was lingering, Schrödinger's box remained closed and both a potentially dead missing person and a potentially living missing person were entangled in a paradoxical legal quantum state. This state of indeterminacy enabled the cases to remain open and investigations to proceed.

X.

Schrödinger's mental exercise in indeterminacy echoes another famous thought image: the idea of the two bodies of the king. In 1957, historian Ernst Kantorowicz described how the bodies of medieval kings were split into a natural body and a body politic.[2] While the natural body was mortal, the body politic, which represented the mystical dignity and justice of the realm, was immortal. While the king was in power, both states were superimposed on his body. He incorporated the nation in a body politic that was immortal and immaterial.

In addition, the king also possessed a natural, material body that was subject to passion, foolishness, infancy, and death. The idea of the twin body of the king became one of the defining factors in developing the concept of sovereignty — ruling power incorporated within a body, in which death and eternal life are superposed.

Neither Schrödinger nor his numerous interpreters took into account the fact that in the twentieth century, his thought experiment was uncannily echoed by new experimental forms of asserting sovereignty. The result was a state that no quantum physicist could foresee.

In the twentieth century — the age of genocide, of racism and terror — the superposition of life and death became a standard feature of various forms of government.[3] In these experiments, Schrödinger's 'box' became a site of lethal detention or mass extinction by radiation and poison gas — as in Schrödinger's original setup — or by explosives, which Albert Einstein eagerly added to the quantum list of WMDs.[4]

Schrödinger even went as far as to explicitly mention the name of the poison gas that threatened the cat's life in 1935: hydrocyanic acid. In 1939, hydrocyanic acid was used in a Nazi gas chamber in Poznan to kill disabled people. Later on, it was produced industrially as 'Zyklon B' by a company called Degesch and employed in the gas chambers of all the major extermination camps of the National Socialist empire.

X.

In 2011, I was in the Spanish town of Palencia, where a mass grave from the Civil War was being exhumed on the site of a children's playground. Volunteers rushed to recover as many remains as possible from the roughly 250 people suspected to be buried there, who were summarily shot by Francoist militias. Funding was going to be cut off within days, so every volunteer was given equipment to participate in the excavation. I was assigned a grave in which a baby's coffin sat on top of the bones of a person who was most likely executed. The arm bone of this person revealed perimortem trauma —a wound sustained around the time of death and an indicator of a violent demise.

But why would a baby be buried on top of a murdered Republican? The archaeologist explained that babies who died unbaptized were (or even still are) believed to go to limbo. The limbo of infants has been a subject of discussion in the Roman Catholic Church since the days of Augustine. The question is whether unbaptized infants can be granted salvation, since their original sin isn't purged by baptism. On the one hand, unbaptized people are supposed to go to hell after they die. On the other, deceased babies haven't had time to commit many sins, so it was thought that their punishment should be rather mild. The solution was the limbo of infants.

The limbo of infants — an intermediary state between salvation and damnation, bliss and torture — is thus not just a place of eternal boredom and hopelessness. In limbo the children might even ascend to a state of ultimate happiness by establishing a different vision of things — being unresolved things themselves,

dumped onto the bodies of people shot as terrorists and insurgents. Things superposed onto other things in a cemetery superposed on a children's playground, as the first Spanish republic shines uncomfortably through the second.

The baby was gone. The crumbling coffin was empty. Its remains had possibly been taken along when the bones of the richer people in the cemetery were moved to a new location. Only a tiny finger bone remained, which mixed with the remains of the executed supporter of the Republic.

X.

In 2011, a plaster cast of a skull said to belong to Gottfried Wilhelm Leibniz was put on display in Hannover. But many doubt whether the skull really belonged to the philosopher.

In 1714, Leibniz developed the idea of the monad. According to Leibniz, the world is made of monads, each of which encloses the whole structure of the universe. He calls them 'perpetual living mirror(s) of the universe':

> All is a plenum (and thus all matter is connected together)
> and in the plenum every motion has an effect upon
> distant bodies in proportion to their distance, so that each
> body not only is affected by those which are in contact
> with it and in some way feels the effect of everything that
> happens to them, but also is affected by bodies adjoining
> itself. This inter-communication of things extends to any
> distance, however great. And consequently every body
> feels the effect of all that takes place in the universe, so
> that he who sees all might read in each what is happening
> everywhere, and even what has happened or shall happen,
> observing in the present that which is far off as well in
> time as in place.[5]

But monads also have different degrees of resolution. Some are more clear in storing information, some less. Like monads, bones, skulls and other objects of evidence condense not only their own history, but — in an opaque and unresolved form — everything else as well. They are like hard disks that fossilize not only their own history, but the history of their relations to the world. According to Leibniz, only God is able to read all monads. They are transparent to his gaze alone and remain vague and blurry to ours. As the only being able to read them, God is in all things.

But humans are also able to decipher some layers of monads. The strata of crystalized time in each monad capture a specific relation to the universe and conserve it, as in a long exposure photograph. In this way, we can understand a bone as a monad —or more simply, as an image. But equally, these objects condense the forms of observation that produce them as durable and individual objects, and snap them back into one distinct state of materiality. This also applies to the plaster cast of Leibniz's skull, as well as to the story of its retrieval. Already at the time of its 'recovery', many people doubted whether the skull triumphantly presented as Leibniz's was really his.[6]

> These doubts were exacerbated by the fact that the church
> documents relating to Leibniz's burial had been lost.
> Eventually, on Friday 4 July 1902, the remains under
> the Leibnitian marker were exhumed. On Wednesday
> 9 July 1902, they were examined by one Professor Dr.
> W. Krause, by order of one Herr Waldeyer. Whatever
> casket had occupied the grave was by then entirely rotted
> away and thus left not a clue as to its original occupant.
> Nevertheless, Krause concluded that the skeletal remains
> were indeed those of Leibniz.[7]

While the origin of the skull is contested, the provenance of the cast seems better established:

> The cast was part of the estate of a former NS civil
> servant. His 90 year old widow offered it for sale 15–20
> years ago, along with 3000 books about racial science.
> A report of the Institute for Germanic Volk and Racial
> Sciences in the Gau capital Hannover indicates that
> Leibniz' grave was opened between the end of 1943 and
> the beginning of 1944.[8]

Leibniz, the co-inventor of mathematical probability, might have computed the likelihood that the skull belonged to him. But could he have imagined that the skull was both his and not his?

X.

Probability became the crucial difference between the experi-

ments in political sovereignty and Schrödinger's experiment. In Schrödinger's experiment, the probability that a live cat would emerge from the box was 50:50. But whenever the metaphorical 'box' of political laboratories was opened, this probability would drop to extreme lows. And whatever emerged wouldn't be a cat, but humans — more precisely, corpses upon corpses. The 'box' became a site for the superposition of death upon death, and a factory for the breathtaking multiplication of victims. The twentieth century radically advanced the development of all kinds of weapons of mass destruction. It took the box and turned it inside out so it would spill all over the planet. Why stop at two dead creatures? Why not millions and millions?

Additionally, the twentieth century also perfected observation as a method of killing. Measurement and identification became tools of murder. Phrenology. Statistics. Medical Experimentation. Economies of Death. In his lectures about biopolitics, Michel Foucault described the stochastic calculus that determined life or death.[9] Counting and observing were radicalized to make sure that anything that entered the box died when the box was reopened.

This development also signified the death of the political idea of the two bodies of the king, one dead, one immortal. Now one had to imagine two dead bodies: not only the natural body, but also the body politic. Not only were natural bodies killed in and outside the insidious boxes of sovereignty. The body politic, which was supposed to be immortal, died as well. The idea of a state, nation, or race incorporated within a single body was radically denied by thousands of mass graves — the fosses communes, which were deemed necessary to violently manufacture a 'perfect' and homogenous body politic.

The mass graves thus formed a negative image of the desired incorporation — and its only tangible reality. Any idea of a natural 'organic body' of the nation (race, state) had to be painfully realized by extermination and genocide. The fosse commune *was* the body politic of fascism and other forms of dictatorship. It made perfectly clear that the 'community' that produced it was a 'fausse commune', a complete and disastrous fake vying for legitimacy.

Schrödinger's innocent if eccentric quantum state of indeterminacy was echoed in political laboratories of sovereignty. Here, gaping political limbos were created in which law and exception blurred in deadly superposition, transforming certain death into a matter of probability. Schrödinger's thought experiment brought to light the mass graves that violently ended many possible superpositions and entanglements of humans and things. And the dream of parallel worlds in which incompossible realities coexisted was transformed into the proliferation of possible deaths and the impossibility of any world other than the one that miserably dragged on existing.

X.

As quantum theory predicts, the state of entanglement is transitional. It can even be exceptionally short — a window of opportunity made to be missed. And as mass graves were successively excavated, states of indeterminacy ended too, forcing decisions between the state of life and the state of death, which — the twentieth century being what it was — overwhelmingly fell on the side of death. Missing persons were identified and their remains were reburied or returned to relatives. And as the bones were retransformed into persons and reintroduced into language and history, the spell of the law over them ceased.

But many of the missing remain nameless. The remains of some of them are stored in the anthropology department at the Autonomous University of Madrid, for lack of funding to proceed with DNA testing. This lack of funding is of course connected to the precarious political situation in which this investigation finds itself. The unidentified skulls and bones speak about anything but their names and identities. They show perimortem trauma and indicators of stature, gender, age, and nutrition, but this doesn't necessarily lead to identification.[10] More than anything, the unidentified remain generic, faceless, all mixed up with combs, bullets, watches, other people, animals, or the soles of shoes. Their indeterminacy is part of their silence, and their silence determines their indeterminacy. They maintain an obstinate opaque silence in the face of sympathetic scientists and waiting relatives. As if they chose not to answer to their final interrogators either. Shoot me all over again, they seem to say. I'm not telling. I will not give it away. But what is the thing they refuse to betray?

Perhaps the bones refuse to reenter the world of relatives, family, and property, the world of name and measure, in which skulls are forced to speak of race and rank instead of love and decomposition. Why should they want to reenter an order that

sustained and strengthened itself over their dead bodies? That had to execute them in the first place in order to keep the realm of belonging, faith and knowledge intact? Why should they want to return from the world of naked matter in which they freely mix with the dust of the universe?

This is what the unidentified missing teach us: even as their bones are carefully handled by forensic anthropologists, they staunchly remain things, refusing to be identifiable in the register of human beings. They insist on being things that decline to be named and known — things that claim the state of potentially being both dead and alive. They thus transgress the realms of civil identity, property, the order of knowledge and human rights alike.

X.

In 2011, Hüsnü Yildiz went on a hunger strike to force the exhumation of his brother, who disappeared in 1997 while fighting as a leftist guerilla. His grave had been located in early 2011 among hundreds of other nondescript mass graves in the Kurdish region of Turkey. Thousands of bodies, most killed during the dirty war of the 1990s, are believed to have been dumped into shallow graves, waste dumps and other places of disposal.[11] As more mass graves are discovered every day, Turkish authorities have for the most part refused to open investigations or even recover the remains of the dead. Sixty-four days into Yildiz's hunger strike, the grave where his brother was suspected to be buried was finally excavated. Fifteen sets of remains were recovered, but as authorities have not initiated DNA tests, Yildiz still doesn't know whether the remains of his brother are among them. In the meantime, Yildiz has declared that not only the fifteen people recovered, but also the thousands more missing are his brothers and sisters. The indeterminacy of remains universalizes family relations. They rip the order of family and belonging wide open.

X.

00:15:08:05

Hito Steyerl — I see one box which does not contain remains.

Luis Ríos — Yes this is...

HS – Can you show it to us?

LR – This is a complex case because this came from the cemetery of Toledo, a city near Madrid, and then the relatives with an undertaker of the cemetery, they went to dig in the common grave where they thought their relatives were. So they did that with a shovel and put all the bones in big plastic bags...
So we have a mess of bones and of these shoes, we don't know if they belong to the people killed or to other, like, normal mortality, and they also went to the common grave... But this, we found, it's very common to find, to find personal objects in the excavations.

HS – What sort of objects? Shoes?

LR – This is the heel of a shoe and that is for the shirts, the buttons, some other buttons and some coins... well, metal objects and... But we have found, this is the... for the belt? Yes, the buckle. So for example all this came from one, from skeleton sixty...[12]

X.

But in the twentieth century and beyond, we have almost always waited in vain to access the other quantum state involved in superposition, the state in which the missing would still be alive – not potentially, but actually. Paradoxically alive, as things in a state of entanglement. In which we could hear their voices, touch their breathing skin. In which they would be living things outside the registers of identity, pure language and the utter overwhelming of senses; things superposing on ourselves as things.
They would form a state beyond any statehood – one in which they wouldn't be entangled with their own dead bodies, but with our living ones. And we would no longer be separate entities but things locked in indeterminate interaction – material extimacy, or matter in embrace.
They would drag us to this place where we would become entangled matter, outside of any categories of identification and possession. We would be waveforms leaving behind individuality and subjectivity to become locked in the paradoxical objectivity of quantum realities.

X.

The mass grave that is supposed to contain the remains of my friend Andrea Wolf is located in the mountains south of Van, Turkey. The gravesite is littered with rags, debris, ammunition cases and many fragments of human bone. A charred photo roll I found on site may be the only witness to what happened during the battle that took place there in late 1998.

Even though several witnesses have come forward stating that Andrea and some of her fellow fighters in the PKK were extrajudicially executed after having been taken prisoner, there have been no attempts to investigate this suspected war crime, nor to identify the roughly forty people supposedly buried in the mass grave. No official investigation ever took place. No experts went on site.

No authorized observer can break superposition, not because there were no observers, but because they have not been authorized. It is an incompossible place, incompatible with the existing rules of political realism, constructed by the suspension of the rule of law and aerial supremacy, beyond the realm of the speakable, the visible, the possible. On this site, even blatant evidence is far from being evident.[13] Its invisibility is politically constructed and maintained by epistemic violence. This is the main reason why the pictures on the charred photo roll remain unavailable for now, pushed into a zone of zero probability.[14] Technical means, expert knowledge and political motivation to investigate and analyze them are unavailable.

But these illegible images can also be seen from a different perspective: as poor images, things wrecked by violence and history. A poor image is an image that remains unresolved — puzzling and inconclusive because of neglect or political denial, because of a lack of technology or funding, or because of hasty and incomplete recordings captured under risky circumstances.[15] It cannot give a comprehensive account of the situation it is supposed to represent. But if whatever it tries to show is obscured, the conditions of its own visibility are plainly visible: it is a subaltern and indeterminate object, excluded from legitimate discourse, from becoming fact, subject to disavowal, indifference and repression.

Poor images take on another dimension when they expand into fractional space.[16] They may be blurred 3D scans, cakes of dirt compressing buttons, bones and bullets, burnt photo rolls, dispersed ashes or lost and unintelligible pieces of evidence.[17] Just as commercial, political, and military interests define the resolution of satellite images of the earth's surface, so do these interests define the resolution of the objects buried beneath it. These indeterminate objects are low-resolution monads, in many cases literally materially compressed objects, fossilized diagrams of political and physical violence — poor images of the conditions that brought them into being. Even if they cannot show the extra-judicial executions, political murders or shootings at demonstrations that they might have recorded, they bear the traces of their own marginalization. Their poverty is not a lack, but an additional layer of information, which is not about content but form. This form shows how the image is treated, how it is seen, passed on, or ignored, censored and obliterated.

Even if its content is destroyed, the charred 35mm roll shows what happened to itself as it went up in flames, doused with unknown chemicals, incinerated along with the photographers' dead bodies. It shows the violence of maintaining this particular state of indeterminacy.

Through their material composition, these poor images reach far beyond the sphere of representation and into a world where the order of things and humans, of life, death and identity is suspended, and 'all is a plenum (and thus all matter is connected together)... And consequently every body feels the effect of all that takes place in the universe, so that he who sees all might read in each what is happening everywhere, and even what has happened or shall happen, observing in the present that which is far off as well in time as in place.'[18]

But who is the ominous reader in Leibniz's text? Is he the ultimate observer endowed with unlimited authority? Whoever he is, he is not up to the task.[19] We cannot leave the task of observation to some obscure monotheist idol, who supposedly reads and knows everything. And we do not need to. The zone of zero probability, the space in which image/objects are blurred, pixelated, and unavailable, is not a metaphysical condition. It is in many cases man-made, and maintained by epistemic and military violence, by the fog of war, by political twilight, by class privilege, nationalism, media monopolies and persistent indifference. Its resolution is managed by legal, political and technological paradigms. A bone which would be abject debris in some parts of the world, a poor image mixed with trash and dumped into landfills alongside broken TVs, could be overexposed in others, scanned in HD or 3D, highly resolved, investigated, tested and interpreted

until its mysteries are solved.[20] The same bone can be seen in two different resolutions: once as an anonymous poor image, once as a crystal-clear piece of official evidence.

Positivism is thus another name for epistemic privilege, assumed by official observers who control hi-tech tools of measurement and are authorized to establish facts. But mistaking this privilege for a solution, when it is just proof of superior epistemic resolution, is sloppy and convenient thinking. It not only denies the existence of expanding pockets of zero probability and gaping limbos in the rule of law. It also shields itself from the unsettling thought that everything could be different and that probability cannot reign in contingency.

If Leibniz's omnivisionary male observer is impotent, then justice is blind to resolution. She carefully runs her fingers over the edges, gaps and rifts of rugged and glossy images, of low-resolution monads left in fractional space, registering their tectonic profile, feeling their bruises, fully confident that the impossible can and indeed will happen.

First appeared at 'The Human Snapshot' conference, organized by the LUMA Foundation in collaboration with the Center for Curatorial Studies at Bard College (CCS Bard) in Arles, 2011.

Notes

1 Thank you to Jenny Gil Schmitz, Emilio Silva Barrera, Carlos Slepoy, Luis Ríos, Francisco Etxeberria, José Luis Posadas, Marcelo Esposito for all information relating to this issue and for their generous hospitality. This first part of the text owes very much to discussions with Eyal Weizman.

2 See Ernst H. Kantorowicz, *The King's Two Bodies: A Study in Mediaeval Political Theology* (Princeton NJ: Princeton University Press, 1997).

3 See Giorgio Agamben, *State of Exception*, transl. by Kevin Attell (Chicago IL: University of Chicago Press, 2005) and *Homo Sacer: Sovereign Power and Bare Life*, transl. by Daniel Heller-Roazen (Redwood City CA: Stanford University Press, 1998). See also Foucault (note 8) on biopower.

4 In a letter written in the 1950s.

5 Gottfried Wilhelm Leibniz, *Monadology*, transl. by Robert Latta (Oxford: Oxford University Press, 1898), p. 251.

6 www.gwleibniz.com/leibniz_skull/leibniz_skull.html.

7 Michael Grau, 'Universalgenie Leibniz im Visier der Nazis', in *Berliner Morgenpost*, September 12, 2011.

8 Michel Foucault, *The Birth of Biopolitics: Lectures at the Collège de France*, 1978-1979, transl. by Graham Burchell (Basingstoke UK: Palgrave Macmillan, 2008).

9 Ibid..

10 Luis Ríos, J. I. Ovejero, and J. P. Prieto, 'Identification Process in Mass Graves from the Spanish Civil War', in *Forensic Science International* (June 15, 2010), pp. 27-36.

11 'Discovery of Kurdish Mass Graves Leads Turkey to Face Past', voanews.com and Howard Eissenstat, 'Mass-graves and State Silence in Turkey', March 15, 2011, blog.amnestyusa.org.

12 Interview with Luis Ríos, September 12, 2011.

13 Thank you to Tina Leisch, Ali Can, Necati Sönmez, Şiyar, and many others whose names cannot be mentioned.

14 In the meantime, this text has been redeveloped into part of a joint performance with Rabih Mroué called 'Probable Title: Zero Probability'. I am deeply indebted to Rabih's contributions, especially in his brilliant text 'The Pixelated Revolution', which gives other examples of low-resolution evidence.

15 I discussed some examples of documentary pictures, mainly from Georges Didi-Huberman's essay 'Images malgré tout', in Hito Steyerl, 'Documentarism as Politics of Truth', republicart.net/disc/representations/steyerl03_en.htm.

16 See Jalal Toufic, 'The Subtle Dancer', p. 24: 'a space that is neither two-dimensional nor three-dimensional, but between the two'. Available at d13.documenta.de

17 'Bones of the Disappeared Get Lost Again after Excavation', bianet.org.

18 G.W. Leibniz, op. cit..

19 For him, whatever is the case is necessarily the best of all possible worlds anyway.

20 This applies particularly to the bones of murdered Kurdish individuals, which get extremely different treatment according to whether they were killed during the Anfal operations ordered by Saddam Hussein in Iraq, or by Turkish armed forces and militias during the civil war of the 1990s. The Anfal mass murders were investigated by world-class military specialists and interdisciplinary teams, whereas the Turkish cases were barely investigated at all.

A Transitional Operation

Samuel Vriezen in Conversation with Christian Wolff

For over sixty years, composer Christian Wolff (b. 1935) has worked at the forefront of experimental music — though without ever quite taking the centre stage. In fact, something about his work has made it remain uneasy and elusive in many subtle ways, and not quite classifiable throughout those years. Over the course of his career, one gets the impression that there have been quite a few Wolffs, and that his work has meant different things to different people. Starting at the age of sixteen, he worked in close proximity to composers quite some years his senior, such as John Cage (1912-1992) and Morton Feldman (1926-1987), who would eventually come to be recognized as central figures in the history of American composed music, but who have both repeatedly cited the younger composer as an inspiration. Along with composers of his own generation such as the pianist/composer Frederic Rzewski (b. 1938) and the British composer Cornelius Cardew (1936-1981), he became known for his interest in the relationship between music and politics. Younger generations today know him as an example for new experimental practices but also as a mentor, through his teaching and through the workshops that he has given. Over the years, extremely diverse musicians, such as composer György Kurtag, expert teacher of classical chamber music performance, and the experimental rock group Sonic Youth, have paid homage to his work.

At the same time, his work gives a very different impression than that of the high-technique professionalism one finds in many avant-garde composers of his generation. Wolff did not formally study composition, save for a few weeks of lessons with Cage. A scholar and teacher of classical literature, he never depended on his composing to pay his bills. As a result, he had the luxury of remaining an amateur as a composer — in the sense of someone writing out of love for the art rather than out of professional necessity. Perhaps partly as a result, his scores do not have the look of technical polish or grandeur that suggests academically trained sophistication. In Wolff, one looks in vain for the grand architecture of Karlheinz Stockhausen, for the advanced mathematical control over acoustic webs and eruptions of Iannis Xenakis, for the extremely subtle and detailed instrumental sounds of Helmut Lachenmann, or for the conceptual rigor and brilliant clarity of Cage. What you get instead are quirky patchworks of ideas, pieces that surprise and delight mostly by their odd twists and turns. A music full of luminous details that don't quite add up, that simultaneously feel familiar and out of joint. Also, quite opposite to the conventional idea of the classical composer who writes down exactly how every note in the piece should be played (loudness, articulation, phrasing) and thereby facilitates an easy performance by industry standard styles of musicianship, in Wolff, you often get baffling notations that look like half-finished sketches, with essential information not being provided — that is, left up to the performers themselves to provide. Playing Wolff means thinking along with Wolff. Some works do not look like scores at all, but more like curiously eccentric games that people might play using sounds; Wolff even pioneered the prose score format, in which all musical notation is replaced by purely verbal instructions that can be interpreted by anybody, regardless of their level of musical literacy.

Because of his unusual career development, Wolff may be thought to belong to two different generations of composers. On the one hand, starting in his teenage years, he was part of the group of composers around John Cage in New York in the 1950s, exploring a high-modernist aesthetics of strange sounds and rhythms, chance, and indeterminacy. This was a group of composers who were interested in freedom, though understood primarily as a freedom of sounds to 'be themselves', as Cage's famous slogan would have it. This is freedom from the necessity to mean something, or to conform to some traditional style or theory. It is a freedom first of all concerned with aesthetics, but it may lead into political concerns too — in the case of John Cage, it combined with an interest in anarchism, and a vision of a world in which sounds, people, and actions could exist together, 'interpenetrate', in a non-centralized way. For other composers, however, 'freedom' ultimately led to very different points of view — Feldman, for instance, ended up celebrating an intuitive approach and a sonic aestheticism that, visionary and original as it may be, seems completely apolitical, and could even be interpreted to be conservative.

Wolff himself became increasingly politicized over the course of the fifties and sixties, in a process that was less ideologically motivated than issue-driven. A pacifist, he found himself opposing American neo-colonial expansionism and the Vietnam War. As a teacher, he found himself helping non-privileged kids in poor black neighbourhoods, which made him aware of the civil rights movement. And through his wife, Holly Nash, to whom he was married in 1965, he developed an interest in feminism. These interests came to a head in the late sixties after the Paris revolts and the Berkeley student uprising, with Wolff joining in the increased politicization that was taking place all over the academic culture which he was professionally part of, leading him to study Marx and Maoism, which for a time seemed to be offering an alternative to the ossified European communist parties of those days. In this, his development was in step with composers of his own generation, including Rzewski and Cardew. The latter had been an assistant to the German composer Karlheinz Stockhausen, and was a co-founder of the British Scratch Orchestra, an ensemble for the performance of experimental compositions in which both trained and untrained musicians could participate. Musically, these composers share an interest in improvisation and in non-classical musical materials, including rock music and political songs.

There was, however, to be some tension between the values of these two generations. Cardew himself had been a European modernist, but his increasing interest in the proletarian struggle led him to renounce his former musical interests in a gesture of Maoist self-criticism, publishing the fiercely polemical *Stockhausen Serves Imperialism* in 1974. Likewise, the aesthetics of John Cage came to be targeted by Cardew for adhering to contentless bourgeois aesthetic values and failing to produce a music that would be useful for the proletarian struggle. Wolff himself, however, never was willing to go that far.[1] Recognizing the need for music to be political and to criticize the aestheticist tendencies in Cage, he never quite wanted to give up the ideals of liberty for the sake of those of a pure collectivity. Finding himself between camps, his music proceeded to seek out a middle ground position in pieces which would be clearly experimental in their formal organization, yet also contain explicit political materials, such as texts or tunes that belong to the tradition of worker's struggles, for example in *Wobbly Music* (1975-1976). Also, the processes of learning the music and of deciding how to play and interpret the compositions together as an ensemble form a political dimension as models for organization in pieces such as *Changing the System* (1972-1973) or the *Exercises* (1973-1975). Political undercurrents and references would remain part of his musical vocabulary, up until the orchestral works of the recent decades of his composing, the latest of which is called *individuals, collective* (Hicks and Asplund 2012).

In recent years, there have been some remarkable revitalizations in leftist politics of the perennial debate between anarchism and communism. For example, the Occupy movement positioned itself between values of radical anti-capitalism and of radically non-hierarchical organization, which made its politics difficult to interpret for many commentators. Similarly, in the works of a leading thinker who has in recent years laid claim to the term 'communism', Alain Badiou, we find a clear post-Leninist, post-Maoist disavowal of the idea of taking over the State, while he at the same time explicitly elevates the value of equality over that of freedom. However, without Party or State to organize this equality, these communist values become something that have to come out of some sort of non-centralized organization, and so should, practically speaking, involve some notion of freedom as well. These days, then, determining the precise relationship between 'equality' and 'freedom' seems to be an important site for thinking politics.

As a composer who has been touched by the musical approach of John Cage as well as the philosophy of Alain Badiou, I have a long-standing fascination with these tensions between equality and freedom, and those between a bottom-up and a bird's-eye view of organization. In Badiou, one finds a communist appeal to equality that rejects following the grand names of leaders;[2] in Cage, one encounters an anarchist who consistently stresses values of discipline and non-intention. It seems to me that these two approaches are compatible to a large extent,[3] and also that the work of Christian Wolff might provide for a key to the relationship between them.

This has to do with the importance in Wolff's music of musical action and interaction. My own first deep engagement with the music of Christian Wolff was being part of a performance of his work *For One, Two or Three People* (1964). This is a work in which no specific sounds are notated, only actions (such as playing a long note, or a sequence of different pitches), which can occur in an indeterminate order and allow many freedoms for interpretation. However, the actions are interrelated, as performers are constantly asked, in many different ways, to coordinate certain actions with whatever it is other performers happen to be doing, which may be something entirely unforeseen because of the piece's indeterminacy. As a result, the score does not give a general structure to be executed, but instead organizes a series of indeterminate dependencies between players. At every moment of the piece, then, all performers are equally responsible, not only for their own actions, but also for the functioning of the ensemble and for the form of the piece as a whole. Here, there is a complete equality of responsibilities, while at the same time there are great individual freedoms in the precise interpretation of the notations (for example, each part can be performed by any instrument). A score like this ends up functioning like a diagnostic device for the ensemble that performs it, as it forces you as a performer to re-examine what your relationship is to the other performers, and to their musical personas. In that way it truly is a piece for *people*, as the title indicates, rather than for instruments. It is also great fun to play, the unpredictability of the structure that you explore as you perform it being as surprising and delightful for the performers as it is for the audience.

The experience of working on this piece has deeply influenced my own approach to musical composition, and so it seemed like a good idea to talk to the composer himself, and see how he thinks nowadays about equality and freedom, or about the tension between experiment or aestheticism and political struggle, how they played out in the seventies and how those concerns have developed in his work since then. An opportunity presented itself in February 2013, as Wolff and Rzewski were the main guests at a music festival in Dijon, France that was devoted to their work and to political music, under the title *Changing the System*.

The festival included a recital by Rzewski in which he played works by Wolff, Cardew and himself. It included a concert by the French Ensemble Dedalus of Wolff's music, including a new work, simply called *Dijon*, and some performances of works of Rzewksi's and Wolff's from the 1960s. A panel was held, chaired by a young French philosopher, who attempted to outline a politics of experimental music by relating the notion of 'noise' in experimental music to the concept of 'dissensus' in the work of philosopher Jacques Rancière, by which an 'aesthetic regime' could be interrupted. The idea here is that the 'noisiness' of much experimental music disrupts the norms of officially accepted harmonic musical languages, and thereby introduces sounds that can't be interpreted or claimed by existing (musical) power structures, and that this radically breaks open the field of artistically valid perceptions. This would constitute a form of politics, even of democratic politics, as it creates a music that can be perceived and enjoyed and interpreted by everybody to suit his or her own situation or needs. In that sense, the artistic use of noise could be interpreted as the contribution of experimental music to achieving equality.

However, during the discussion, the composers themselves turned out to be somewhat sceptical of such an equation of art and politics, and insisted that their music making was not to be seen as inherently having political effects. As Rzewski observed, he had seen very little evidence that his music had ever had a serious effect on people's political convictions and actions. If anything, music and politics seem to be drifting apart further, as he observed that these days, in big political demonstrations, hardly any new political songs are heard that could become part of the collective consciousness.

Yet I had come to discuss the politics of music, even to explore what the concept of justice might mean within the context of Wolff's musical aesthetics, expecting that somebody whose work has so explicitly addressed both political issues and the politics of ensemble playing itself would have something to say about that. Clearly, however, he was not going to make any grandiose claims, and perhaps the whole notion of aesthetic justice itself might prove too abstract. Indeed, the night before my interview with Wolff was scheduled to take place there had already been a minor confrontation with Rzewski over this exact point. Always enjoying a provocation, he had asked upon my mentioning of the term aesthetic justice: 'What the hell is that supposed to mean?' My answer was that I was hoping to find out, too. Then he told us how one day, most likely in the sixties or seventies, he and Morton Feldman were walking on the street in New York. Rzewski was talking about some artistic-political point, when suddenly the aesthete Feldman interrupted him: 'You know what your problem is? You believe in justice. There is no justice!' To my ears, this sounded almost like a statement of poetics: the aesthetic craftsman Morton Feldman, for whom freedom first of all means letting sound proceed according to its own logic and composing intuitively, rejecting the overly intellectualist idealism of a younger Marxist composer. However, when the next day I started the interview with Wolff discussing the anecdote, he came up with a somewhat different interpretation. Asking him whether he would agree with Feldman's remark, Wolff said:

In the abstract sense, yes. But I'm trying to think what
Feldman really meant by saying that. I think maybe
what he meant was you can't expect to get justice. Which
doesn't exclude the possibility that there is some larger
justice out there, depending on how you understand
justice. I've a feeling Frederic was complaining, and
Feldman was saying, there's no point complaining, just
do what you have to do, and see what happens.

At first, this surprised me. Surely, an intellectual with such a clear leftist point of view should believe in justice? Wolff had been interested in Maoism. In a 1973 talk, he had brought up the aesthetics of Mao's *Yenan Forum,* which called for critical thinking about the level of complexity that new art should have when the purpose is to serve a proletarian audience, and Wolff had compared those positions with some polemical views about music in Plato's dialogues, which discuss the pernicious effects of a 'new music' that is needlessly refined and complicated. These critiques would combine to provide a critique of contemporary art music. So much of it seemed to disconnect artistic content (compositional construction, in Plato: melodic refinements) from real, social content (social struggle, in Plato: forming a support for the words of the text).[4] Now, for somebody using Plato, for whom the Good had an absolute and eternal existence, it is strange not to believe in the existence of Justice. But Wolff's position was always more refined. If justice does not exist, that is so because it always has to be created — it has to be brought to the context within which one operates. Wolff's Platonism, and indeed his Maoism, were far from the inhumane, monstrous theoretical abstractions that conservative interpretations would have them be. Instead, they were fully practical.[5] Typically, when he did set a Maoist propaganda text to music in the 1972 piece *Accompaniments* for a speaking pianist, he chose as his text an account by a veterinarian and his wife dealing with daily problems related to sanitation which were seen from a political perspective, rather than some abstruse piece of political theory.[6]

Wolff consistently stresses doing what you can within the situation in which you find yourself over any grand theories. Politics for him is fully situated, and in his case, that means it is related to his work as a teacher and as a composer. His first involvement with the Civil Rights movement coming out of teaching kids

in poor black neighbourhoods is one example. Later, teaching at
universities, it led him to join political groups and protests on the
campus, but also to apply insights out of Marxist theory to readings of Euripides and Plato. Musically, it means dealing with the
situation in which you find yourself as a musician: how you deal
with music-making itself, but also with the audience.

Samuel Vriezen — Did your political activity have an effect
on the music you were doing?

Christian Wolff — In the seventies, we would use texts that
had political implications, and were most concerned that
they were somehow going to appear in a musical context
that wasn't going to undercut those texts, or would
somehow block it. And that meant a kind of music which
would be recognizable to other people as music.
　　　　So we suddenly decided that we should make
a music that was not so esoteric as this avant-garde
stuff we were doing, that should be more accessible,
that whatever politics were in the music would be more
available to more people. Now, this was also the time
when completely non-political composers were suddenly
discovering modality, were returning to harmonic
systems, and all the rest. There was this whole neo-
romantic movement at the time, so there's a combination
of music history and political musical history that comes
together in a weird way.
　　　　But we were quite explicit about the need to make
a music that was not self-enclosed, that was outgoing, and
that had the possibility of at least interesting people who
might not have otherwise come to new music concerts,
and in which there might be some political content. Or
the music could be used for some political occasion.
Frederic might do a concert at a gathering of a union
organization, playing *The People United*,[7] and still people
might be a little bit surprised. The paradoxical case
was Nono,[8] who didn't change his style, but still made
La Fabbrica Illuminata. When that was performed, the
workers for whom it was performed were very polite
about it, but I'm sure they could not in any way relate to
it whatsoever; that stuff is really crazy. Whereas Frederic

was trying to make a music that they might relate to. Cornelius went a step further. But he did it in a way that seemed really forced somehow. That's the way he was. He pushed himself to the next point, whether or not it really suited him. He tried to make a kind of pop music with political content, for which there at least was the precedent of folk music, of political folk music, which we were all also interested in and tried to relate to in some way. Cornelius actually formed a band where they would sing traditional political songs, mostly Irish ones, and then they got new ones which were suitable to the issues of the day.

SV – But you had the idea that what he did was a bit forced, so it didn't really catch on?

CW – Well that's the question. To write a good pop song is a skill too, and it's not one for which we were trained. On the other hand, Cornelius was willing to give up everything in order to do that, and that's quite remarkable. Completely radically changed his style. I was with him in Berlin, and we were going to go out to eat, and he made a special point of not going to some rather nicer restaurant; we went to some working class restaurant where the food was rather awful, but he felt he should be in there eating it with these other folks. So, you have to say this for him, he's completely consistent about it.

There was one particular situation which was quite painful. It was in Berlin, 1974, where Cardew had been in Berlin on a DAAD[9] grant two previous years and had done a lot of political activism, especially around one issue, which was a public clinic that was going to be discontinued and turned into an artist's centre. Classic! It was in Kreuzberg, which at the time was a working class neighbourhood, mostly Turkish. The left took up that cause, and tried to block the cultural authorities from doing this. And Cornelius actually wrote a very beautiful song in connection to that, which is in the political songbooks of the period.[10]

There was a German composer, Erhard Grosskopf, who's also into these political things, and

Frederic was around, and we decided to do a concert
to raise money for this cause. Which was really quite
contradictory, because we were all being paid by the
DAAD, who were really pissed off with us for doing so.
But anyway, we did it. And then the question was where
to do it, and we did it in this pop music/jazz/folk club.
Fairly large, kind of noisy, but where you could get a beer
and sit at tables and somebody would go and play. And
we all made an effort; we decided we really had to make a
music which would work in a context like that. And there
was even a rock group available. I made a piece for this
rock group, a song based on words by Rosa Luxemburg
– the idea is so crazy! And Frederic did something, and
Cornelius. It was a disaster. It was a complete disaster.
These people hated the music; they shouted out at us, it
was a fiasco.

SV – You made an attempt to go into the musical
vernacular...

CW – Yes, and it didn't work, at all.

SV – It's funny, because later on, of course, you worked
with Sonic Youth.

CW – Well, that's a different world. And that had nothing
to do with politics. But if I had come on with Sonic
Youth, or the equivalent of Sonic Youth at that time, it
probably would have worked. The rock band was not very
good. And we had no rehearsal time, there were these
technical issues – I think if we had been more together, it
might have been okay.
  But something happened there which was really
interesting. The song that I mentioned, that Cornelius
wrote – it was a political folk song. And he wrote
variations on it for piano, and he played it. And as he
started, people in the audience started to sing in, because
they knew the song. But then he went on into these
variations, and then they couldn't follow it anymore, and
the whole thing collapsed! That was almost, you know,
the exemplary situation. Total contradiction. Even though

the music that he made had a very accessible style, kind of quasi-romantic, Beethoven style... but for that audience...

Clearly, musical language as such is no guarantee that some music will be politically effective — or even that it will communicate in the intended way at all. The assumptions of the classical concert form itself, which are needed to make it logical to listen to lots of variations after you have heard the tune itself, here were an impediment to successful communication. The didacticism of such a set-up has to end up a failure, since it does not sufficiently take into account the freedom of the audience *not* to understand the musical language, or the musical ritual that is being offered. Involving people within the musical process on a level that could be meaningful in any way, let alone on the political level, must involve much deeper notions of freedom than having them simply be in the passive position of a proletariat that has to be enlightened by an elite. To activate them, into musical participation or proletarian struggle, must also mean to already presume their liberty.

Following this line of thinking, I decided to address the relationship between equality and liberty directly. This led into the tight connection that exists in the work of Wolff between practice, philosophy, composing and teaching.

> **SV** — More generally, there's the possibility of a tension between values of liberty, of being free to be the person you want, and values of equality, by which we all get to have the same possibilities, but which implies an ordering of society. Again, those might imply different thinking. Since both drives are part of your musical work and politics, I wonder how you relate to that?
>
> **CW** — What's the term I like to use... accessibility. Everyone should have a chance to be able to do what they want, what they think they want, on the one hand. In the States, still, black kids don't finish school in much larger numbers than white kids. Has to do with all kinds of social issues. Obviously you can do something about that. It will take money, it will take organization, it will take dedicated people and so forth, but something could be done. On the other hand, it doesn't guarantee that

whoever has new educational opportunities will be able
to do much with them. There will be some who otherwise
might not make it. A very smart kid who lives in a bad
neighbourhood might even get shot, whereas if you take
him out of that neighbourhood... On the other hand, that
particular kid is an exception; out of twenty there may
just be one like that, and the others may just be ordinary
people, and they'll do whatever it is that will make a life
for them. So on the one hand, the opportunities should
be very equal; on the other hand, you recognize that
people have very different capacities. And ideally, each
of those capacities should be realized to the greatest
extent possible.

This, by the way, is straight out of Plato's *Republic*.
I mean, he uses it as a justification for a class system,
which is a little bit more uncomfortable. Because he
assumes there will be an elite, and the elite will control
everything. So that's more problematic.

SV – That also goes back to an idea that there exists an
ideal organic organization of society.

CW – Right. And somehow this thing will come out
that everybody will be functioning in what is their
best capacity.

SV – Interestingly, Plato is using musical metaphors, even
comparing such ideal organization to musical harmony.[11]
Perhaps if somebody like John Cage is stressing the
importance of discipline in relation to his work, he's
talking about something similar?

CW – Yes, I think so. When you talk about freedom,
that's a very problematical issue. Cage is a very good
example from the aesthetic point of view. There's this
familiar image that people have of Cage that since he's
an anarchist, anything goes, and you don't really have to
pay attention to the score, you just do whatever you feel
like doing. And that's when Cage turned around and said:
'This is very important, you have to do exactly
what it says.'

SV – But if freedom only becomes possible on the basis of discipline, you get into the paradoxes of Plato's *Republic.*

CW – Yeah, you have to impose discipline. Now Cage's notion would be that the discipline has to be self-imposed. But you have to teach that.

I mean, it's not obvious to everybody. As you know when you raise children, they don't automatically do the right thing, they go crazy, they'll do this and that and you have to say, no I'm sorry, at dinner time we'll all sit at the table and eat together. You can't go off and start playing now because you feel like that. So obviously there has to be some structural matrix within which you function.

SV – In Cage, the structural matrix is usually extremely precisely defined in the score. This brings me to your music, because you tend to under-define responsibilities. You leave a lot open to performer freedom. At the same time, you do recognize that there is the necessity for teaching and for discipline, and I wonder how you see that tension?

CW – There is an element of idealism in what I'm doing. I'm hoping that people who want to engage with my music will be serious to begin with and will not just want to do anything. Or put it this way, are willing to undergo the kinds of discipline you need to undergo in order to do the music. But those disciplines are much vaguer. In Cage, as you say, it's very precise. Whereas in my case, it varies.

What I like to do in scores is to run a gamut between very precise determination and complete freedom. You don't have consistently the one or the other. And then the whole spectrum in between, various degrees of my control, or of things that you have to observe, up to the point where there's nothing you have to observe, coming from where it's everything that you have to observe. It's a teaching strategy. You discover the range of possibility within a free situation. In some cases, you have to just do this, no question, just do that. And then suddenly you're in a situation of "do anything". But when you come to the point where you do anything you have

had as it were the experience of preparation. The problem
with letting people do anything is that they really do not
know what to do at that point, but if you sort of prepare
them for that, by specifying various degrees of what they
might do, then they have a notion of what they might
do when in fact they don't have any specification. So my
music isn't really as free as it looks in some ways.

SV – You have a reputation for refusing to tell performers
what to do, to answer questions, basically.

CW – Right. If they assume I have some image in my
head as to how it should sound, I don't want to encourage
that. I remember being shocked really, long ago when I
used to hang out with pianists a lot, because it's when I
thought I was going to become a pianist. And these were
mostly traditional pianists. There was some young person
who was quite gifted technically and so forth, and he had
a gig, he was going to play the Liszt *First Piano Concerto*,
and he went and got a bunch of recordings of it and
listened to them, to see how it should go. And I thought:
'No! What are you doing, this is totally wrong.'

SV – But if you're working with an ensemble, like
Ensemble Dedalus playing *Dijon* just yesterday, how do
you see your own position, when you're sitting in on the
rehearsals? You don't tell them much about how to do it.

CW – It depends. If I hear something I don't like, I will
first of all check that they're doing it correctly. And more
often than not, there's some misunderstanding of the
score. Or else they just decided to do something that I
don't like, I mean that's pretty simple.

SV – For some people the fact that you don't say much
can be a bit of a frustration.

CW – I know, that drives them crazy. One way I deal
with that is that I say, "Just play the notes." I think
usually, they worry about what is it they should be
expressing, and then I think just do the notes, see

what happens and let the music as it were find its own expression. Now, obviously it's subjective. I have my preferences, no question. And then it's a matter of judging to what extent is the performer doing what they're doing because of some kind of conviction of their own. Is it the way they are, the way they do things, or is it because they're not really into it seriously? If that's the case, then I try to improve.'

SV – Then the teacher in you awakens.

CW – Exactly. On the other hand, if it's just what this person does, then I'll take it. Because that's what in a rough way you could call self-expression. But filtered through all this other stuff. And that's fine, that's good. You go hear five pianists play the same piece, and what kind of musicians they are will be very evident from the way they do the piece.

SV – So you tend to interpret practice, both in politics and in music, in terms of teaching?

CW – Yeah. Teaching is very important. And it's a certain kind of teaching. It's not lecturing. You don't make pronouncements *ex cathedra*. It's what we call Socratic teaching, question and answer. In other words, it's a teaching where you try to activate the student rather than tell them what to do. Obviously sometimes you do have to tell them what to do; if there's information that they don't have, you've got to give it to them. But the best kind of teaching is to get people to think, and to do it themselves.

SV – What do you think of the authoritarian position of the teacher? You invoke Socrates. He is always speaking from the position of somebody who might not know the truth as such, but at least knows that you are not there yet. Which can be a manipulative position to put yourself in.

CW – Yeah. From one point of view that's almost inevitable. You are the one in authority, you have

control – you give students grades, which are important
to them. Plus, you're older. Those are givens, you might
say. On the other hand, of course you know more. You
have more experience. You may not be smarter, you
may find students smarter than you are, but who simply
don't have had as much time as you have to collect the
information and process it etcetera, so you try to help.
But it's true. That's the danger of the student-teacher
relationship, that the teacher is the authority.

SV – Can you reconcile that with the idea of justice
and equality?

CW – I think so. Maybe in a simple way, which is that
the student will leave you. Your authority does not extend
indefinitely. And therefore the student will be released,
and will do whatever they're going to do, and you no
longer have any control over it.

SV – And how does that relate to the situation with a
score, and a composer?

CW – The music is out there, people do with it what they
are going to, and I can't control that. And that's a good
thing. I'm not always happy about that, because some
people will do weird things to the scores, but yes, you
have to let go. Teaching is always a transitional operation.
Maybe that's the key.

SV – Is it a transitional operation for your own position as
a teacher at the same time?

CW – It could be. Famously, teachers learn a lot, too.
Partly because you have to prepare yourself, you have
to learn. I made a special point of this, because I was
in three different departments, which sort of happened
partly by accident. I was in classics, I was in music and I
was in comparative literature. And what that meant was
that I had to do a wide variety of courses. The standard
model of teaching is that so-and-so is a specialist in
seventeenth-century English poetry, and that's basically

what they teach. Which means they're going to teach the same thing over and over again for twenty years, and that to me was a total nightmare. So the idea was that I might teach the course on Greek tragedy one year, but I would do different things for the next two years, and by the time I came back to it, I might have new ideas. In some ways it's not efficient because I had to start all over again — well, obviously not all over again, but I do reread these things and think again. So it kept me awake, and that was good.

Thus, the balance between freedom and equality is to be found in self-discipline, the conditions for which can be helped by teaching, provided the teaching itself is primarily a transitional operation that accompanies and opens up the spaces for liberty, for students or performing musicians alike. If there is a sense of justice in the work of Wolff, it must reside in this transitional process of developing self-discipline. Something that empowers you as a student, or a musician, to do the right thing in whatever contingent circumstance you may eventually come to find yourself. Such a notion is completely consistent with the idea that justice as such does not exist as a given thing in the world, but only as something one can work towards, doing the best you can do given the circumstances.

Still, this seems like a process that functions within small circuits. And we cannot expect everybody who is interested in music to be a dedicated performer themselves. Towards the end of our conversation, I tried getting back to the relationship between musicians (and composer) and the broader audience, for an idea of how experimental musical knowledge might be transferred beyond its primary boundaries. Also, I was curious how Wolff's perception of the audience question had developed since the seventies.

> **SV** — Continuing with the question of audience, in that time you were very concerned with trying to find this more accessible musical language, but that turned out to be problematic. Then, if I read interviews with you from the nineties, your ideas about the political potential of music seem much more modest than in the seventies.

CW – Well, in some ways it goes way back. When I was starting in the fifties, the audience response, at least the audience that would come from a musical background, was very negative. It was really a confrontational situation. So I was used to a very negative feeling in a concert situation. And I decided just not to worry about it. Because I figured there is nothing I can do about it, and I'm not going to change my music. My music is what it is, and if they don't like it, okay, that's too bad. So I decided, you can't think about the audience. You just have got to do what you're going to do, and hope for the best. And then of course you're never going to tell who's going to be there, you have no idea. You might by some weird accident have a bunch of older people who came to hear Brahms, and instead they get Wolff or Cage – you can't predict that. On the other hand, you might have a bunch of kids who just came in off the streets and are interested, ah this is kind of cool, you know, there's no way to control that. So you just have to relax about it.

SV – So what would you say is nowadays the role, or what would you like an audience to do, or to produce, so to say? Why in fact the concert form, why do we need an audience? Before, comparing with the teaching situation, you were very much talking about the relation between the composer and the musicians, and that seems to be a very important nucleus of the musical process. So what is the audience to do in this constellation?

CW – Well it's nice to have one. Music seems to me a social activity. Cage at some point said that your piece is not finished until it's performed. In other words, until it becomes part of the social situation. You may only perform for one person, but it moves out. That's just a given. And then, my feeling now is just, you do what you can, I write music with the best quality that I can produce, and then we just have to see what happens. I don't have to do it for millions, get famous and rich.

But still, you want to do it for more than a little coterie of five people. And somehow, in a weird way, that seems to be happening. One of the things that's

very encouraging was for years, we didn't have much of
an audience, but now, in New York, we play the small
venues, but we always pack them out. It's a recent thing,
maybe from the last ten, fifteen years. And what's really
interesting is that three quarters of the audience is under
thirty or is thirty-ish. And that's very pleasing, that there's
a whole generation out there that is interested. I mean,
you'd think — Wolff, that's last century, that's sort of
history, forget it, we want what's now. But no. This stuff
somehow seems to have something in it which interests
them. It's very encouraging. Makes it worthwhile. There's
a kind of demand. It's all very modest. What I think of
as the whole situation of experimental music seems to
me to have fallen into a kind of niche, which is like folk
music, or even jazz. I mean, these are not highly popular
genres by any means, but they carry on. They have their
tradition, they have their musicians, some of them very
good, they have their audiences. What more do you want?

SV — Do you still feel this has a kind of political — well,
I won't use the word impact, but importance?

CW — I think so, just by the fact that it's there. I still like
to talk about experimental music, even though many
people would say that it's a non-category now. These days,
the formula that I come up with is that experimental
music, quite apart from its actual technical procedures
and all that, is a kind of music which suggests to people
the possibility of change. That things don't have to be
the way they are, to the extent that the way they are is no
good. So you kind of make a model, if you will. You do
this kind of music, it's done in this kind of open way, and
there are things in there that some people like to listen
to, maybe other things that they do not relate to so well.
Also, witnessing how these musicians work together, and
that somehow that communitarian spirit of the music
conveys itself to the audience, and suggests to them this is
different, not even like Boulez or some high-glitzy, high-
end modern music, never mind pop music or something
that's commercially viable. So it's a kind of modest,
underground, alternative image of things.

SV – Which keeps the idea of change alive.

CW – Exactly. Now it's not much, but...

SV – And going back to justice?

CW – It's part of that image, part of that notion. As I say, you do what you can. And there may not be a whole lot you can do. Some people get very pessimistic, but I'm not quite so despairing. I like to hope, I mean, hope is unreasonable, but it's necessary.

Notes

1 The episode is recounted more fully in Michael Hicks and Christian Asplund, *Christian Wolff* (Champaign IL: University of Illinois Press, 2012).

2 See for example Alain Badiou, *La relation énigmatique entre philosophie et politique* (Meaux : Germina, 2011).

3 For a more extensive exploration of this theme, see Samuel Vriezen 'Rituelen van de Contingentie', in Ernst van den Hemel and Joost de Bloois (eds.), *Alain Badiou. Inesthetiek: filosofie, kunst, politiek* (Amsterdam: Octavo, 2012). An English version of the text exists and, at the time of writing, is due to be published in the online journal, *Theory & Event*.

4 See Hicks and Asplund, op. cit. p. 58.

5 Of course, at the time when he was using Maoist materials, like many Western Mao-enthusiasts, Wolff was unaware of the repressive politics that the Cultural Revolution had ended up as, in Chinese reality. During the interview, Wolff mentioned that Maoist politics 'seemed at the time, [a] very enlightened and intelligent and useful way. And not until later did we realize what a horror show that all was, really dreadful.'

6 For a discussion, see a.o.: Christian Wolff, *Cues: Writings & Conversations / Hinweise: Schriften und Gespräche* (Cologne: MusikTexte, 1998) p. 134.

7 *The People United Will Never Be Defeated*, Rzewski's 1975 virtuoso piano variations on a Chilean communist protest song, combining a Beethoven-like large-scale form with political references, modernist styles, as well as improvisation and stylistic references to popular music.

8 Luigi Nono (1924-1990), Italian composer and Marxist, associated with the European post-war avant-garde circles of the Darmstadt School. His works are characterized by a highly refined sonic sensibility and a sense of discontinuity and fragmentation, as well as being motivated by deep, abstract political ideas. *La Fabbrica Illuminata* is an electro-acoustic work from 1964, which had been performed for factory workers. According to Nono himself, the noisy elements of the work did not prompt any discussions over musical esthetics; rather, the workers noted that the noises were not half as bad as the sounds they were accustomed to working to in their normal factory conditions, and so helped them become more aware of their labor conditions.

9 DAAD: Deutscher Akademischer Austauschdienst, an agency organizing academic and artistic international exchange programs within Germany.

10 Cornelius Cardew: *Bethanien Song* (1974).

11 See book VI of Plato's *The Republic*.

The Invention of Aesthetic Law

An Experiment on the Aesthetic Horizon and the Art of Living Beautifully

Gerald Raunig

The Aesthetic Horizon

In 1750, Alexander Gottlieb Baumgarten published the first part of his *Aesthetica,* thus founding the philosophical discipline of aesthetics. In the very first sentence, Baumgarten describes aesthetics as *ars pulcre cogitandi,* the art of thinking beautifully. From the beginning, aesthetics was not solely a theory of sensuous cognition and a philosophical classification of the perception of the beautiful, but rather also a search for a different way of thinking. The 'art of thinking beautifully' is not simply aestheticism, a mannerism of the philosopher, or the way one thinks and talks about beauty. Rather it is a technique, a skill, an art of thinking beautifully in the sense that this is a completely different and special way of thinking.

'Thinking beautifully' — the beautiful is not intended here as an adjectival supplement and subordination, but rather as an adverbial, therefore wilful, autonomous quality of an 'inferior' thinking that eludes logic, the 'superior capability of cognition' and joins it at the same time as its dark, obscure, confusing side — and even goes before it in a certain sense. The thinking involved here is not simply beautiful, but rather it emerges in a beautiful way. Aesthetics as the art of thinking beautifully means more than 'beautiful' thinking or thinking about beauty; it attempts to break open thinking and to newly imagine it, reinvent.

For Baumgarten, the starting and friction surfaces are the zones of cognition of what is dark and confusing. With a stance of apparent devotion, the inventor of aesthetics approaches the hierarchical tree pattern of the Leibnizian levels of cognition, in order to acknowledge it and to undermine it at the same time. He does so by introducing a philosophical concept, which he takes up from the canon of epistemology and simultaneously removes it from its contemporary use. This concept is that of the horizon. In Paragraph 6 of the preliminary remarks of his *Aesthetica*[1], Baumgarten already remarks on one of the possible objections to the assumption of aesthetics as its own field of cognition: 'One may object to our science that the sensuous, imaginations, fairytales, the confusions of passions etc. are unworthy of the philosophers and lie beneath their horizons.'

But what does this *infra horizontem*, 'beneath the horizon of the philosophers', mean? Obviously there are 'lower', 'dark' things that are not only unworthy of philosophers, but also threaten to elude them. Baumgarten responds first to the objection to his new sphere of cognition: 'A philosopher is a human being among human beings, and it is not seemly for him to believe such a large part of human cognition is not his proper sphere.' In the same passage, the lecture transcript provides the ironic image of the philosopher as a cliff that rises high above the clouds — sublimely above all that is sensual. What is below the clouds, below the horizon, is not worthy of his sublimeness. Yet at the same time, he does not see it either. This blind spot of the philosopher as a specialist in reason is a first indication of Baumgarten's interest in what is dark and confusing, as well as of his subversive strategy.

Baumgarten continues to use the term of 'superior cognition' for reason and that of 'inferior cognition' for sensuous cognition. Implicitly, however, this hierarchy tips in the course of his argumentation, and the vertical arrangement becomes horizontal. And this is clearly expressed in Baumgarten's use of the concept of the horizon. For Baumgarten the horizon is no longer only a line, a homogeneous boundary of human cognition or a boundary between forms of cognition, but rather a sphere (*sphaera*).[2] For this reason, in Baumgarten's terminology there is not only an 'over' and a 'beneath the horizon', but most of all the question of what is 'within the horizon' — *intra horizontem*.

This kind of spatialized notion of the horizon can already be found with Leibniz, but Baumgarten goes further. At the beginning of the section on the abundance of material , Baumgarten begins to speak of a folding of the horizon concept, a spatial-social division into a territory which is the sphere of a *horizon logicus*, and a territory which is the sphere of a *horizon aestheticus*.[3] These two horizons are no longer to be understood as an absolute boundary of cognition, but rather as two mutually touching, even overlapping spatial-social spheres. The two spheres are, in turn, horizontally arranged, and they are not total, they do not encompass everything. There are matters that lie *infra horizontem aestheticum*[4], and there are those that are *supra horizontem aestheticum*.[5] However, there are also those that are common to both horizons.[6]

The horizon is thus no longer boundary, end, *finis*, that which sets a limit to our gaze or our cognition, in the sense of the Greek word ὁρίζω as an absolute and insurmountable limitation of immanence; yet it is also not the transcendental or even utopian echo of what is on the other side of the boundary, an indication of what eludes our gaze. And finally, the horizon is also no border

space between two areas overlapping at their ends, no *con-finium* as the place where in scholastic philosophy the human soul or the human being altogether is located between nature and cognition.

For Baumgarten, the horizon itself is something in which one moves as in a sphere : but it is a particular sphere that nevertheless goes beyond cognition and nature.[7] The particular sphere of the aesthetic horizon is also subjective in the sense of situativity. Baumgarten writes : 'Everyone has his horizon in aesthetics as well, and it can be something particular within the aesthetic horizon of many, which is nevertheless not within mine, but which either surpasses that horizon or is held down by it or is in any case outside it.'[8] In this context, Baumgarten speaks of subjective abundance, *ubertas subiectiva*. Everyone has their own horizon, above and below which they should not remain (157).[9] Indeed, the mode of subjectivation is respectively singular, the horizon is flexible, blurring even subjectivity as an individual. 'As the horizon appears in geography sometimes wider, sometimes narrower, my aesthetic horizon can retract, it can expand(149).'[10]

No longer simply the inferior sphere of lower cognition, the aesthetic horizon is capable of displacing, shifting, changing the logical horizon. The task of the aesthetic sphere is to expand the logical horizon (also envisioned as a sphere) into what is measureless, immeasurable, incommensurate, specifically as a never-ending process. The horizon as aesthetic horizon becomes itself a chaosmos, a completely immanent and yet other world, which confronts the clear and determined, measuring and measurable cosmos of the logical horizon with invasions of the obscure and the confusing.

Aesthetic Law

Law is not necessarily always only a preserving power, the handmaid of a force long since constituted, tool of established institutions, instrumental means of a state apparatus. One line of the possible non-servility of law — breaking through the conventional reading as a dependent application of law — is the broad field of jurisprudence. This does not operate at the level of terms like 'state under the rule of law' or 'universal human rights', but instead achieves a new actuality with each new judgment. It thus moves not at all in the terrain of a sovereignty situated wherever, but rather goes far beyond the static force of purely safeguarding and reinforcing law, of preserving the law. This applies to the decisions of ordinary courts and all the more to the spheres of constitutional court jurisprudence, of informal law, of community law, of truth commissions or of indigenous jurisprudence.

The Eurocentric-colonial genealogy of law inscribes law as part of the logical horizon, a thoroughly striating and striated logic, at the same time the logic of property and the primacy of the individual. The preconditions of Eurocentric-juridical discourses include the instance of a responsible and indivisible individual, a legal person, who can also assume undivided responsibility by means of being identifiable. Law and property are tied to an individual subject on the one hand, to a territory on the other. The construction of individual rights has not only been seen since modernity as the basis of every possible law, it is also projected onto the laws of antiquity, especially Roman law.

Just as the primacy of the individual has extended discursively into the past, it is also supposed to colonize present becoming. Even where ideas have emerged in recent decades, particularly from a broader ecological perspective, about non-anthropocentric law, the basis for these ideas does not distance itself at all from the fundamental reference to the individual. As the South African environmental lawyer Cormac Cullinan develops his theses in the manifesto *Wild Law*, for instance, he starts by opposing the false dichotomy between the wild and the law, between nature and civilization.[11] His stance, however, remains a deeply universal-humanist one, with a benevolent look at the human being as a good wild being, the good wild animal, the good wild nature. On the other hand, he can only imagine including the wild in law in a process of recognition as a subject. Just as companies, associations, and other 'legal entities' gain a legal status in the construction of the juridical person following the pattern of the individual, the vague notion that other entities, such as animals, trees, the deceased, divinities, and the earth as a whole, should 'have rights', works analogously.[12] Even though some states have made progress in this direction, for instance in the context of animal rights, the linear success story of the individual is also continued here: as a continuous further expansion of the struggle against exclusion from individuality, initially against slavery as exclusion of the human being (here the temporal parallel of the imposition of colonization and slave trade with the invocation of universal human rights is notable), then against the exclusion

of animals, then against the exclusion of other life forms from the individual sphere of law.

Undoubtedly, these first steps in the new terrain of an ecological law, in the broadest sense, are extremely difficult. In the limited holistic positions on expanding rights, however, the wild remains imprisoned in an organic paradigm (and its new hierarchies, as with Cullinan, such as that of 'Great jurisprudence', 'Earth Jurisprudence' and 'Species Jurisprudence').[13] Instead of a topos of the wild in keeping with the orgic-machinic ecology of bodies/spirits, things and socialities, as developed by Félix Guattari in his essay 'The Three Ecologies', this organic paradigm couples critique of civilization with a superficial critique of capitalism. With 'nature' as a universal point of reference, where imitating its order is basically recommended, in Cullinan's organic paradigm the legal position is shifted simply from object to subject. What eludes this perspective are relationships, positing relations, socialities as primary reference points of law, which could all engender completely different modes of subjectivation before and beyond identification as an individual or the structural analogy to individual law.

The critique of this significant and thoroughly internalized genealogy of law — as a component of a more general radical critique of Eurocentrism — first of all regards law and aesthetics as being mutually exclusive. In this perspective of an attack on the logical horizon of the striating law and its possessive individualism, aesthetics, perhaps also the 'aesthetic justice' that gives this volume its title, would assume the role of being outside the law, in an extreme case that of a law-*destroying* power. Under these conditions, aesthetics would become a power external to law, which as a transcendental instance attacks law as a sphere of constituted power serving only to preserve law, seeking to destroy this law and its genealogy. It is possible, however, that this figure of the mutual exclusion of aesthetics and law is fundamentally false or at least in need of complements.

Yet who says it is not possible to posit the subversion of Eurocentrism specifically at the beginning of the influential dispositive of knowledge of aesthetics as a component of modern European epistemology, and without discounting its involvement in colonial regimes, as called for by de- and post-colonial theorists such as Anibal Quijano, Shalini Randeria or Dipesh Chakrabarty? Who says it is not possible to detach Baumgarten, in an eccentric reading, from the dominant interpretation as the origin of a discipline that discursively accompanied and supported colonialism? Similar to the way Baumgarten's concept of aesthetics counters the superior field of cognition not only with aesthetics as a less valuable inferior field of cognition, but also conceptualizes the logical and aesthetic horizons as overlapping, a different relation of aesthetics to law could be considered: not as something entirely different from law, but rather as a flowing sphere capable of radically changing this law from the inside.

Before taking a closer look at the possibilities of aesthetic law, a further delimitation must be drawn: the ideas of aesthetic law do not imply that a measurelessly flowing sphere of the aesthetic horizon is a paradisiacal landscape. Nor, however, should it be disambiguated and equated with processes of domination and disfranchisement, the introduction of conditions of lawlessness, or the governmental instrumentalization of the informalization of law. Instead, it is necessary to recognize the ambivalence of the aesthetic horizon as potentially overcoming Eurocentric law in its own terrain, but also as a potential appropriation by it and as an extension of the state to areas outside the state. How the relation between formal and informal, between aesthetic and logical takes shape, can only be decided in each specific case.

In his early texts, Boaventura de Sousa Santos already called the informalization of law part of a process of 'disorganization on community level': 'What is new in current informalization and community programmes is that while up until now the oppressed classes had been disorganized at the individual level, that is, as citizens, voters, welfare recipients, in the future they will be disorganized at the community level. I suggest that state sponsored community organization will be the specific form of disorganization in late capitalism.'[14] That was in 1980, and with the increasing valorization of informal labour and approaches to order via civil society, up to today's invocations of big society, the disorganization steered by the state has reached an incredible extent. De Sousa Santos' text has an anticipatory quality here, also in the way he uses the term 'chaosmic'[15] to explain disorganization through informalization: 'To the extent that the state... tries in those reforms to integrate the sanctioning power inherent in the ongoing social relationships, it is indeed explicitly connecting its cosmic power to the chaosmic power, which up until now had been outside its reach.'[16] The situation of a clear separation

between the cosmic power of the state and the chaosmic power of social relationships turns into an increasingly one-sided subservience: in De Sousa Santos' interpretation following Foucault (and implicitly Guattari), the over-coding of chaosmic power by the state apparatus is to be understood as an expansion of the state. Where the state purports to withdraw, it expands; what appears to be de-legalization is actually re-legalization.

What is called aesthetic law here is not intended to deny these processes of de- and re-legalization and their ambivalence. The following, however, focuses on the emancipatory sides of the developments within law, which target changing its colonial determination and which — as suggested above — are not to be understood as an intervention from outside, but rather as an immanent movement. An aesthetic law understood in this way would no longer only be law-destroying, but would also be part of a law-making power at the same time, questioning and attacking given concepts of law, but also making law in a new way.

This aesthetic mode of law-making would apply to the contents of the respective law, as that which is dark, measureless, unstriated would repeatedly thwart the logical horizon, its juridical standards and the components of striation, of property, and of individualization. This would be a law, a constitution, not based on individuals and their property, but rather on the singularity of manifold ecologies beyond property and individualization. On the other hand, however, aesthetic law would also transform the *forms* of law-making at the same time: even the moment of instituting is virulent for all further constituting. In this sense, aesthetic law starts with the instituent act of every constituent process, with its form, its offers of participation, with the crucial difference of whether this instituent act is posited by a sovereign representing the counted mass, or a manifold process of the countless many.

It is only in the interplay of the forms and contents of law-making that an aesthetic law can be imagined that is both law-destroying and law-making, which attacks the dominant law of individual and territory as property and invents new modes of dividual law-making at the same time.

Law and the Art of Living Beautifully

It is probably not surprising that our search for an actualization of the possibility of an aesthetic sphere of law today takes us especially to Latin America. Following the highly symbolic marches of the Quinto Centenario de la Conquista in 1992, the Zapatista revolt in Mexico in 1994, the rebellion of Quito in 1999 and many other social struggles against dictatorship and neo-liberal transformation, there were leftist election victories all over the continent, which consequently also resulted in crucial breaks in law-making.

When Hugo Chávez won the presidential election in Venezuela in 1998 and took office in February 1999, he initiated elections for a constitutional assembly, which developed the new 'Bolivarian Constitution' through an extended procedure of activating the population and giving the people a voice over the course of one year. It was exactly this form of broad participation that radically opposed the usual forms of representation, such as the institution of a limited body that was supposed to represent groups of the population. With this machinic-social form of instituting, Chávez thus set two parallel processes in motion: on the one hand, a social upheaval was to be impelled from below; on the other, a process of newly founding institutions.

The contents of the new constitution were not only broadly discussed, but even went far beyond conventional constitution texts in some points in their emancipatory potential. The constitution introduced a progressive form of 'participative democracy' and the 'protagonist role' of the population, and it contained a complex version of human rights, women's rights, indigenous rights and environmental rights.[17]

In Ecuador, work started on the constitution in 2007 with the discussions of a constitutional assembly.[18] The Constituyente convened from November 2007 to July 2008, and its proposal was accepted in September 2008 with nearly 64% of the votes. Here too, the people's participation, especially on the part of the social movements, was central. Magdalena León T. accordingly sees the two determining features of the constitution in the 'cosmovision and practice of the indigenous peoples' and in the 'feminist and ecological economy of recent decades'.[19]

It was in the negotiations of the constitutional assembly and the surrounding discourses that a version of the family of terms associated with the indigenous term of *sumak kawsay* appeared for the first time in the context of a constitutional discussion. *Sumak kawsay* (Spanish *vivir bien*) describes the principle of a good life and living together in abundance, in exchange and

reciprocity among all living creatures.[20] Rooted in the indigenous demands for autonomous self-administration (including justice and economy), the close connection of the existential territory (as a living space inherited from the ancestors and space of the *pachamama*), and political, legal and economic autonomy becomes clear. With a view to limiting the exploitation of natural resources, the material aspect of the territory covers not only the land (in the sense of legally attributed ownership of land), but also the air space and natural resources. Here the existential territory also has a temporal component, the chaosmic concatenation of the here and now with what is long past, of present becoming with passing. Conjoined with these temporal concatenations, immaterial rights all the way to knowledge production, to science and technology are also part of an idea of happily living together.[21]

There are many ways in which the conjunction of living together and a form of reterritorialization that is not simply retrospective are manifested in language: *suma qamaña* (Aymara in Bolivia), *sumak kawsay* (Quechua in Ecuador), *bien* or *buen vivir* in Spanish are complementary terms emphasizing different aspects. Translating them is difficult, because entire world views are transported with the terms, which are in turn hard to render in other languages. Francesco Salvini points out that it may be specifically the untranslatable nuances in the translations *between* the indigenous versions, but also among their European relatives, *sumak kawsay,* suma *qamaña, la buona vita, el buen vivir, the beauty of living, la vida en plenitude, convivium, commons, commonfare, commune, etc.,* which open up a new territory of imagination.[22]

Kawsay is not a noun, so it does not mean 'life', as for instance in Italian 'la buona vita', but rather 'to live'. To live means here primarily living together in the sense of *convivencia*, a non-individual perspective of mental, social and environmental ecologies. The meaning of *sumak* oscillates between good and beautiful, and the adverb is not subordinated to the verb *kawsay.* In analogy to Baumgarten's definition of aesthetics as the art of thinking beautifully, *sumak kawsay* could also be called the art of living beautifully.[23] However, this is not a matter of a good, beautiful life in the sense of an individual way of life that follows certain, ever so strict ethical and aesthetic norms. To live beautifully refers instead to *a* life as a singular assemblage of modes of subjectivation, which is at the same time a dividual life, never whole, but always before the whole, before that which is indivisible, undivided (which also implies the negation of dividing), in manifold exchange with all living beings.

The concept of *sumak kawsay* already appears in the Ecuadorian constitution in the preamble as a goal of society: '*Decidimos construir Una nueva forma de convivencia ciudadana, en diversitad y armonía con la naturaleze, para alcanzar el buen vivir, el sumak kawsay.*'[24] This claim is explained in more detail in further articles as the right to live in a healthy and ecologically balanced environment (Art. 14), also with an explicit reference to indigenous justice (Art. 171) and indigenous territorial districts (Art. 257).

Indigenous justice and how it is anchored in the constitution actually gains the function of an aesthetic horizon here. As that which is measureless, that which is not to be grasped and measured entirely, it works inside the logical horizon of law, of property territory, and of the individual. Seemingly coming from the outside, from below, it shifts what is dark, confusing, into the sphere of state law. In a study on the reflection of overlapping practices of state and indigenous justice in Bolivia and Ecuador that he coordinated in 2012, Boaventura de Sousa Santos proposes two central concepts: the first terminological proposal applies to *interlegalidad*, the knowledge that can emerge under certain circumstances, when people can decide between two forms of justice. The second terminological proposal applies to *híbridos jurídicos*, legal terms and procedures that take up aspects from different legal systems:

> Hybrid justices, in its turn, are concepts or procedures in which the presence of varying legal cultures can be identified. For example, the concept of the Right of Nature is a form of hybrid justice. The concept of this justice stems from Eurocentric culture and from modern law, but its application to nature, conceived as Madre Tierra (Mother Earth) or Pachamama, is a contribution from original Andes culture. The use of indigenous law forms and acts can be considered as another hybrid justice. By recourse to writing, indigenous justice seeks to improve its memory, register recidivisms and avoid double judgements.[25]

De Sousa Santos speaks here of a bilinguality in matters of law.[26] This, however, does not resolve the two problems of the relations between the aesthetic and the logical horizon — disfranchisement/lack of rights *between* the two orders and appropriation/over-coding of chaosmic power, the social relationships by the state apparatus. Yet, instead of a rigid and mutually exclusive duality of indigenous and state law, what can also emerge here is an *ecología de saberes y de prácticas jurídicas*, a complex ecology of forms of knowledge and juridical practices (35).[27]

In the development of interlegality and juridical hybrids, it becomes clear that the figure of the mutual exclusion of aesthetic and classical law does not hold. It is the aesthetic law of indigenous justice, which potentially shifts the constitution as well as the practice of jurisprudence from the inside, especially in relation to the primacy of the individual. The law of *sumak kawsay* is understood as law that is not limited to being simply a continual further expansion of law, classically based on this primacy of the individual, to all human beings and all living beings beyond humans. Instead, it carries out the decolonization of living together as the fundamental condition for inventing a non-capitalist life. The law of *sumak kawsay* is no civil law, not limited to the citizen, to the human being, nor to individual living beings. The law no longer depends here on the two aspects of property and individual. The territory is no longer that of land ownership along with its rigid land registry of even past ownership (which also goes hand in hand with the irrelevance of the memory of earlier owners). The claim to self-administration of the existential territory tends to break through the logic of possessive individualism. This break does not put just other, collective identities in the place of the individual, but rather the necessity of rights based on the between of singular modes of subjectivation, on the middle of dividual ecology.

Decoloniality and the Ethico-Aesthetic Paradigm

A dividual ecology, which is before the individual and at the same time to be made to emerge post-individually again and again, takes into consideration human subjectivity (as mental ecology), the between of sociality (as social ecology) and finally also ecology as the environment in the narrower sense. These three levels are 'three modalities of praxis and subjectivation that correspond to three types of assemblages of enunciation, which in turn comprise equally the psyche, human societies, the living world, the machinic species and, in the final consequence, the cosmos itself.'[28]

This complex accumulation of ecological modalities also helps us to go beyond essentialist connotations of nature, earth and cosmos. It is the snares of anthropological exoticism that lead to misinterpreting *sumak kawsay* as an esoteric primitive belief. It is not a retrospective movement in the direction of a community of forefathers, the invocation of the soil or other essentialist figures that are the basis of the hybrid and complex ecology of *sumak kawsay*. When the argumentation revolving around *sumak kawsay* refers to a past before colonization and subjugation, then this is primarily to emphasize their temporary character. Before this, however, there is the primacy of struggles, the division and the dividual constitution of the social, historically always mutable and yet ineluctable. The current fields of struggle necessarily develop from the lines of flight of the indigenous and ecological and feminist struggles: monopolist land ownership, strategies of displacement, and the renewed colonization of immaterial commons call for decoloniality and the constituting of new modes of subjectivation that no longer take recourse to the primacy of the individual.

The ecology of *sumak kawsay* emerges, most of all, as the eternal return of the experience of anti-colonial struggles, of decolonial critique, of resistance against colonial genealogies. This eternal return is actualized in the precarious politics of an unfashionable present that develops the art of living beautifully from the struggles. The present becoming, the extended here and now of *sumak kawsay* is thus not at all without history, but nor is it just the experience of a transition, as it is read in some interpretations of *sumak kawsay* close to the state.[29]

The present becoming of *sumak kawsay* emerges on the one hand in the anti-linear leaps that break open the continuum of colonial and even anti-colonial historiography and found other narrations, other assemblages of events, other modes of writing and story-telling. These leaps do not deliver us from the past like zombies, undead spirits demanding satisfaction for the disruption of their eternal rest, and they are also not just 'our' leaps, a voluntaristic appropriation of the past that is simply available to us. The return of the leap in time takes place instead between the times, between present becoming and passing. And at the same

time, it emerges from and in ever new forms of resistance, of becoming-minoritarian even in the own existential territory, the lines of flight from the immanence of machinic capitalism and its state apparatuses.

A similar figure of the leap between the times is also the figure that Guattari calls a 'new aesthetic paradigm', whereby 'new' does not refer here to a linear logic of development and progress. For the new composition of a present aesthetic paradigm, Guattari is also not seeking to pave the way for a return to the holistic ecologies and the 'territorialized assemblages of expressions' of the proto-aesthetic paradigm. Certain aspects of this 'polysemic, animistic, transindividual subjectivity' can also arise in today's worlds of childhood, madness, love or artistic imagination, but: 'Magic, mystery and the demonic will no longer emanate, as before, from the same totemic aura. Existential territories become diversified, heterogenised.'[30]

Instead of the totality of the territory — be it ever so polyphonous, so tending to closure — in the organic-proto-aesthetic paradigm, instead of the deterritorializing segmentation and sectoralization of territories in the bipolar-modern paradigm, the new aesthetic paradigm involves the diversification and heterogenesis of a multitude of existential territories. The aesthetic paradigm overlaps here with ethical aspects. The good and the beautiful are not to be separated from one another. Aesthetic production has ethico-political implications, not least of all, according to Guattari, because creation as making also always means a responsibility on the part of the creating instance for the created thing, turning the state of the things, a bifurcation beyond previously determined schemata. The new aesthetic paradigm thus becomes an ethico-aesthetic paradigm.[131] 'But this ethical choice no longer emanates from a transcendent enunciation, a code of law or a unique and all-powerful god.'[32]

Immanence, multitude of existential territories, diffusion of aesthetic law within the code of law: the chaosmos of *sumak kawsay* is a variant of this ethico-aesthetic choice, a variant which clarifies that living well also means living beautifully. *Sumak kawsay* shifts the aesthetic horizon into the logical, bringing the measureless all the way into the constitution, but its chaos is a composed and composing chaos. This composition and recomposition corresponds to its emergence from the forms of indigenous struggles and knowledge of the cosmovision and those of the leftist movements of Latin America. The existential territories that emerge in today's social struggles also produce the spheres of aesthetic law, from which new chaosmo-visions can grow. Perhaps constituent processes will unfold at the same time not only for the Latin American region, but also as an expansion of decolonial critique in the originating geographies of colonialism as well. The passing in the present becoming of *sumak kawsay* then corresponds to the coming spectre haunting Europe and searching for its form and name in the raging middle of multiple crises.

Thanks to Nikolaus Linder, Isabell Lorey, and Francisco Salvini.

Notes

1   Alexander Gottlieb Baumgarten, *Ästhetik I/II, Lateinisch-deutsch*, transl. and ed. by Dagmar Mirbach (Hamburg: Meiner, 2007).
2   Ibid., p. 119.
3   Ibid., p. 119.
4   Ibid., p. 120.
5   Ibid., p. 121.
6   Ibid., p. 123, 567, 843.
7   Ibid., p. 840.
8   Ibid., p. 149.
9   Ibid., p. 157.
10   Ibid., p. 149.
11   Cormac Cullinan,*Wild Law* (Devon: Green Books, 2011), p. 30. See also the Earth Democracy movement in India and the Earth Justice movement founded in South Africa.
12   Ibid., pp. 95-98.
13   Ibid., p. 112 and further.
14   Boaventura de Sousa Santos, 'Law and Community: The Changing Nature of State Power in Late Capitalism', in *International Journal of the Sociology of Law* 1980, 8, pp. 379-397, here p. 390.
15   The term 'chaosmos' is already found in James Joyce's *Finnegan's Wake*, and then beginning in the late 1960s in the writings of Gilles Deleuze and Félix Guattari, see especially Guattari's last book *Chaosmosis. An Ethico-aesthetic Paradigm* (Bloomington: Indiana University Press 1995).
16   De Sousa Santos, 'Law and Community', p. 391.
17   On Venezuela, see Dario Azzelini's works, which further develop Antonio Negri's concept of constituent power, among other ideas, and apply it to the Bolivarian process in Venezuela.
18   Another example of a constituent process is Bolivia, where Evo Morales was the first indigenous person elected to president in 2005. Here too, the procedure of law-making through a new constitution was chosen in 2009. On 22 April 2009, due to Evo Morales' initiative, the same day was declared 'International Mother Earth Day' by the UN General Assembly. At a 'People's World Conference on Climate Change and Mother Earth's Rights' a year later in Cochabamba, the Universal Declaration of the Rights of Mother Earth was proclaimed.
19   Magdalena León T., 'El "buen vivir": objetivo y camino para otro modelo', in Irene León (ed.), *Sumak Kawsay / Buen Vivir y cambios civilizatorios* (Quito: FEDAEPS 2010), pp. 105-123, here p. 107.
20   In the words of the chairman of the constitutional assembly, Alberto Acosta: *'El Buen Vivir es entendido como una vida en armonia de los seres humanos consigo mismos, con sus congeneres y con la naturaleza. Asi como tenemos que defender y fortalecer los derechos humanos — y lo venimos haciendo ya 60 anos-, es importante pensar en la Declaracion Universal de los Derechos de la Naturaleza. Si no entendemos que la naturaleza es la base de la vida no podemos ni siquiera comenzar a defender los derechos humanos'*Alberto Acosta, 'Respuestas regionales para problemas globales', in Irene León (ed.), *Sumak Kawsay / Buen Vivir y cambios civilizatorios*(Quito: FEDAEPS, 2010), pp. 89-104, here p. 100. In my formulations I purposely do not use the term of 'nature' (nor that of 'culture' or 'Mother Earth') central to Latin American discourses, because massive conceptual shifts would be needed to divest these terms of the essentialist connotations. However, Acosta explicitly points out that in the references to indigenous spirituality there is no idea of a mere return to a state before colonization (ibid., p. 99).
21   See León T., 'El "buen vivir"', p. 114.
22   Francesco Salvini, 'Sumak kawsay or the Politics of Joyful Living', http://eipcp.net/n/1384760094.
23   Francesco Salvini (ibid.) uses the free translation 'beauty of living together'.
24   'We decide to build a new order of cohabitation for citizens, in its diversity and in harmony with nature, to achieve *buen vivir, sumak kawsay.*'
25   Original Spanish text: 'Los híbridos jurídicos, a su vez, son conceptos o procedimientos en los que es posible identificar la presencia de varias culturas jurídicas. Por ejemplo, el concepto de Derechos de la Naturaleza es un híbrido jurídico. El concepto de derecho viene de la cultura eurocéntrica y del derecho moderno, pero su aplicación a la naturaleza, concebida como Madre Tierra o Pachamama, es una contribución de la cultura andina originaria. El uso de formularios y de actas en la administración de la justicia indígena puede ser considerado otro híbrido jurídico. Mediante el recurso a la escritura, la justicia indígena busca mejorar su memoria, registrar las reincidencias y evitar dobles juzgamientos.'
Boaventura de Sousa Santos, Cuando los excluidos tienen Derecho: justicia indígena, plurinacionalidad e

interculturalidad, in *Justicia indígena,
plurinacionalidad e interculturalidad en
Ecuador,* Boaventura de Sousa Santos and
Agustín Grijalva Jiménez (eds.), (Quito:
Abya Yala, 2012), pp. 13-50, here p. 39.
26   Ibid., p.46.
27   Ibid., p. 35.
28   Félix Guattari,*Chaosmosis. An Ethico-
aesthetic Paradigm* (Bloomington:
Indiana University Press 1995), p. 108.
29   See René Ramirez, La transición
ecuatoriana hacia el Buen Vivir', in Irene
León (ed.), *Sumak Kawsay / Buen Vivir y
cambios civilizatorios* (Quito: FEDAEPS,
2010), pp. 125-141, here p. 141.
30   Guattari, *Chaosmosis*, p. 105.
31   Guattari already uses the term in *The
Three Ecologies* Here, however, the
aspects of the ethical (obligation, influence
on instances) and the aesthetic
(reinvention) are still analyzed relatively
conventionally and separate from one
another.
32   Guattari, *Chaosmosis*, p. 107.

Part 2

Justice on Stage, Justice Reframed

The Always Yet-To-Come

Aesthetic Justice from the Theatre Stage to Outer Space

Niels Van Tomme

> ... in any case we have our being in justice I have never
> heard anything to the contrary — Samuel Beckett[1]

When the American philosopher Monroe Beardsley originally coined the term 'aesthetic justice', he wasn't thinking about
critical artistic positions that would challenge and re-define our
understanding of this composite concept, as this book modestly
sets forth to do.[2] Instead, Beardsley was aligning himself with an
age-old Western tradition of philosophical inquiry that connects
notions of justice to experiences of beauty, broadly engaging a
harmonious relationship of the individual to society. Referring to
different 'world events', such as Antiquity, the French Revolution,
and World War II, literary scholar Victor Kocay emphasizes and
continues this rich tradition, highlighting specific texts from these
periods which 'underscore the importance of aesthetic notions...
for the formation of opinions concerning social and individual
justice'.[3] Along similar lines, Beardsley, in devising 'aesthetic justice', intends to connect the issue of aesthetics to the theory of social justice, thereby specifically addressing the distribution of aesthetic welfare in society, suggesting that 'aesthetic justice should
be conceived of as a distinct and independent domain of justice
within which the problems of the distribution of goods have to
be assessed with sensitivity to the peculiarities of the specific domain of aesthetics'.[4] In his vision, aesthetic justice becomes a theoretical framework to describe a harmonious relationship, rather
than a critical tool that raises urgent and uncomfortable questions
about the possibility of forging new ideas of justice. Through examining investigative artistic practices and innovative theoretical positions, it is the latter, which is explored throughout this
text and volume.

Considering the writings presented in this book, which
taken together present a kaleidoscopic view on the somewhat
defiantly from Beardsley appropriated and re-interpreted term,
'aesthetic justice', it should become clear that the relationship
between aesthetics and justice cannot be solely based upon neat
ideas of beauty and harmony. Aesthetics can, and perhaps should,
one might argue, be messy and decidedly un-aesthetic when concerned with the representation of ongoing struggles for justice.
In its current proposition, aesthetic justice should be primarily seen as dealing with issues of representation and the myriad
ways in which works of art can challenge and redirect social and

political imaginaries, proposing potential alternatives for a more just future rather than merely critiquing a contemporary status quo. Addressing the great under- and misrepresented areas of social and political life, forms of aesthetic expression hold the potential to open up a space between imagination and political reality in a way other fields of knowledge cannot, as it is not bound by the restrictive frameworks and moral deontology of most professional endeavours.

When confronted with aesthetic justice, the issue of representation becomes an issue of *just* representation. 'Just', not so much in the sense of adhering to a politically or morally correct depiction, but in the sense of actively exposing and questioning the very mechanisms of representation at work in present-day society, and perhaps finding a way to reverse, or temporarily undo, current dominant power structures associated with it. Viewed as such, the rejoining of the terms 'aesthetics' and 'justice', instead of describing a forcedly harmonious relationship between two seemingly mutually exclusive terms, proposes a new reading of the phrase.

Rather than establishing a strictly theoretical framework to advance a potential conceptualization of aesthetic justice, something done with more precision and thoroughness elsewhere in this publication, this text will evoke two recent art works that challenge dominant modes of representation, thereby fittingly emphasizing the questions outlined above. In doing so, these works open up new possibilities for the concept of justice, no matter how tentatively and speculatively it is framed. While vastly different in approach as well as subject matter, both French choreographer Jérôme Bel, in his series of choreographies *Disabled Theater* (2012 – ongoing) and Palestinian artist Larissa Sansour, in her video *A Space Exodus* (2009), shed light on the dynamics of inclusion and exclusion relating to complex issues of aesthetic representation. Engaging popular cultural tropes, these artists appropriate the language and formal characteristics of popular performance and pop staging on the one hand, and science fiction and displaced Afrofuturism on the other, ingeniously subverting the way we read and interpret these popular tropes in their habitual contexts. Beyond evoking some of the main issues these art works address, this text will emphasize that an idea of justice can perhaps be best developed through artistic praxis, as it has proven to fail when applied in legal or normative frameworks.

Disabled Theatre

On an unidentified empty theatre stage, a young man wearing a white t-shirt against an all-black backdrop is framed in a medium shot. He talks slowly but decisively, his speech demarcated by remarkable punctuation. The English subtitles to his words, delivered in German, read:

> I am far too slow. This is my handicap. Slowness doesn't disturb me. But I get on my mother's nerves. My handicap is called as well Down syndrome. The Down is a doctor. He discovered this handicap. That's why the name Down syndrome. My handicap is called as well Trisomy 21. This means that I have one chromosome more than you in the audience.[5]

After this short speech, which already allows for an unusual sense of frankness and directness regarding the protagonist's condition, we see the man in a long shot standing perfectly still until a popular Euro house tune starts playing, to which he starts to dance intuitively. His movements are unrestrained and uncontrolled, challenging the usual constraints of 'good taste' or 'skill' to be displayed on the dance floor. Such constraints clearly suggest limited physical freedom due to social restrictions and precise culturally conditioned instructions as to the correct movement and posture of the body in a particular social context that is the dance floor. These ideas were powerfully cemented in the early period of Western thought. As theorist Anca Parvulescu explains, these types of conditioning were first introduced by Erasmus of Rotterdam in *De Civilate morum puerilium* (*On Good Manners for Boys*) from 1530, one of the main textbooks on the subject that was referenced throughout Europe in the sixteenth century, and more precisely in the chapter 'On the Body'.[6] Overtly controlled and disciplined sites for the production of civility, such as schools and workplaces, eminently create the norm for sameness of the body, in the sense of precise prescriptions of how, when, where, and for how long certain bodily movements and behaviours can and must be executed or repressed. As thinkers such as Georges Bataille and Michel Foucault have repeatedly emphasized, such conditioning through the establishment of prohibitions is 'in a dialectical relation with [its] transgression', that is to say, creating the very conditions for its exact opposite to emerge: Otherness.[7] The theatre stage, as powerfully exploited by choreographer Jérôme Bel, might just be such a site of transgression, a preeminent stage on which historically framed bodily difference, defining those which fall outside the norm as 'Other', can be contested and negotiated.

In staging *Disabled Theater* and collaborating with the mentally disabled actors of Theater HORA from Zurich, Bel is concerned with an inherent transgression of boundaries, challenging the rules of dance, theatre, and bodily performance and the ways in which they can be analyzed and put on display. To do so, Bel uses a wide range of formal strategies, such as having the performances be accompanied by immediately recognizable pop tunes to 'seduce' the audience and involve them in an otherwise potentially uncomfortable performance. Through these efforts, he raises uneasy questions about the mechanics of representation and the ways in which views habitually regarded as 'progressive', such as those of theatre and contemporary art, deal with direct confrontation of significant otherness. Putting the handicap at the very centre of the performances, both visually and thematically, Bel staged a version of *Disabled Theater* at dOCUMENTA, while simultaneously screening a video of the piece named *2 Dances* (2012), both presented in a formerly derelict but for the occasion repurposed film theatre in Kassel. Realizing the thought-provoking on-stage presence of actors with mental disabilities, Bel implicitly yet inevitably contrasts their physical and mental difference with the (it is assumed) intellectually sophisticated and privileged audience of dOCUMENTA. In doing so, he not only realizes the social and political but also the aesthetic potential of staging this kind of confrontation, considering it as central to an understanding of radical difference and the ways in which such conflict negotiates social hierarchies. Working with disabled actors, Bel touches upon major issues surrounding contemporary theatre and art, most significantly with regard to issues of representation and invisibility. As the choreographer states: 'People with... disabilities have no representation and there are very few discourses about them. They don't exist in the public domain either. They're excluded from society. The gap between the majority and this minority is unfathomable.'[8] With urgent clarity, Bel implicitly suggests that society's acceptance of disability only works as long as it is constrained within the limits of politically correct representation. Yet the moment it asks questions about the way in which deep-rooted normative structures function in society by Othering disability, it becomes the threshold against which what is acceptable and habitual becomes defined.

To contrast Jérôme Bel's reminiscent use of mental disability which confronts politically correct modes of representation, it seems useful to evoke the work of Belgian-born filmmaker Jaco Van Dormael, who in highly popular and critically acclaimed films such as *Le Huitième Jour* (The Eighth Day, 1996), offers a sympathetic and sentimental portrayal of people with mental and physical disabilities. Perhaps Van Dormael's overall attitude towards disability is best exemplified in *The Kiss* (1995), a charming one-minute film he made prior to *Le Huitième Jour* as part of the *Lumière and Company* project.[9] In this silent, poetic filmic statement, Van Dormael shows a man and a woman with Down syndrome framed intimately close while both look straight into the lens of the camera. They turn their head to one another and look into each other's eyes, after which they smile and kiss, nuzzling happily. After a while, they turn back to the camera, smiling while holding each other, after which they start kissing again. Unlike Jérôme Bel's stark confrontation with individuals, Jaco Van Dormael achieves quite the opposite representational effect in his kind-hearted portrayal of disability. Instead of a staged performance highlighting difference, the actions captured by Van Dormael's camera are to be understood as a confirmation that the disabled characters in his film are much like us. As this short portrait shows, they fall in love like us, kiss like us, and in fact are also superior to us. Evoking yet another tired stereotype about mental disability, the gesture of spontaneity captured in the film suggests that they are able to express these feelings in decisively more innocent and open ways than we are. Indeed, signs of irritation, slowness, or other negative yet strikingly frank emotions as expressed by Jérôme Bel's subject described above have no place in this idyllic vignette. In the work of Van Dormael, in other words, the Otherness of the disabled is erased in favour of a more humanistic and politically correct representation, safeguarding the viewer's securely sympathetic emotions while watching the film. Importantly, such an approach keeps the disability, which is at the very core of these people's social and political being, and which also marks them as decisively different in any other real-life context, at all times at a safe distance, behind the veil of politically correct tolerance.

Slavoj Žižek's well-known tirades against the idea of multiculturalism as promoted in neoliberal states seems relevant to evoke in this framework. Žižek has repeatedly pointed out that in today's multicultural liberalism the 'experience of the Other [is] deprived of its Otherness', becoming what he calls 'the decaffeinated Other', while revealing how 'multicultural tolerance and respect of differences share with those who oppose [it] the need to keep others at a proper distance'.[10] Opposing Van Dormael's veiled representation, Jérôme Bel's engagement with disability is infused with a radical adherence to highlighting Otherness as a constitutive expression of identity, as the choreographer is foremost interested in 'opening up a space where disability is not expelled from visual and discursive practices, or hidden behind the screen of political correctness', but instead becomes 'internal to a discourse that has a strong bearing on both the political and aesthetic dimension'.[11] Viewed as such, Bel's fierce confrontation reverses the supposed respect of difference as promoted by politically correct discourse, opposing at all times the need to keep those who diverge from the norm properly isolated. Žižek's more general critique of multiculturalism can thus be extended to other instances of marginalization, installed by those in positions of power, who dictate the rules of living together in a diverse society. In this regard, it seems useful to evoke Judith Butler's influential idea of Otherness as the normative limit against which categories of normalcy are defined, and her theoretical conceptualization of justice as an ongoing process in which one's responsibility lies in the understanding of the always vulnerable relationship to the Other, to which one is always inextricably bound. The work of Bel, then, becomes a conduit through which we should not merely question issues of representation, but create an opportunity to understand others as decisively different, becoming 'the basis of a "non-normalized" sense of responsibility, one that seeks to protect the other against destruction', as Butler eloquently states.[12]

A Space Exodus

Also engaging popular cultural tropes, albeit in an entirely different cultural, political, aesthetic, and representational framework, Palestinian artist Larissa Sansour, in her short film *A Space Exodus*, portrays herself as a space traveller on an imagined permanent journey through the universe. The video echoes the visual and aural language of Stanley Kubrick's well-known *2001: A Space*

Odyssey (1968) film, here creatively interspersed with orientalist accents. With a sense of deviant provocation, Sansour's piece implements the idea of a first Palestinian being launched into orbit. Playfully referencing Neil Armstrong's historic landing on the moon, she plants a Palestinian flag on this newly conquered space, and in a voiceover declares this proposition as 'a small step for a Palestinian, a giant leap for mankind'. Sansour then waves to planet Earth, and finally floats and fades away into outer space, while repeating the word 'Jerusalem'. Although seemingly straightforward in structure, *A Space Exodus*, a carefully crafted work that is part political commentary and part science fiction fantasy, is a relatively complex film that draws inspiration from Palestinian political history.

The exodus of the title clearly references the removal of the Palestinian people from their homeland after the Second World War. By evoking this moment in the recent history of this conflicted region, it points to the ways in which the prevalent Israeli perspective on this historical moment has greatly influenced the international representation of the Palestinian reality. Not incidentally, the shaping of Israel's very own exilic mythology is not in the least aided by popular tropes, notably the Hollywood narrativization of this history through the popular 1960 film *Exodus* directed by Otto Preminger, widely known and celebrated as a 'Zionist epic'. In his book *The Iron Cage,* Palestinian-American historian Rashid Khalidi, asks if 'it is not possible that the Palestinian people will continue to exist indefinitely into the future... in a stateless limbo', and more radically, if we are 'perhaps too obsessed with the very idea of a state, in our attempts to place the state at the centre of the historical narrative?'[13] Proposing an entirely fictionalized world that is even more surreal and absurd than the everyday political reality of her native land, Sansour posits the idea of a Palestinian state into outer space, the ultimate, final frontier and well-known realm of fictional fantasy. Contextualizing this event in a popular visual language, while appropriating the moon landing as 'a Palestinian triumph', the piece gives a sense of agency and self-determination to the Palestinian people, even if it is interspersed with moments of implied grief and anxiety about the impossibility of ever returning home again, hence its above described evocative last scene. As the artist points out, 'the pain of the real, forced exodus of the Palestinians is doomed to remain a private grief, forgotten by the rest of the world'.[14]

Over the years, Larissa Sansour's work has evolved in remarkable fashion, from a straightforward documentary approach to conceptually and formally more rigorous engagements addressing a wide range of issues she is interested in exploring. Often incorporating science fiction tropes with dystopian elements from techno-culture, she opts for a number of stylistic blurs that are often genre-bending, and which further enhance and underscore the challenges associated with adequately representing the politically charged subject matter she addresses. Recently, Sansour's work has been included in a large-scale exhibition at the Studio Museum in Harlem, which surveyed wide-ranging artistic practices through the lens of Afrofuturist aesthetics and philosophy. Presented in this specific context, an interesting question emerges: in which way can an artist working so specifically with issues related to the representation of Palestinian identity align her practice with another cultural mode of expression, equally deeply bound to a particular set of societal and aesthetic concerns, such as Afrofuturism? According to South African scholar and artist Tegan Bristow,

> Afrofuturism uses science fiction and cyberculture in a speculative manner, just as cyberfeminism does. It is an escape from the externally imposed definition of what it means to be black (or exotically African) in Western culture, and it is a cultural rebellion drawing on techno-culture, turntables, and remixes as instrumental forms. By placing the black man in space, out of the reach of racist stereotypes, Afrofuturism allows for a critique of both the history of the West and its techno-culture.[15]

Although Larissa Sansour, in *A Space Exodus*, does not directly evoke turntables or remixes as instrumental forms, she does creatively change the recognizable music scores of Kubrick's celebrated film's iconic scenes set in space, adding electronically enhanced Arabesque elements that match the surreal visuals of her video. Redefining and recontextualizing a number of immediately recognizable cultural tropes, both visually as well as aurally, Sansour intelligently exploits a sense of double cultural displacement, using creative techniques associated with Afrofuturism to delineate a Palestinian identity in space. The question of whether an Afro-background is an essential element to being an Afrofuturist, as asked by curator Zoé Whitley, is coun-

terbalanced by her statement that 'issues of alienation, anxiety, social acceptance, national identity, and personal belonging', which she considers as essential a part of the Afrofuturist vernacular as the speculative and technological imagery, 'persist worldwide'.[16] It is perhaps through the urgent relevance of these very challenges to Palestinian identity that Sansour's work appears so well suited to establish a creative dialogue with the aforementioned aesthetic sensibilities.

One of Afrofuturism's strongest assets is its ability to critically disrupt and unsettle a widerange of dominant intellectual discourses, ranging from Francis Fukuyama's triumphal insistence on 'the end of history' to the hopeful pessimism of Franco 'Bifo' Berardi's 'after the future', as well as 'what Stuart Hall calls "the racialized regimes of representation", such as anthropology, ethnography, and art history', to quote Kodwo Eshun.[17] For Afrofuturism — a fundamentally peripheral philosophy, since its origins lie in marginalized black culture — the future still holds ideological, political, and technological potential as a liminal zone that reimagines broader issues of justice. As Eshun further states, 'Afrofuturism demoralizes the automatic promise carried by the future in favour of a renewed attention to the ways in which predictions, projections, and speculations operate as chrono-political instruments that seek to capture the future by modelling its variations over time.'[18] Placing Larissa Sansour's *A Space Exodus* in this lineage suggests a different determination for the Palestinian people, a people habitually deprived of self-determination. It produces a strong alternative image that holds the potential to drastically reformulate Palestinian reality, using sci-fi and the above-mentioned themes normally associated with Afrofuturism as political allegory. In this sense, Sansour's work, and Afrofuturism in general, is a collection of speculative possibilities and desires that are projected into the future, one that sidesteps dominant modes of representation and agency as maintained throughout mainstream media, Western academic discourse, and the majority of art history.

The Always Yet-To-Come

Intelligently bypassing and offsetting dominant modes of representation, Jérôme Bel's *Disabled Theater* and Larissa Sansour's *A Space Exodus* provide opportunities to look at the subject matters these artists address in novel and surprising ways. Two highly diverging cases with regard to thematic and aesthetic pre-occupations, they nevertheless share an opposition to strictly delineated and restrictive modes of representation, either as victims or threats, which are rarely produced from within. Joining a broader struggle for justice and for a more just representation, these art works vehemently address the idea that marginalized groups indeed have a right to speak, appropriating the language of popular culture to express and enhance such statements, thereby playfully negotiating relationships between high and low culture.

When Bel, in his video *2 Dances* (2012), shows a mentally disabled woman dancing erratically but enthusiastically to Abba's 'Dancing Queen', one of the most iconic pop songs of the past forty years, the song creates a sense of familiarity to most viewers, while her erratic dancing produces a sense of difference and captivating disorder, unsettling the habitual contexts within which we are used to hearing it. The ambiguous familiarity within the viewer is thus interspersed with a sense of alienation, which clashes with his or her own politically correct framed ideas of disability as something which should be considered in an egalitarian framework. When the woman finishes dancing, she is shown in a medium shot saying: 'I am...mongoloid. I'm a fucking mongo as well. Sometimes yes, sometimes no. It hurts me', thereby defiantly appropriating the very term that condemns her as an inferior human being while simultaneously engaging the complexities and contradictions of her being as an individual. The latter is embedded in her statement through which she confusingly describes herself as 'sometimes' being 'a fucking mongo' and 'sometimes' not. While this contradiction can be read as a factual description of how the outside world does or does not describe her, it can equally reference her own conflicted and complex self-image, withstanding simple classifications and pre-defined understandings of her being.

A gesture of ambiguity also pervades Sansour's video, most clearly articulated in the last shot where we see the astronaut figure, which is the artist herself, suspended in space for 'eternity', as suggested by the open ending of the piece. While playing with the iconography of national expansion in outer space, the piece nevertheless shies away from clearly designating a territory that could effectively become a physical manifestation of this provocative idea. Sansour seems to suggest that the

Palestinian state will indeed continue to exist indefinitely into the future, as was suggested earlier by Rashid Khalidi, without any reasonable solution or alternative immediately at hand.

Justice, both in the work of Jérôme Bel and Larissa Sansour, is a temporal projection rather than a clearly defined goal, something which we should always strive for, rather than attempt to fully achieve. Seen as such, the power of these works lies in their ability to position highly subjective approaches towards justice into the collective realm, negotiating the terms by which groups of marginalized people can gain agency and a mode of (self-) representation, rather than straightforwardly propagating an absolute, or universal idea of justice. Using a highly complex and differentiated amalgam of artistic and aesthetic approaches, as this text has shown, these works underscore Cornel West's thought that 'aesthetics [can] have substantial political consequences'.[19] As West states, aesthetics, when applied effectively, can emphasize the ways in which 'one views oneself as beautiful or not beautiful or desirable or not desirable [with] deep consequences in terms of one's feelings of self-worth and one's capacity to be a political agent'.[20]

Viewed against this light, these works should be seen as ways in which an habitually marginalized group of people can be reimagined politically — the disabled woman becoming a successful dancing queen and the Palestinian a brave female space traveller. Providing an opportunity to explore agency from below, these two highly diverging examples of aesthetic justice undeniably keep the hope for justice alive, no matter how tentative and speculative its framing. This justice powerfully hinges on aesthetic modes of expression, joyfully escaping any legal or normative societal frameworks. Seen in this way, theirs can be considered a justice that is always yet-to-come. As Judith Butler points out when writing about the late Jacques Derrida, this doesn't mean we shouldn't aim for it, as that would be 'as mistaken as believing that one has already arrived at justice and that the only task is to arm oneself adequately to fortify its regime'.[21]

Notes

1 Samuel Beckett, *How It Is* (New York: Grove Press, 1994), p. 135.
2 Monroe C. Beardsley, 'Aesthetic Welfare, Aesthetic Justice and Educational Policy', in *Journal of Aesthetic Education*, Vol. 7, No. 4, October 1973, pp. 49-61.
3 Victor Kocay, 'Is Justice an Aesthetic Notion?', in *Canadian Aesthetic Journal*, Vol. 7, Fall 2002, www.uqtr.uquebec.ca/AE/Vol_7/Aes&justice/1-Kocay.html, last accessed October 9, 2014.
4 Hanna Matilla, 'Aesthetic justice and urban planning: Who ought to have the right to design cities?', in *GeoJournal*, Vol. 58, Issue 2-3, October. 2002, pp. 131-138.
5 Jérôme Bel, *2 Dances,* 2012, www.youtube.com/watch?v=jdxvTj3n7SE, last accessed December 16, 2013.
6 Anca Parvulescu, *Laughter: Notes on a Passion* (Cambridge: MIT Press, 2010), pp. 24-25.
7 Ibid., p. 8.
8 Jérôme Bel, artist's website, www.jeromebel.fr/eng/jeromebel.asp?m=3&s=19&sms=5, last accessed December 16, 2013.
9 To celebrate the 100th anniversary of cinema, *Lumière and Company* (1995) was a collaboration between forty international film directors who each made a short film using the original camera invented by the Lumière brothers. Working under conditions similar to those of the Lumières, there were three basic rules: the film could not be longer than 52 seconds, no synchronized sound could be used, and no more than three takes could be made.
10 Slavoj Žižek, 'Liberal multiculturalism masks an old barbarism with a human face', in *The Guardian*, October 3, 2010, www.theguardian.com/commentisfree/2010/oct/03/immigration-policy-roma-rightwing-europe, last accessed December 18, 2013.
11 Jérôme Bel in *dOCUMENTA (13), Das Begleitbuch / The Guidebook, Katalog / Catalog 3/3* (Ostfildern: Hatje Cantz Verlag, 2012), p. 414.
12 Judith Butler, 'The Claim of Non-Violence', in *Frames of War: When Is Life Grievable?* (Brooklyn and London: Verso Books, 2010), p. 177.
13 Rashid Khalidi, *The Iron Cage: The Story of the Palestinian Struggle for Statehood* (Boston: Beacon Press, 2006), XIX.
14 Quoted from email correspondence with the artist, February 7, 2011.
15 Tegan Bristow, 'We Want the Funk: What Is Afrofuturism to Africa?' in *The Shadows Took Shape*, Naima J. Keith and Zoé Whitley, eds. (New York: Studio Museum Harlem, 2013), p.81.
16 Zoé Whitley, 'The Place is Space: Afrofuturism's Transnational Geographies' in *The Shadows Took Shape*, op. cit., p. 20.
17 Kodwo Eshun, 'Stealing One's Own Corpse: Afrofuturism as a Speculative Heresy' in *The Shadows Took Shape*, op. cit., p. 117.
18 Ibid, p. 119.
19 Cornel West in *Breaking Bread: Insurgent Black Intellectual Life*, bell hooks and Cornel West (Cambridge MA: South End Press, 1991) p. 117.
20 Ibid..
21 Judith Butler, 'Jacques Derrida', in *London Review of Books*, Vol. 26, No. 21, November 4, 2004.

An Argument for Something Else

Dieter Roelstraete in Conversation with Kerry James Marshall

Dieter Roelstraete — I'm interested to hear more about the intersection of your development as an artist with more broadly political developments. Growing up in Alabama in the 1950s, the 1960s certainly must have made an impact to begin with...

Kerry James Marshall — As a child, I was initially only minimally aware of what was going on around me. For instance, my family lived in an all-black neighbourhood of Birmingham, and I didn't really get to see many white people — they just didn't factor much in our lives, except at school. My mother worked for some white folks who lived far from where we lived, the Brittens or Brittins they were called. One time we rode with my father to pick up my mother from work, and their neighbourhood looked like a scene out of *The Wizard of Oz*: it's a black-and-white movie until Dorothy opens the door and then everything is suddenly Technicolor. I mean, the grass in this white neighbourhood was *so* green... You know, everything on TV was black and white as well — I'd never seen anything quite as bright as that green lawn.

Anyway, I began to understand how volatile the world was with the assassination of John F. Kennedy in November 1963. After that came the 1965 Watts Riots, the 1968 student uprisings, the murders of Martin Luther King Jr., Robert Kennedy, Malcolm X and so on. It was just one thing after another! At my junior high school there were daily walkouts and rallies. One day I saw about twenty of my classmates bend the main flagpole down to the ground and tear off the American flag. Somebody was throwing garbage cans through the windows of the school buildings, and the principal's office was set on fire — and that's just junior high! The police charged into a sit-in at the administration building and ended up beating up fourteen-year-olds. I witnessed a group of fourteen-year-old girls beating up the vice-principal, Mr Naseef, in turn... It was just crazy! I didn't take part in any of that; I was just an observer. Now, much of what was happening was connected to the Black Student Union out of Berkeley; one of the demands being made was for black history to be taught as part of the school

curriculum. Ironically, my first 'Negro History' teacher
was a Japanese man from Okinawa called Mr Kowano.
He was a member of the Central Avenue chapter of the
Black Panther Party who came to school wearing army
boots and military fatigues. That Black Panther office on
the corner of 41st and Central later became the scene of
a massive shoot-out with the LA Police Department... We
were obviously all thinking: what in the world is going on?

Look at this book — *Great Negroes Past and Present.*
This is where I first learned about Charles White... I
must have been in fifth grade or so. I hadn't seen this
book since then, but I found this copy, all beaten up and
held together with duct tape, in the drawer of a desk
left behind in the first studio building I bought here in
Chicago. That was so uncanny, since Charles White
was born in Chicago. When I opened that drawer, I just
couldn't believe my eyes.
     When I was in seventh grade, Mr Romity picked
me to take a summer drawing class for teens at the Otis
Art Institute. One day the teacher, George De Groat,
took us downstairs to a lecture room where he showed
us pictures from a book titled *Images of Dignity: The
Drawings of Charles White.* Afterwards, he told us that
Charles White actually taught at Otis and that he even
had a studio on the third floor, which we could visit. I
was completely blown away when I first set foot inside
that studio. I had never seen anything quite like it, a
place where real art was made. There were finished
paintings next to sketches, drawings at various stages of
the process. Just seeing how things start out and how
they end up — that was really important for me. Back in
the drawing class I was copying his drawing of Frederick
Douglass when one day Charles White himself walked
into the room... From that day onwards I was determined
to get my art education at Otis and nowhere else.

DR — So what were you painting at the time? How and
when did you find your subject matter?

KJM — At first I was just trying to master different

techniques. I was painting still lifes, dolls, using oil pastels, watercolours... Those were the kinds of things I had put in my portfolio when I applied to get into Otis. Now with regard to subject matter – when I showed you that first painting, of the two men behind bars, painted in the style of early Charles White, that was the first oil painting I ever made. I painted that in 1971. That picture is an example of me trying to say something about injustice or such. But it was much too early for this to be considered meaningful work – I was still developing my skills. As a young artist going to the library and looking at all these different books... How do you figure out which path to follow, which approach to take? When I came across Egon Schiele's work, for instance, I'd try copying that for a little while. James Ensor, the German Expressionists, Gustav Klimt, Maxfield Parrish, Diego Rivera: same thing. I'm looking at all this stuff and trying to figure out how it's done, because I want to do something that's just as good. This is how you develop your own style, your own voice. And it really only started to fall in place around 1978, when I did a series of collages after having looked at Romare Bearden's work for some time. I was still at Otis, and just about to graduate. The advantage of collage is that you don't have to spend a lot of time drawing out your composition, and it is easy to work with narrative 'content' when you are working in that manner. Some of these collages included references to black cultural history, while others registered a kind of naive dissatisfaction with the way the world works... One of the first collages I made was titled *Thirty Pieces of Silver* and dealt with artists who 'sell out'. I did another collage around the same time about white folks moving out, *White Flight* – stuff like that. I also started to do some genealogical research on my family, going back to Birmingham to interview my grandmother and compile all these stories I had heard my mother and my aunt tell. From that history came a collage titled *Yellow Quarters*, the subject of which was my maternal grandfather's murder in a notorious place in Birmingham called Yellow Quarters... Under Charles White's influence, I always knew that I wanted to make work that was about *something*: history, culture, politics, social issues... It was just a matter of mastering the skills to actually do it.

DR – You mentioned the German Expressionists, Ensor, Klimt, but also Hammons' body prints and so forth – clearly the human figure and the broader issue of figuration were always going to be there.

KJM – Indeed, early on I made a commitment to drawing figures, to mastering the art of figuration. This did not exclude the possibility of exploring abstraction and so forth, but it seemed essential to me to actually master representation before abandoning it. Furthermore, since the overwhelming majority of the bodies on display in art and advertising are white, producing images of black bodies was important to offset the impression that beauty is synonymous with whiteness. It is not hard to see how one's interest in being part of the Western art-historical tradition conditions you to *perpetuate* the models and values it privileges. It sounds crazy to me now, but it's simply because I hardly ever saw black people as the subject of art that I initially didn't know how to conceive of works that would have black people in them – especially in a narrative sense, except perhaps in the way Charles White would depict them, i.e. in a more emblematic manner, mostly as single figures in particular situations. I had never seen a grand, epic narrative painting with black figures in it, and that's the kind of painting that I became interested in making – pictures in the grand manner.

DR – So this must have been when you realised you were onto something new – that you had found a calling, so to speak.

KJM – Except that I had not yet found the appropriate narrative material. I knew *how* I wanted to paint, but not yet *what* I wanted to paint. You have to realize that there wasn't such a thing as 'Black Studies' until the 1970s. I didn't even know what, say, the African equivalent of Grimms' fairy tales was. Sure, we were taught the history

of slavery and so forth, but I did not know of any stories
of black heroism for instance. I knew about Charles
White's murals but never saw any of them in person —
and the same was true of Hale Woodruff; I never saw
any of his murals either. And I couldn't go see them in
the museum because they weren't in any. That's pretty
much how I felt back then: I am nowhere and I have no
idea where to go to from where I am. Which is why in
the meantime, at least, I just focused on techniques and
processes, on mastering the craft, so that I'd be ready to
proceed when the day came that I would finally know
where to go.

DR — And that day eventually came, of course.

KJM — Yes, and reading Ralph Ellison's *Invisible Man*
had a lot to do with it. It must have been sometime
around 1978. I had been making these abstract collages
for a little while and had been receiving some attention
because of them, but it never completely satisfied me. I
had been pushing around paint for some time as well,
and had become fairly good at it but I felt like I had
reached some kind of dead end. Until I read Ralph
Ellison — his description, in the introduction to *Invisible
Man*, of the condition of invisibility literally changed
everything for me. What I was reading there, the notion
of being and not-being, the simultaneity of presence and
absence, was exactly what I had been trying to get at
in my art work. That's when I decided to leave behind
both the collages and the abstract work and made my
first figurative painting, titled *Portrait of the Artist as a
Shadow of his Former Self.* That was the first time I used
a black silhouette against a nearly black background:
simultaneous presence and absence, where you can
alternately see and not see the figure in the painting.
This was the first time I was able to put into practise
everything I had learned so far by studying the art-
historical record. So sometime around 1979, 1980, that
was the moment of crystallisation for me. Not only did
I finally grasp the dialectic of absence and presence but,
just as importantly, I now also really understood how

to put into practise all the formal devices used by the
classical painters. For the first time I was completely
conscious of what I was doing, all the way through.

DR – And executed in egg tempera on top of that.

KJM – That was important, yes: using a technique and
material taken from a period in art history to which the
figure rendered with it was utterly foreign. Even though it
was structured on a classical frame, I felt the picture to be
completely modern.

DR – It's interesting you should say that because in
a sense the art world appears to have been at a bit of
a crossroads in the early 1980s. The conceptual art
movement had clearly exhausted itself, painting was
readying itself for a triumphant return to art's big stage,
yet in the meantime the Pictures Generation artists were
continuing conceptual art's critique of the image and
spectacle. And here you are, leaving abstraction behind,
and returning to figuration.

KJM – It's true that Los Angeles in particular seemed
to be at the epicentre of what was then referred to as
a 'crisis of representation'. If you think of what John
Baldessari or Chris Burden were doing at the time... But
that was all very far removed from what was happening
in black artist communities. I was aware of this 'other'
LA art world, but it didn't mean anything to me. Once
again, you have to see this in the larger perspective of
what was happening in the US as a whole at the time: the
assassination of JFK, the Watts Riots, the murders of
Martin Luther King Jr. and Robert Kennedy, the killing
of Malcolm X, the police assaults on the Black Panthers...
With everything that was going on in the streets at the
time, how could a black person be concerned with an
art for art's sake? The notion of a crisis of representation
felt particularly alien to me as I was just then beginning
to master the *means* of representation. I also had to ask
myself *whose* representation are we talking about exactly
when we observe this so-called crisis? Here's how this

notion played out for me: I go to a museum... look at all the art that's there... and all I experience is *absence*. Not only are black people largely absent from the history of representation that is on display there, we are also outside of the domain of mastery. *My* crisis was actually a crisis of *under-representation* — a very different crisis from the feeling of exhaustion that the Western European tradition seemed to suffer. Unlike you, for instance, I did not grow up in the shadow of the 'oppressive' perfection that, say, the Van Eyck brothers embody. Magnificent images of my 'type' were not everywhere in the museum. For me, *that* history of representation always felt distant, remote and unassailable; I was outside of it. It's hard to be anxiety-ridden about the state of art except when it relates to your marginalisation in it. If Picasso's *Demoiselles d'Avignon* was the first salvo, then Duchamp's ready-mades and conceptual art were the final barrage that annihilated the representational regime. Now, to me those moments do not really constitute an actual crisis of representation. It is true that they opened up the field for more different kinds of production to be read as art, but what remains is a vast trove of historical images that are still the foundation of artistic understanding. I wanted to see more pictures of black people in art, and more paintings of black people in particular. The atmosphere in the art school environment being what it was at the time, I quickly learned that I'd be on my own there. Again, that's very much what making that first painting, the *Portrait of the Artist as a Shadow of his Former Self*, was about. There I was, wanting to learn all these techniques, wanting to master the art of constructing pictures, and the first thing I hear is that I no longer need to know all those things because nobody is doing that kind of stuff anymore!

DR — What were some of the works that followed from the breakthrough you mentioned earlier?

KJM — I made *Two Invisible Men (Naked)* and *La Venus Negra* soon after. Then I started making pictures using gold paint, with hand gestures that clearly referenced medieval religious paintings. They were fairly simple pictures with a single figure in the ground, and they were somehow related to an earlier statement that I had made to the effect that all great art was in essence religious art. I also started working on a much larger scale, in drawing in particular at first. Not all of those works have survived however.

DR – We are talking about the early 1980s now, the early days of the Reagan era – a very different time from that of the formative experience of your witnessing the rise of the civil rights movement. Did those changes filter through to your work in any way?

KJM – One thing I learned witnessing all those epochal changes, all the social upheaval all the way from the mid-1960s to the early 1980s, is that you come to realize how little power you have as an individual to change things. No matter what you do, it just won't have any effect whatsoever. Also, if you look back at the history of the civil rights struggle, Martin Luther King Jr., Malcolm X, the Black Panthers... It really didn't matter what strategy you chose, militant or non-violent, you'd get killed anyway. Sure enough, many people acted as if the world would end if Reagan got elected. It didn't. I understood then that it didn't matter any longer who was president. That's when I stopped fretting about it.

DR – You mentioned that your earlier painterly work had a decidedly emblematic character, but sometime in the late 1980s, early 1990s, the narrative dimension in your practice clearly gathers strength. Could you talk a little bit about this transition? No doubt the shift to working on a larger scale must have played a part in this.

KJM – It is partly a matter of scale indeed. It wasn't until I got a larger studio space that I began working on the first big paintings, such as *Lost Boys* and *De Style*. Before that I worked in my room at the YMCA, then in our apartment in Hyde Park. My first studio was a 350 square feet office space closer to downtown Chicago, and that's where those two paintings were made – those pictures were real breakthroughs. Everything that I had been practising since making my *Portrait* could now finally be executed on the scale I had been looking to work on for a long time. At this point it really became a matter of engineering, of building pictures and making sure all of their parts fitted together in the way I wanted them to. *Lost Boys* and *De Style* were the pictures I had always imagined myself being able to make. And sure enough, one of those paintings, *De Style*, was purchased by LACMA, the first museum to acquire a major work of mine. That was my boyhood dream come true: to see my own work in the very first museum I visited as a child.

I never really liked the idea of working in series, but the first cohesive body of paintings I made was the *Garden Projects*, when I was living near Stateway Gardens and Wentworth Gardens here in Chicago — public housing projects that had been built with utopian notions of beauty and good living in mind, but were unable to maintain the promise of their pastoral-sounding names. I very much had the tradition of the pastoral in mind (think of Giorgione's *Concert Champêtre* for instance) when I was making these pictures. People eating lunch and listening to music in a bucolic setting — only this time the setting is a public housing project for African-American families. The *Garden Projects* were followed by a group of elegiac works called *Mementos* and *Souvenirs*. These paintings were first shown at the Renaissance Society in Chicago in 1994 and functioned as some kind of requiem for the civil rights movement and the Black Liberation Struggle... In all these works, whether serially conceived or not, the overarching principle is still to move the black figure from the periphery to the centre and, secondly, to have these figures operate in a wide range of historical genres and stylistic modes culled from the history of painting. Those really are my two overarching conceptual motivations. I'm using African-American cultural and social history as a catalyst for what kind of pictures to make. What I'm trying to do in my work is address Absence with a capital A. This is also why the *Rythm Mastr* comics project exists, and why the work uses the language it does.

If you believe that the struggle of the civil rights movement essentially revolves around the acceptance of black people as equals, and that non-violent resistance alone won freedom for black people, you essentially gloss over the history of resistance that black people have been engaged in from the moment they got here *centuries* ago. I'm interested in showing that such a history of resistance has always existed, and that for this history in particular 'success' is not assimilation *per se*, it is *competition* — that is to say, the ability to compete head to head in every arena, and to achieve recognition as a capable people, not just as individuals. There exists a constant pressure to reject consciousness of blackness as difference; I use blackness to *amplify* difference as an oppositional force, both aesthetically and philosophically. Black consciousness means emphasising the historical particularities of being black in the world over notions of what it means to be American, or simply 'human', i.e. to be *assimilated*.

The goal is to try and break the pattern of weakness and dissipation that led to, and was exacerbated by, the Atlantic slave trade and imperial colonisation. That really is the underlying premise driving almost everything I do, and that's why I keep looking back at African and African-American history and culture to locate moments of resistance and rebellion. It is also why I have an eye on the present; I'm always looking for ways to propel a black presence, forcefully, into the future. Take the exhibition organized at the Secession in Vienna in 2012, 'Who's Afraid of Red, Black and Green', a reference to Barnett Newman's series of paintings *Who's Afraid of Red, Yellow and Blue*, but also to the colours of Marcus Garvey's Pan-African flag — that's why the exhibition also includes portraits of the Stono Rebels, who led an early eighteenth-century slave rebellion, or people like David Walker, an outspoken abolitionist from the nineteenth century. I want people to know that resistance has existed from the very beginning. Rebellion wasn't something that started with the civil rights struggle; it started in the eighteenth century, and the goals of that struggle are yet to be realized.

DR – And one of those goals is to be able to compete – not be merely equal.

KJM – Absolutely. The goal is competitive parity in every arena. That is why the notion of *belatedness* that Jeff Wall wrote about so convincingly in his catalogue essay for my exhibition at the Vancouver Art Gallery in 2010 is so relevant. When black people were first brought to the Western hemisphere from Africa and put to work as slaves, they were already competitively disadvantaged in lots of ways: they had no ocean-going ships, no explosive armaments, and no state economies that compelled adventure-seeking in search of wealth and resources. We were vulnerable on all those fronts. The dominant Western concept of art developed formally and philosophically, all the way from the fifth century BC to the nineteenth century AD, without any theoretical contributions from black scholars or practitioners. The development and perfection of realism in art, for instance, all the way from Jan van Eyck to the Photo-realists, wasn't in the least driven by African economies or African aesthetics. None of the important developments that gave rise to modernism were led by black people, despite the fact that approaches borrowed from 'primitive' and 'tribal' art inspired the radically transgressive gestures that defined much of modern art. Again, this is why for black people the crisis of representation is different from the crisis of representation experienced by whites. And the problem that African-American artists in particular were having is that by the 1950s people were saying that the game was essentially over while we were just getting started. We still don't get to decide what kinds of things will or will not be recognized as works of art, or what can or cannot enter the museum. All my life I've been expected to acknowledge the power and beauty of pictures made by white artists that have only white people in them; I think it's only reasonable to ask other people to do the same *vis-à-vis* paintings that have only black figures in them. That is part of the counter-archive that I'm seeking to establish in my work. In fact, I would have to qualify

even that notion, as my work is not an argument *against*
anything; it is an argument *for* something else.

DR — I'd like to dwell on this notion of a counter-archive
for a moment. Because if your work constitutes a critique
of the dominant visual culture of the last five hundred
years or so, it also does so by way of taking recourse
to that culture's most paradigmatic art form, namely
painting in the grand manner. Obviously there's a bit of a
contradiction there.

KJM — Here's why I'm perfectly comfortable operating
within the realm of painting with the goal of entering the
museum as it is currently structured: if I don't do it, or if
other people like me don't do it, we will be condemned
to celebrate European beauty and Europe's artistic
achievement in perpetuity.

DR — Thus perpetuating the self-same condition of
invisibility...

KJM — And that's precisely why I stopped making
abstract work — because white figures in pictures
representative of ideal beauty and humanity are
ubiquitous. The truth of this reality is almost everywhere
taken for granted. And to me that's unacceptable. I have
lots of young nieces and nephews — they should encounter
a broader representation of human ideals than the post-
imperial models I had to work against. I think it is safe
to say that museums around the world are not going to
get rid of their Titians, Goyas and Van der Weydens any
time in the foreseeable future. Those pictures are going
to stay right where they are, anchored in a narrative that
begins in ancient Greece, Rome and medieval Italy, and
is carried through all the way to Robert Rauschenberg,
Jasper Johns and Andy Warhol. The custodians of this
history are happy to tell you that sometime in the late
1980s a space was opened up for all these different groups
of people, all these other identities, to come in — but
what does that mean? In all this, it really doesn't matter
what we think of Velázquez, Matisse or Lucian Freud.

What *does* matter is that if no one is out there working to produce paintings with a racially different set of figures in them that are as interesting, as challenging and as *good* as those historical masterworks, non-white people will always be in trouble. So *that* is why I keep making pictures that aim to make their way into these museums. When one day the Prado will start collecting contemporary art, I want to be in a position to have one of my works considered. That matters.

DR – Could you talk a little more about your interest in the comic as a viable art form in its own right? I'm interested in the relationship of that particular form to the subject of our discussion.

KJM – The superhero-centred comic book is a very popular art form that has rarely featured black characters in the lead role – yet more invisibility. And of the few black characters that have appeared, none of them is the product of a black artistic imagination, and none has achieved the status of Superman, Batman, Spider-Man or the Fantastic Four. So that presents yet another challenge... Without a paradigmatic hero figure, and no heroic fantasies to speak of that can be transmitted over generations, black youth are as trapped as black adults are in an image world that privileges white persons as both heroic ideals and ideals of beauty. So I developed the *Rythm Mastr* comic project starting in 1999 because there was just too little out there featuring black people at the centre of it all. Although the project was originally conceived as a conceptual work about black absence in daily newspaper comics for the 1999 Carnegie International, the objective is to see its development through to a full-blown graphic novel, and ultimately an animated feature film.

DR – It is worth noting that the comic strip has, historically at least, not only been overwhelmingly white, but also overwhelmingly male-dominated. It's not the first instance where your work intersects with questions of gender and masculinity as much as it does with questions of race.

KJM — Of course, we still have to contend with the fact that the shape of the world as we know it has been determined by and large by the prototypical white male adventurer. For black men, because my primary concern is with black culture, the picture becomes even more complicated because of what the dominant culture is willing to tolerate as far as demonstrations of a hyped-up masculinity are concerned. There are certain acceptable arenas in which black men can exercise the dominating tendencies of their masculinity, like athletics and entertainment. But intellectual and material invention, especially in areas such as weaponry and advanced technology, remain effectively closed off to black competition worldwide. Even the essentially soft-power domain of innovation in the visual arts has largely eluded our ambition.

DR — And of course as soon as some headway is made towards cracking the art world's glass ceiling, as soon as you're able to take a place at the table where it seems art history is written, you're told that art is dead and that art history is over...

KJM — Exactly right. Yet even if we accept that the game is over, we are somehow compelled to push on, because there are still plenty of useful moves to be made, even in endless endgames. And this is where the demographic changes in much of the Western world come into play: those peoples who were left outside while the canon was taking shape are now allowed inside to look at what the canon wrought, and of course they find that they are completely under-represented in it, and that the game is pretty much over — history has been written without them. But it is important that they continue to challenge the dominance and perceived naturalness of that canon regardless.

DR — We have to always be reminded of the particular social, economic and political conditions that determined how art was produced and how art history was written.

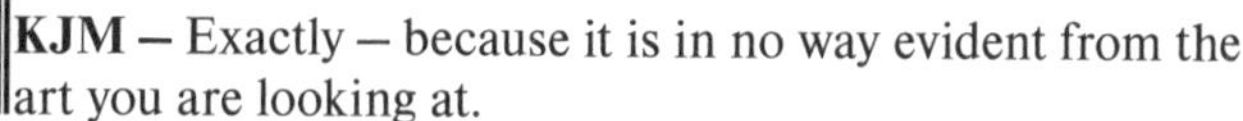

KJM – Exactly – because it is in no way evident from the art you are looking at.

This is an excerpt from an interview first published in Nav Haq (ed.), *Kerry James Marshall: Painting and Other Stuff* (Antwerp: Ludion 2014)

Lament of the Images
A Lament of Justice

Julia Svetlichnaja

How can we think of art and justice together? This relation has always been on the agenda, and today many argue that, in search of social justice, artistic practices are obliged to transform into quasi social services. Indeed, socially-engaged art is still on the rise: 'NGO' and 'Activist', 'Art of Over-Identification' and 'Interventionist', 'Relational Aesthetics' and 'Street Art' — the list can go on. What all these artistic practices have in common is a desire to repair and humanize the social. They fight poverty, social exclusion, internal and external domination, authoritarian regimes — they demand justice. The talk about the 'Other' has become one of the most pertinent subjects in the contemporary art discourse. Furthermore, this 'Other' is usually someone deprived, wronged, repressed, and in need of help and guidance, compassion and inclusion. For example, the eleventh edition of Documenta, an institution focused on democracy and justice, identified its goals as bringing humanism back on the agenda.

The crucial question, however, is what kind of link one can establish between a practice of art and a conception of social justice. It seems, given the emphasis placed by contemporary artistic practices on the 'Other', that we are rooted in the modern liberal understanding of justice that posits the priority of that which is right and presupposes an inclusive formula to measure fairness in any society. Such a conception of justice postulates that individuals are equal because of their fundamental humanistic qualities and that therefore, by including and reconciling differences, justice as a desire for fairness could and should be achieved. The 'wronged' lives of others could be put right if we recognize and engage with them. However, is injustice simply the absence of justice, a mere victimhood, or is it something more complex? Shall we approach the issues of justice in terms of equal rights based on humanistic ideals? We know that some rights exist because others have been suppressed and excluded. Hence, differences, which are constructed as relations of subordination, are the result of moral agreement embodied in the liberal conception of justice. It could be said that justice is made because we a priori accept that there are differences, that any society is based on acts of exclusion. If there were no differences, then justice itself would be needless; yet, the common notion of the concept of justice is situated around the idea of fairness.

To be sure, justice as fairness is only one among many interpretations of the political principles of liberty and equality. In his *Spheres of Justice: In Defense of Pluralism and Equality*, Michael Walzer, for example, takes issue with the idea of 'simple equality', and instead argues for a pluralist conception of justice which recognizes a connection between the plurality of criteria for justice and equality. According to Walzer, the problem of justice is better understood in terms of a 'complex equality' that is based on the separation of spheres of justice with their respective distributive principles and their pluralization.

There are also others who do not take up the traditional question of justice as a politically independent concept. For Alain Badiou, for example, justice is 'the name by which a philosophy designates the possible truth of a political orientation'.[1] This disinterested understanding of justice views justice not as a distributive concept but as the marker of the truth of a particular political orientation. For Badiou, a political event based on political truth must be rooted in a concept of justice.

It seems that assigning the idea of justice to any grounds or general principles is problematic, and instead of searching for a solution to the problem of justice, we should probably focus on providing as many interpretations as possible. Reflecting on the many conflicts and contradictions of justice, Judith Butler places its subject matter within the ethics of the political. In her *Frames of War: When is Life Grievable?*, Butler maintains that because violence and 'non-violence' are the constitutive possibilities of the subject, 'non-violence' (or justice) cannot be a set of principles or a position but an 'ethical' appeal to preserve the life of the other. Such a form of justice as a call for 'non-violence' has to be based not on the injurability of all but on an understanding that 'who we are' is a shared precariousness. While, according to Butler, 'there are no conditions that can fully "solve" the problem of human precariousness', what is at stake is to minimize it by assuming responsibility, which involves questioning the prevailing 'frames' of recognizability within which some lives are perceived as 'grievable' or worthy of protection and some are not. For Butler, what is at stake in the issue of justice is to grasp the universal precariousness as a dependency on social conditions through which life becomes liveable, to realize that 'life requires support'.

Dwelling on Butler's 'discourse of life' as an obligation to minimize precariousness in egalitarian ways, what comes to mind is Russian philosopher Nikolai Fyodorov's humanistic project of resurrecting all of the dead. Fyodorov argued that the struggle against death is the only common cause capable of uniting all people and thus neutralizing existing antagonisms. According to Fyodorov, our responsibility towards all humans who have ever lived constitutes the frame of justice to come. What Butler and Fyodorov's thinking seem to have in common is the idea that 'a man is the measure of all things'. Our unity comes alive when we identify with the Other, when we preserve or improve lives — this ethical appeal is based on the idea that justice is an ongoing realization of our humanity by combating the precariousness of our social condition. The difficulty here is that we are supposed to minimize something that we fundamentally share — precariousness — and that life is supposed to overcome its social conditioning in order for justice to be done. To be sure, the political principles of liberty and equality should be at the core of a theory of justice in a democratic society; however, it seems to be problematic for equality to be achieved under the common denominator of humanity. Jacques Lacan has repeatedly argued that humanism is fraudulent and that the only 'essence' to be found in man is the lack of it. For Lacan, there is no subject which is not always already a social subject. In other words, there is no life without social conditions.

It is common sense to argue that the social constitutes the depository of the representations used by the psyche; that human life depends on society. The question then is how one views the socio-political plane. According to Lacan, it is not interdependence but division and disharmony that construct social reality. The subject, which is always a subject of lack, seeks its absent fullness in the locus of social reality. However, because the symbolic order, or what Lacan calls 'the big Other', is also structured around a central lack, the social field reveals itself on the basis of the exclusion, repression, and reduction of an impossible real. Such a view of the socio-political dimension dislocates the very idea of any positive identification with Otherness.

We are not interdependent subjects but divided, says Lacan. Instead of sharing some humanistic essence, we can only share the 'structure' of lack. The condition of precariousness then appears to be not a problem to overcome but something which is constitutive of our society that we need to come to terms with. Our ordinary condition is one of utter precariousness. However, it seems that this is where our most essential possibility lies. If all identities are necessarily precarious and unstable, then they always can be transformed. Thus, instead of minimizing precariousness, perhaps we should think about creating a bigger space for it to exist. Rather than proclaiming 'non-violence', it seems to be more productive to welcome violence, to make society more radically open to disagreement; since, if we follow Lacan, there is no society and social reality without exclusion; without it, the world falls into a psychotic realm.

For example, while the mainstream strategy of dealing with homelessness presupposes its eradication through various schemes and projects, the strategy informed by Lacanian ethics would allow homeless people to live the way they do in a more comfortable and normalized way. Such an approach would make their exclusion less powerful and attractive and also bring the 'closed' and shameful aspect of our society into the open, allowing us to see that there is no such a thing as a 'wronged' life needing to be recognized, but rather, the plurality of existence. The radical innovation of Lacanian ethics consists of a lack of ideals, without 'wrong' and 'right'. Rather than reducing society to a place of a 'positive' or 'negative' identification, what is at stake is to make identification itself problematic, to radicalize existing differences in terms of showing their limits.

What would it look like to make more room for antagonism and violence in our society? Again, if we follow Lacan's ethical framework, such openness would be based not on the recognition of difference or of the Other, but on identification with a lack of the Other. In this way, what seems to be at stake here is the possibility of animating symbolic gestures that institutionalize social lack and enacting visions of the human subject and subjectivity, which involve a different understanding of the bond between people, the bond which confronts ideas of individual liberty and, at the same time, provides a different framework for equality. For example, a work of art generally suggests a different kind of 'bond' between individuals, since it does not emerge from a common purpose or good but from its own singularity, which, at the same time, is also addressed to the public. Thus, the work of art creates a 'bond' which is not based on the communality but on the ability of the art work to transcend its author's subject. When we identify with a work of art, we identify not with the artist's subjectivity but with its transcendence. As Joseph Brodsky once noted, 'the eye identifies itself not with the body it belongs to but with the object of its attention.'[2]

Reflecting on artistic practices which might identify with a lack of the Other, which do not seek certainty and the satisfaction of belonging but rather create the conditions needed to carry on living without support, traversing the turbulence and violence without an illusion of 'non-violence', what comes to mind is the work of a Chilean-born architect and filmmaker by profession and artist by vocation: Alfredo Jaar. Jaar's artistic device broadens the zone of exclusion by bringing together what is missing and silenced, and what is present and voiced, onto the same plane of blindness. One cannot identify with the Other, Jaar's work shows, without experiencing radical otherness. Through Jaar's artistic strategy of the 'inability to show everything', the possibility of identification with the Other is seriously compromised. Equality, for Jaar, is something that cannot be achieved but is fundamentally presupposed. Justice here acts as an artistic device enacting ethics of subjectivity, which transcend differences without the possibility of reconciliation.

For Jaar, the increasingly precarious state of global society, in which people live under the conditions of uncertain, hostile and indifferent environments, reveals just how secure, sure, strong, and undoubted the existing power structures are. A post-political condition of precariousness, for Jaar, is not based on innocence, on leaving behind the old ideological conflicts in order to concentrate on competent management and administration but on a dangerous complicity, against which no other action remains but to recover the courage of our minds and a sense of individual responsibility. It is from figures like Pier Paolo Pasolini and Antonio Gramsci that Jaar takes his inspiration. No such space exists, Jaar argues, where power could be liberated from its own blindness about itself. To think that we can abstract ourselves from the mechanisms of power, its supposed field of action, would be to conceive of a realm beyond the forms of political functioning, described by Gramsci as 'consensus and coercion'. Meanwhile, critical art means more than just saying what people do not want to hear or showing what they do not want to see. The power of what is articulated, in this case, transcends the use of criticism as a direct accusation. Rather, Jaar argues, in the face of the blindness of power, critical art brings into play a way of visual thinking that constructs a recognition of the blind spots, identifying some of the zones of denial on which our image of the public realm is based. Such spots are always very uncomfortable places. By breaking the relationship between the image and its system, Jaar constructs a different regime of visibility where the lack of images creates its own intolerability and constructs an ethical dimension of identification with a lack of the Other.

Jaar's installation *Lament of the Images* (2002) creates precisely a vertigo dimension where all simultaneously is excluded. Three texts glow upon the wall in a semi-obscure room. The first text tells the story of the twofold blinding of Nelson Mandela: by the sun reflected on limestone in the quarry where he served his sentence and by daylight, seen in the photograph of his release. The following text describes how millions of images, including the one of Mandela, were bought by a company owned by Bill Gates and buried in a limestone mine. The third text states that the US Defense Department has acquired the rights to all satellite imagery of the war in Afghanistan. 'There is', it declares, 'nothing left to see.' Still dazzled by the glowing texts, the viewer's eyes are drawn towards a dim corridor and the faint glow at the end of it. As one walks through the corridor, a feeling of uncomfortable expectation rises — we want to see what is hidden. However, suddenly, we find ourselves facing a screen of cold white glare, which, instead of revealing, obscures and blinds our vision. It is not that the pictures are missing, that they are excluded from our field of vision, but that field of vision itself is problematic. The idea here is not about missing images of the Kabul bombardment — Jaar does try to make 'an invisible visible'. Rather, becoming involved in the narrative, we too, blinded like Mandela, are seeing nothing because there is no image left for us to see. The empty glare makes us imitate what we see and recognize ourselves in the peering eye. It also forces us to acknowledge the artificial character of all images — they are elusive, inadequate, and incomplete. The momentary loss of sight caused by the glare of a stroboscopic light somehow suggests that 'true' visibility would be impossible to bear, that the only thing revealed here is the suppression and concealment of every record, of every image.

While the original scene can never be documented, shown, or reconstructed, the 'mental' picture which we create out of our own experience with this narrative reveals not just what we think is hidden but also what we do not question — our visual system of perception, which only though the loss of sight allows us to restore the ability of the contemporary viewer's jaded eye to look. The lament conveyed by our eyes stands for the whole 'lament of

the images' — images having long since been transformed into 'agents of blindness'. Jaar's question, in our view, concerns not so much the problem of making the 'invisible visible', what is included and what is not, but the problem of what is visible. Jaar's visible involves a relative non-visibility, when one must look without seeing, constructing a narrative which does not come from the images but from our experience of this narrative.

Only the way we look can change how we see things. While there is always something to see — but actually we cannot see anything unless we have this experience —, we are involved and we look. *Lament of the Images* demands a perception which is based on equality rather than including what is excluded from our field of vision. Jaar purposely does not include the missing pictures of a suffering community, in order to produce a feeling of a shared society where equality is understood as supplying equal visibility and progressively moving from the invisible oppressed to the visibility of guilt, sorrow, and the final satisfaction of our curiosity and need to identify with the other in order to feel secure and comforted. Why do we want to see these missing pictures? There is no specific strategy of visibility of the oppressed for Jaar, because aesthetics for the artist are always about ethics — an ethical dimension of intellectual emancipation, which is the same for the oppressed and the ruling, for the rich and the poor.

Here, Jaar takes his lead from Gramsci's argument that 'All men are intellectuals, one could therefore say: but not all men have in society the function of intellectuals', i.e. all men are thinking actors and 'non-intellectuals do not exist'.[3] This is an idea of intellectual emancipation: that there is always some point of equality. Gramsci argues that, contrary to the understanding of the role of the traditional intellectuals, 'The problem of creating a new stratum of intellectuals consists therefore in the critical elaboration of the intellectual activity that exists in everyone...' in order to construct a 'foundation of the new conception of the world'.[4] This approach resonates with Rancière's understanding of equality. He states:

> In the 1820s there was a lot of concern about how we can educate the people, slowly, progressively: but that was not the point, the idea of starting from inequality to reach quality; it's impossible because in the very process, you ceaselessly recycle practices of inequality. You must not

go towards equality, but must start from equality. Starting from equality does not presuppose that everyone in the world has equal opportunities to learn, to express their capacities. That's not the point. The point is that you have to start from the minimum equality that is given.[5]

This is where Jaar starts in *Lament of the Images* – from the equality of the impossibility of any such place where power is liberated from its own blindness about itself, to the idea that it is possible to progress from the realm of the invisible and the oppressed into the realm of the visible and therefore the liberated. Your lament, says Jaar, cannot be satisfied; it can only be exchanged with another grief, the one that is common for all. There is no position of superiority, neither for the viewers nor for the artist. Jaar explains, 'I put these images in your world, but always in a fragmented form, so that my inability to show everything becomes part of the work.'[6] The installation mingles the themes of captivity, that of people and that of images. It stages the paradox of excessive visibility; which, by accumulation, means that we ultimately see nothing. 'Progressing' from missing pictures to the loss of sight, one can grasp that we can only move from the equality of invisibility to the equality of the impossibility to see, of the experience of the limits of what can be achieved, shown or said. One has to start with equality and not finish with it.

Dwelling on Jaar's works, it is clear that there is always something missing, fragmented, silenced, separated, imbalanced, or destroyed. In *Real Pictures* (1995), images of the Rwandan genocide in 1994 have been supplanted by their descriptions on the black box; in the *Skoghall Konstall* (2000), the wood and paper museum is inaugurated with the Swedish authorities in attendance, only to be burned down the next day to illuminate the total absence of art in Skoghall; in *Untitled (Water)* (1990), Jaar shows only fragments of the sea and people – some of the photos that that artist took on the ships used by the immigration authority. The combined use of the seductive tourist advertising format of imagery of the sea which promises an exotic cruise and the projection of a different kind of journey embodied in the images of 'travellers' behind the bars is a reflection on political problems of global dimensions: stability on the one side and uncertainty, confinement on the other. The borders are open to goods but not to people. *Untitled* makes you suspicious

of Hardt and Negri's hopes for mass global mobility as a 'counter-empire', as microphysics of resistance. The people behind the bars hardly look like new revolutionaries — they are smiling, they just want to be on this ship, to join in the 'empire', to stabilize their displaced lives. Again, Jaar does not address the 'Other' as the realm we have to be sympathetic to or identify with but rather shows the visual imbalance of the picture, which seems to be full and promising but never is. In contrast with the mainstream of contemporary art, which has become a place to define the 'Other', Jaar allows the latter to define itself as identities that are never pre-given in the first place.

Hence, Jaar constrains normal visibility, revealing through the lacking fullness of image the lacking reality. There is never a full image, positive or negative; there is always something missing, and the artist cannot fulfil these absences, silences, lack of visibility, and inclusion. Jaar not just identifies the zones of denial but shows his inability to represent reality in its entirety; as the artist says, his 'inability to show everything' is his work of art. Jaar's regime of visibility shows that the present society is always lacking something; and the recognition of this lack is the precondition of social critique, not inclusiveness and recognition. While an art work can never replace the lack of a 'true' reality, it can, based on the perspective of that lack, present itself as an image of 'intolerability' that stands in opposition to itself and the reality that it is supposed to represent. This notion of the image standing in opposition to itself corresponds to what Lacan terms an 'identification with the symptom'. To say that power is blind and so is the image is to acknowledge the limits of positive identification with the Other. Jaar's artistic device of an 'inability to show everything' to satisfy our desire for the recognition of so-called 'wronged lives' does not argue for the exit of a suspension of identities. On the contrary, it constructs a space where they are living in the same moment where the line between 'victim' or 'perpetrator', 'good' or 'bad' in moral terms, cannot be drawn. Jaar's device not only recognizes exclusion, it shows that inclusion is also not attainable.

Through symbolic gestures, which institutionalize social lack, Jaar's works enact a type of subjectivity that flows from identities that are re-constructed via the art work. This subjectivity has problematic relations with the Other, since it cannot escape experiencing radical openness itself. Justice here could be understood not only as the recognition of something hidden, silenced and excluded but also as the incorporation of injustice into subjectivity. While for Butler the goal is to minimize precariousness through an ethical appeal of 'non-violence', Jaar calls for making life even more precarious, so to speak, by broadening the plane of vulnerability and uncertainty. The question of justice for Butler is about how do we object to human suffering — how do we decide whose life is grievable and whose is not, and how do we preserve the life of the Other. Jaar's aesthetic device, meanwhile, highlights the limit of the recognition of otherness, thus undermining the traditional ethical strategy, and, instead, focuses on maintaining the visibility of the social 'emptiness'.

There is this very difficult question of how justice can be understood and achieved in a society whose entire existence is based on injustice — acts of power that bring exclusion, division and antagonism. Jaar approaches this question aesthetically. We know that whereas ethics and aesthetics both express order, ethics presupposes principles, while an aesthetical order constructs itself from disordered material. The matter of aesthetics concerns more profound problems of form, of relations with the given sensible world—it is like an order without laws that deals with the visible configuration of the given by constantly showing that so-called 'rules' are flawed. That is why new art works are constantly created — there are no limits to how the sensible can be reconfigured. While ethics judge, aesthetics demonstrate the structural impossibility of any judgment. Kant long ago pointed out that an aesthetical 'agreement' such as 'this rose is beautiful' merely indicates an imagined shared reality, because there is no such thing as a *sensus communis* and therefore the latter must be constructed in a form we can all agree on. Kant teaches us that to make an aesthetic judgment is to fundamentally disagree with the possibility of any agreement. Hence, aesthetic critique is better understood not in terms of a judgment per se but in terms of how these judgments are performed. Jacques Rancière, for example, calls this 'the aesthetic agreement on the disagreement'. For him, the praxis of art shows how we should judge generally — to expose the flawed nature of any agreements. Hence, aesthetics understood in these terms would approach the question of justice, the matter of equality and unity, in a different way. 'Aesthetically' performed 'justice' would provide a different framework for equality. Given the conceptual impossibility of any agreement, this 'aesthetic justice' would not seek to include and reconcile but rather to exclude all.

That is why Jaar's aesthetic strategy of the 'inability to show all' is such an effective device, aimed at creating an equality of radical exclusion from the outset.

For Jaar, justice is not about attending to the suffering of others, but about a fundamental critique of justice. Staging an unsituated and non-objectifying regime of visibility — the vision of lack without the image — produces a new scene of equality where identities, instead of being endlessly exchanged, are excluded. Rancière's longing for the 'emancipated spectator' would certainly resonate with Jaar's notion of radical exclusion. Rancière argues that, 'Emancipation begins when we challenge the opposition between viewing and acting; when we understand that the self-evident facts that structure the relations between saying, seeing and doing themselves belong to the structure of domination and subjection.'[7]However powerful 'the intolerable' image is, attending to true horror and suffering, it always belongs to a particular system of visibility. Rancière writes, 'The image is pronounced unsuitable for criticizing reality because it pertains to the same regime of visibility as that reality, which by turns displays its aspect of brilliant appearance and its other side of sordid truth, constituting a single spectacle'.[8] What is at stake here is 'the shift from the intolerable in the image to the intolerability of the image...'[9] and this is what Jaar's regime of visibility performs. What the artist endlessly attempts is to not assert any authority in supporting any given system or narrative by satisfying the uncomfortable spots. For example, rather than satisfying feelings of guilt or outrage, Jaar prefers to envisage public space itself as a memorial, as a symbolic graveyard of many voices, identities, of life itself.

As mentioned above, Butler seem to deal with the issue of justice through defining what is human and what is not, which life is grievable and which is not. In her *Frames of War*, Butler talks extensively about the importance of public grieving as recognizing a life as having been worth living and thus bringing about justice in the form of public mourning. She states, 'An ungrievable life is one that cannot be mourned because it has never lived, that is, it has never counted as a life at all. Open grieving is bound up with outrage, and outrage in the face of injustice or indeed of unbearable loss has enormous political potential.'[10]

Rather than marking loss with public mourning, Jaar envisages public space itself as a memorial. For him, justice does not come about with the recognition of a life but by coming to terms with the idea that public space itself exists out of 'gaps' and 'silences', articulations that never took place, lives which were ignored so that the public space could be maintained. For Jaar, this public consensus is never based on innocence and a desire to recognize the life of the Other, but on a dangerous complicity to cover up the absence of fullness and to silence or ignore the irresolvable antagonisms that Chantal Mouffe has placed at the centre of political life. Jaar's ethics refuses any transcendence of power and antagonism in the name of something higher, for example, humanity. For him, as for Lacan, a man is not the measure of all things — what we have in common is only this lack of fullness or commonality. Chantal Mouffe argues that:

> While there is no underlying principle of unity, no predetermined centre to this diversity of spaces, there always exist diverse forms of articulation among them and we are not faced with the kind of dispersion envisaged by some postmodernist thinkers. Nor are we dealing with the kind of 'smooth' space found in Deleuze and his followers. Public spaces are always striated and hegemonically structured. A given hegemony results from a specific articulation of a diversity of spaces and this means that the hegemonic struggle also consists in the attempt to create a different form of articulation among public spaces.[11]

Recognizing that any given public space exists because of exclusion and incorporating, underlining, the excluded to public visibility rather than maintaining the 'smoothness' of a given public space via including, is what Jaar has in mind when he contracts public spaces as a memorial. Following Jaar's conception, what is to be mourned is public space itself, since it is fundamentally barred (or prevented) from being open.

Jaar's vision of public space is always one which activates a sense of mourning and a warning of articulations that did not take place. For example, one of Jaar's preferred techniques for creating public space is through the image of a memorial or a monument (from the concept of *monitus*, which means 'warning') that stands as a substitute for many discourses that did not occur. Jaar's installation *The Geometry of Conscience* (2010), for instance, is a below-ground-level memorial for people who died or

disappeared during Pinochet's regime. As the room becomes fully, blindingly lit, the viewer finally sees that on each side of hundreds of silhouettes there are mirrors, so the effect is that the wall of faces goes on into infinity. Then the lights are abruptly turned off. The viewer experiences the faces of the victims and survivors literally being burnt onto their retina for several long moments. Similarly, Jaar's memorials include earlier works such as *The Cloud* (2000), an ephemeral monument to the memory of those who lost their lives trying to cross the Mexico-USA border, where for 45 minutes viewers can mourn more than three thousand people and then balloons are released; or *Lights in the City* (1999), where a 'photograph' is taken every time a human being asks for help — a light flashes as if a photograph is being taken and then a red light in the Cupola warns the city of Montreal of a condition that within the context of one of the richest cities in North America is clearly unacceptable: its endless homeless people passing by.

These memorials are speaking of something that no one else wants to speak of, or can no longer speak of since their voices have been silenced, ignored or rendered incapable of speaking by becoming locked into amnesia. It is the most invisible and unheard voices who are offered a chance to speak for themselves here rather than being included and recognized. They stand on their own — not allowing the positivity of the public space to prevail, to mend the 'wounds'. To envisage a public space as a memorial rather than a mourning of individual victims is to say that history will always repeat itself, that bad things will happen again, because division and exclusion are constitutive of the social. While this is not the most positive approach to the question of justice, this is the one which Jaar considers to be most productive. He argues, 'I have no illusions and, like Gramsci, I am an intellectual pessimist. But also like him, I have an optimistic will.'[12] There is an ethics of harmony with a vocabulary that includes justice, democracy, responsibility — this ethics aims at reconciling with the lack of unity. There is, also, a different type of ethics — a Lacanian ethics of disharmony. This ethics does not focus on portraying victims and seeking responsibility. It does not attempt to create unity by recognizing the Other. Rather, it is engaged in the possibility of constructing symbolic configurations and spaces that institutionalize social lack and incorporate the ethical recognition of the impossibility of social positivity.

In this light, what becomes fundamental for the question of justice is incorporating injustice by maintaining the visibility of this constitutive lack, and this is what Jaar's aesthetics do. Rather than appealing for 'non-violence', Jaar's artistic device aims at abandoning the idea of a society beyond antagonisms and violence. It animates symbolic gestures which resist the idea of a bond between ourselves and the Other based on the recognition of differences. The bond that Jaar envisages comes out of a failed unicity and identification with the lack of the Other per se.

According to Jaar's aesthetic thinking, the issue of the blindness of power cannot be attended by portraying suffering and endless calls for responsibility. What his work articulates is that there is a more complex set of relations between 'wronged' lives and 'good' ones, the included and the excluded, the visible/ pronounced and the invisible/ silenced. The power relations and the very logic of power by which any given society is maintained are permanently in need of the Other and its justification. This justification is achieved through a desire to recognize, include, and take responsibility; to fight a system we are part of.

In this way, Plato's wish to ban weeping poets mourning injustices from the Republic to avoid public outrage and disorder is misplaced and unnecessary. Contrary to Plato's convictions, when citizens constantly watch tragedy and attend to the suffering of others, this provides stabilizing and consolidating influences. What would really threaten Plato's Republic is the poets' silence and a lack of outrage, since order cannot exist without disorder. What follows is that injustice is not simply the absence of justice or mere victimhood, but the condition for the existence of justice. That is why, instead of appealing for justice, Jaar's aesthetic devices are aimed at dislocating the very conception of justice as the possibility of recognizing the Other under the umbrella of commonality and fairness. What is common here is only lack of communality. Such a device does not deal with the 'disorder' side of the order — i.e. 'wronged' lives, victimhood, etc., but threatens the very relationship, the very system based on the presence of the Other. It broadens, radicalises exclusion and thus alters identities, which came to attend to suffering, to reconcile — and this in itself is a moment of power. This moment of power disarticulates and re-articulates pre-given identities, it restructures the exclusion in the way of 'excluding all', by denying the desire to see 'the missing picture', to identify with victims.

Butler envisages the concept of justice through the prism of an ethical appeal for 'non-violence'. However, what does violence mean? Strictly speaking, it means an unjust use of power. Following this logic, 'non-violence' then would entail a just, fair use of power. By showing that power is blind to justice, since its very mechanisms entail division and exclusion, and that it forgoes the notion of fairness presupposed in the liberal understanding of justice, Jaar rejects the idea of justice and power having a harmonious relationship.

Power is fundamentally unjust, and what justice means for Jaar is making its traces visible; bringing all that is missing, excluded, and invisible into its own right; not recognizing and thus satisfying our desire for the Other but placing 'them' and 'us' on the same plane; sharing the same moment of equality. Jaar's 'vision without an image' attends to a notion of justice without victims, making us assume responsibility for our multiple accommodations to power structures on the cognitive and affective levels. To put it in Lacan's terms, it forces us to 'identify with our symptom', to return to our own attachment to what ensures our servitude instead of identifying with the Other. Jaar's symbolic registration of lack produces an ethical form of aesthetic appeal that creates a sense of inner conflict and forces us to question our desire for justice. Such a trajectory has a true potential for injustice to be symbolically incorporated.

Notes

1   Alain Badiou, 'Philosophy and Politics', *Infinite Thought*, transl. and ed. by Oliver Feltham and Justin Clemens (New York: Continuum, 2005), p. 53.
2   Joseph Brodsky, *Watermark* (New York: Farrar, Straus and Giroux, 1992), p. 111.
3   Antonia Gramsci, 'The Problems of History and Culture', in *Selection from the Prison Notebooks*, transl. by Quintin Hoare and Geoffrey Nowell Smith (London: Lawrence and Wishart, 2007), p. 9.
4   Ibid..
5   Jacques Rancière in conversation with Fulvia Carnevale and John Kelsey, 'Art of the Possible', in *Artforum*, March 2007, online: http://findarticles.com/p/articles/mi_m0268/is_7_45/ai_n24354911/?tag=content;col1.
6   Alfredo Jaar is quoted in: Adriana Valdes, 'Don't Think Like an Artist, Think Like a Human Being', in *Alfredo Jaar: Santiago de Chile 2006* (Barcelona: Actar, 2007), p. 56.
7   Jacques Rancière, *The Emancipated Spectator*, transl. by Gregory Elliott (Brooklyn and London: Verso Books, 2009), p. 13.
8   Ibid., pp. 83-84.
9   Ibid., p. 84.
10 Judith Butler, *Frames of War: When is Life Grievable?* (Brooklyn NY and London: Verso Books, 2009), p. 39.
11 Chantal Mouffe, 'Artistic Activism and Agonistic Spaces', in *Art & Research*, Volume 1, No.2, Summer 2007, www.artandresearch.org.uk/v1n2/mouffe.html.
12 Alfredo Jaar's interview with Luigi Fassi, *KLAT* Issue 01, Winter 2009-2010, available online: www.alfredojaar.net.

Justice Terminable and Interminable
Rachid Bouchareb and Michael Haneke

Arne De Boever

The Problem of Living

J.M. Coetzee's novel *Disgrace* starts with the sentence: 'For a man of his age, fifty-two, divorced, he has, to his mind, solved the problem of sex rather well.'[1] The man in question is David Lurie, professor of communication studies at Capetown Technical University, and a specialist of Romantic Literature. In its measured prose — which starts off what one critic has referred to as the novel's 'relentless'[2] focalization through Lurie —, the first sentence states what is the central problematic of the book: not so much 'the problem of sex', but the problem of such a problem itself — in other words, a problematic — and the question of whether it can ever be solved.

Indeed, when it comes to the problem of sex, *Disgrace* seems to be about how this problem is opened up again, this time interminably so. For when the solution Lurie has found for the problem of sex — the prostitute Soraya — disappears from his life, he has trouble coming up with a new solution, even if he is offered another prostitute also named Soraya. Sex gives Lurie so much trouble, in fact, that he wonders whether he should not, perhaps, 'give up, retire from the game': 'At what age, he wonders, did Origen castrate himself?... A simple enough operation, surely: they do it to animals every day.'[3] Ultimately, he will begin an affair with one of his students. When the affair sours and it turns out he has falsified attendance and grade records, he leaves his teaching position and retires to the countryside to live with his daughter Lucy.

However, sex is only one of the problems evoked in the novel's opening pages. Lurie's desire, obviously, is to be 'post' the problem of sex: either because he is having the sex he wants (with Soraya, for example), or by having eradicated his desire for sex altogether (castration). But given the location where this problem is played out — post-apartheid South Africa — it is difficult not to read 'race' instead of 'sex' in the opening line of the novel, and to consider this white man's desire to have solved the problem of sex as allegorical for South Africa's desire to have solved the problem of race. One 'post' evokes the other, and the novel shows that in both cases there is a wound that persists underneath the 'finiteness' of its solution — including the solution of South Africa's new national sovereignty. Consider, for example, how in the second part of the novel, Lurie and his daughter Lucy are attacked by two black men and a boy. Lurie is badly beaten and burnt; his daughter is raped. In the conversations they have about the attack afterwards, the question of South Africa's violent history — colonialism and apartheid — is never far away.

Both in the case of sex and in the case of race, *Disgrace* therefore seems to suggest that whatever solution may be found for these problems (a prostitute; castration; a new national sovereignty) is ultimately always only temporary, and thus part of the interminable management of what could be called *the problem of living*. In the face of this problem's concrete and present violence, but especially also in view of its historical legacies, it seems difficult to believe that a definitive, terminable solution could ever be found. Whatever therapeutic effects a proposed solution may achieve, it seems doubtful that it could ever be considered 'complete'. Instead, we learn to live — individually, collectively — *with* the problem of living, and we are more or less successful at it. When this project fails, we seek help. Failure can be triggered by an event that opens up an old wound that resists closing — that persists, insists, pulses. Like life itself.

Therapy?

Some may counter that seeing life as 'learning to live with the problem of living' is a tragic and pessimistic view of the human condition — and they may fundamentally disagree with me for this reason. However, while I might agree with the use of the qualifier 'tragic' to describe the position I have laid out, I would not call it 'pessimistic' (and this constitutes, in fact, the core of the problematic of aesthetic justice as I present it here): there is no reason to cast the interminableness of one's solutions to the problems of sex, race, or life in a negative light — in the same way that there is no reason to think negatively of the interminableness of our attempts to be good in a world that often appears otherwise. Instead, the incompleteness of our attempts to definitively settle this or that problem could also liberate us from our dogged labour for final solutions, opening up instead an era of non-final solutions in which a creative, moderately happy, interminable play of problem-solving might come about. The history of humanity is arguably nothing other than this — and it is ultimately up to each and every one of us to decide whether this fills us with unhappy resentment or with (at least) moderate joy.[4]

In my discussion, I have been rehearsing some of the terminology of one of Sigmund Freud's last psycho-analytic

writings, the 1937 essay titled 'Analysis Terminable and Interminable'.[5] While the position Freud takes up in the text — namely that psycho-analysis is ultimately not *entirely* therapeutic in the sense that the problem of living that it tries to solve is ultimately never *completely* solved and may emerge again — may appear to be a pessimistic one, it is not entirely clear why this should be the case. The tone of the text is certainly not particularly pessimistic. It is, rather, a realist piece that acknowledges the problem of living and adds the question mark after therapy, drawing into question — several years before Georges Canguilhem — the distinction between the normal and the pathological, exposing that whatever we think of as normal was always nothing but the interminable management of the problem of life: i.e. a normal inhabited by the abnormal.

In an article that was published in *The Journal of Aesthetic Education*, I have discussed how Freud's relation to the work of art, like his psycho-analytic practice, pushes toward interpretation and communication, thus leading away from the riddle and the incomprehensible, and saddling him with what I playfully called an 'aesthetic Oedipus complex'.[6] It is an Oedipus complex because if Freud's ideal is to solve the riddle (music famously frustrates him because he finds there is nothing to solve there...), his hero is arguably Oedipus. But what is Oedipus' reward for solving the riddle, if we look at the tragedy? True, he becomes king. But he also has sex with his mother, after he had already murdered his father. It is a strange, dubious heroism to be sure — and if the Oedipus story arguably teaches us anything, it is *not* to reproduce this tragedy... by *not* solving the riddle.

It certainly seems that such a 'solution' — a non-final, interminable one — was an option for Freud, not only at the end of his life, after he had already dedicated himself to broader civilizational problems, but even at the very beginning. For in a letter to Wilhelm Fliess from 1900 that is mentioned in the introduction to 'Analysis Terminable and Interminable', Freud refers to the 'career' of one of his patients as a 'riddle' that is '*almost* completely solved', adding that the 'treatment' for the patient's condition is in reality 'interminable' and was terminated only by a decision from the patient in consultation with the analyst.[7] While outsiders may find this a disappointment, Freud notes that to him it is actually 'a matter of indifference', and that he will 'keep an eye on the man' to see if any problems return.[8]

These are not the thoughts of an Oedipus who has *solved* the riddle but of an Oedipus for whom the riddle is *almost* completely solved. Note that such a position does not come at the expense of *trying* to solve the riddle. I am not advocating passivity in the face of the problem of living. Instead, the work of trying to solve the riddle, and the desire that is invested (sublimated) in it, are redistributed here. Again, while this perspective might still be tragic, I do not think it is pessimistic. At the very least, it opens up a breathing room in the aesthetic space of tragedy — tiny but significant — where something else — a tragic ethics and politics, to evoke the individual and collective 'doing' of 'creative, moderately happy, interminable problem-solving' — can come about.

Bouchareb and 'The Police'

It is through this lens that I approach two films dealing with France's colonial past, but in drastically different ways: Rachid Bouchareb's *Indigènes* (Days of Glory, 2006) and Michael Haneke's *Caché* (Hidden, 2005). Both films engage France's relation to its former colonies (specifically, Algeria). But whereas Bouchareb's film offers a Hollywood aesthetic that ultimately appears to focus on financial retribution for the discriminated, colonized North Africans who fought for France during the Second World War (a project that is worthwhile enough and that I do not want to discredit), Haneke's film raises the question of justice at another, psychopolitical level — at the level of a trauma that no financial retribution can relieve. This position is hauntingly captured in the film by the (unexplained) point of view of a surveillance camera, recording the daily life of a Parisian family whose history will turn out to be related to the 1961 massacre of Algerians in Paris. It is through the adoption of this peculiar aesthetic —this speculative, but disturbingly realist (in other words: *horrific*) point of view — that in Haneke's film some kind of justice is delivered, even if it may not be a satisfactory one.

If poetic justice generally refers to the fact that a fitting reward is coming to whoever practices virtue or vice, aesthetic justice upsets this logic of the reward in order to in fact

accomplish something more political, and, in this case, psychopolitical: the uncomfortable, unfitting, and not necessarily successful working through of a historical trauma that shakes the very foundations of Western, bourgeois family life and indeed of the Western, bourgeois nation-state. It deals in the horror of what is hidden rather than in the ideology of glory.

At the end of *Indigènes*, there is a text that translates the film's narrative into a concrete call for justice: while North-African and sub-Saharan soldiers like those shown in the film fought for France in the Second World War, they are not getting the same retirement money as French soldiers, and this situation should be adjusted. All of the problems that the film has been addressing — which are not limited to post-colonial issues but also involve, of course, the problematic of war as such — are thus reduced to this concrete and practically realizable concern with compensation for the gift (the sacrifice) that these soldiers have made. And not without effect: generally considered a political work, the film and its Hollywood aesthetic moved French President Jacques Chirac to adjust the soldiers' pensions to the same level as that of their French colleagues, a policy change that was heavily criticized by Nicolas Sarkozy, at that time Minister of the Interior, for costing France tens of millions of Euros. This fact is often quoted as evidence of the film's politics, of its transformative, political effect 'in the real world'.

As Alec Hargreaves in an article about the film has remarked, it is worth noting, as far as the definition of politics that is implied in this assessment goes, that Bouchareb's politics, and also that of its lead actor Jamel Debbouze, is 'conciliatory' in this case 'rather than recriminatory': 'the injustices suffered by yesterday's colonial soldiers and today's postcolonial minorities' should not be 'pretexts for destructive behaviour'. 'This was in contrast,' Hargreaves notes, 'with the recriminatory position taken by an organization established early in 2005 [i.e. before *Indigènes* was released] calling itself Les Indigènes de la République (Native Subjects of the Republic) arguing that violence was a justified response to the racial and ethnic discrimination endemic in French society. 'During the riots of November 2005,' Hargreaves notes, 'Les Indigènes de la République came to the fore in arguing that violence was a justified response to the racial and ethnic discrimination endemic in French society.'[9] Violent or non-violent, conciliatory or recriminatory politics? This is, of course, an old issue, and my aim here is not to reopen it — even if it remains an important one.

I *am* interested, however, in the separation that this question presents to the extent that it pertains to the finite or infinite, terminable or interminable nature of the politics that one is confronting in this context. For the fact of the matter is that there are two kinds of politics that come into play here: there is, first of all, the conciliatory politics that seeks to secure 'a rightful place in French society' for those 'minority ethnic youths' whose ancestors fought in the Second World War.[10] This kind of politics is arguably finite. It has a terminable project: securing a place in French society for minority ethnic youths. But there is also another politics in the film, one that much less easily leads to conciliation and that is, possibly, interminable. That politics would continue even *after* one's rightful place in French society has been secured: the psychopolitics of a spirit that has been scarred by the violence first of all of colonialism, and secondly of war. Whereas the first politics is still of an economic order and can be solved within the logic of political economy, the second escapes the measure of such a conciliation and demands another type of justice — one that might, in the end, be impossible to deliver. For what compensation, what *economic* solution, could make up for the theft (colonialism) or the gift (sacrifice) of life (in war)? There is a debt here that can never be repaid. This is not only about paying North-African and sub-Saharan soldiers the same retirement money as French soldiers. It is also about how one can *ever* repay the gesture of putting one's life on the line in a situation of war. At this level too, there is arguably no final, economic solution — instead, another approach is asked for.[11]

Let me start with the conciliatory, terminable, and — as I present it here — economic politics of the film. In an article entitled 'Incorporating Indigenous Soldiers in the Space of the French Nation', Panivong Norindr has already criticized this particular dimension of the film. Norindr argues that despite its popular success and its unprecedented achievement as a militant film-event that will earn its place in film history, *Indigènes* fails to respond to the urgent need for public debate about French colonial history because it represses a more unpalatable truth that contributed to making France what it is today.[12] This 'repressed truth' — note the psychoanalytic language — returns in various guises in Norindr's text. He points out, for example, that the film

remains entirely within the 'glorious' logic positing that in order to be part of the French nation, one must 'show [one's] credentials' and prove one's 'worthiness' and 'commitment', to the point of wanting to 'die for' the French nation. There is an assimilationist project that is uncritically promoted in the film, and one that cannot be separated from France's colonial project — even if the film leaves their connection unaddressed. Related to this, Norindr points out that the film's focus is entirely on 'the loyal Maghreb soldiers who fought for France: it does not consider 'the consequences of French colonial violence in the Maghreb and other occupied territories'.[13]

In addition, Norindr discusses the film's uneasy status between narrative film and documentary, exposing how *Indigènes*, in spite of the fact that it was partly based on testimony and historical research, ignores some historical truths, for example by suggesting at the beginning that the impoverished Maghrebis 'volunteered to serve under the French flag'.[14] As Norindr points out, historian of Algeria Benjamin Stora has challenged this revisionist aspect of the film, which erases conflict from the story in favour of a more conciliatory politics. In his final assessment of the film, Norindr does not mince words:

> *Indigènes* will ultimately be remembered as a mediocre war film, in large part because it borrows a Hollywood model, from its narrative structure to its diachronic temporality, that fails to account for the ruptures and discontinuities of history.[15]

To be clear, I do not want to dismiss the film's politics. I am not saying that the film cannot be called a political film on these grounds. Like other critics — Hargreaves and Norindr included — I think that what the film has achieved, politically, is important. However, the film's final focus on the economic issue of the pensions risks to overwrite a politics, also evoked by the film, that is of another order. This is the politics of making visible, and remembering, the violence of France's colonial history. It is on this count that Norindr argues the film fails.

I would add to his argument that this is a violence that ultimately cannot be compensated for, that no pension adjustment or other financial redress is ever going to make disappear. Instead, it is the violence of the 'interminable' analysis that Freud is writing about. From this perspective, the film is decidedly less successful (whatever 'success' can still mean in this context): its 'polished, unoriginal' aesthetic in no way addresses the rupture of this historical trauma, one that arguably continues today, precisely in the unsecured place of those 'minority ethnic youths' in French society, for whom there might never be 'a rightful place in French society'.

Indeed, isn't there a problem with keeping the desirability of such a place, the object-ideal of such a place and its operation of inclusion/exclusion, intact as a place of value? Instead, these youths mark *through* their unsecured position the violence of France's history and there is arguably no amount of positive discrimination, affirmative action, or whatever other 'economic' compensation we can think of, that is going to make that scar disappear. Moreover, this is arguably the political mark of all of us — because no one rightfully belongs anywhere. *Indigènes* ultimately risks to promote the political ideals that produced the very exclusions it sets out to address.

The scar of these retired soldiers as well as these 'youths' then becomes the scar of a conception of politics: not as consensus or agreement but as dissensus or disagreement, coming from a state of internal exclusion or exception generated by the distributions of the sensible that politics challenges. While the terms consensus and agreement and dissensus and disagreement may not *exactly* match the terms 'conciliation' or 'recrimination' that I used earlier — there is no reason why disagreement would need to come with the recrimination of destructive violence — they can still be used to mark the difference between two kinds of politics: one in which an initial disagreement would ultimately be defused into a conciliation, and another where such a conciliation may not be possible.

In a book called *Disagreement*, Jacques Rancière defines politics in opposition to what he calls the police. Rancière proposes to call 'police' what is generally called 'politics', namely 'the set of procedures whereby the aggregation and consent of collectivities is achieved, the organization of powers, the distribution of places and roles, and the systems for legitimizing this distribution'.[16] Politics, on the other hand, is a term he reserves 'for an extremely determined activity antagonistic to policing: whatever breaks with the tangible configuration whereby parties and parts or lack of them are defined by a presupposition that, by definition, has no place in that configuration – that of the part of those who have no part'.[17] Whereas the police, in other words, refers to what is considered one's 'rightful place in society' – Rancière's criticism of this logic in fact goes all the way back to Plato's carefully distributed layout for a just society in his *Republic*–, politics is an activity that would be antagonistic to the logic of this order. It 'does not recognize relationships between citizens and the state' but only 'the mechanisms and singular manifestations by which a certain citizenship occurs but never belongs to individuals as such'.[18] Combining Norindr's criticism of *Indigènes* with Rancière, one would have to conclude that *Indigènes* is with the police, that it confirms the police order rather than antagonizing it. The redistribution of the pension funds that it achieved may mark a certain kind of politics, but it is not the politics that Rancière lays out in *Disagreement*.

It is at the very end of Rancière's book that this theorization of politics becomes concretely tied up to France's colonial history, and specifically France's relation to Algeria, that is central to *Indigènes*. There, Rancière mentions the bodies of the Algerians that were thrown in the Seine by the French police in October 1961, and that the police and the government tried to hide from view.[19] In its attempt to bring Algeria back into view, *Indigènes'* aesthetic paradoxically continues to hide it, and thus the film ultimately fails to deliver the justice that France's history demands – even if, at the level of poetic justice, the justice of a 'fitting reward coming to whoever practices virtue or vice', it was arguably successful.

So the question, as far as justice at this level goes, is: Can it be delivered? How? How does one respond ethically, politically to a historical issue like colonialism and the violence it has wrought? What is the relation of such a response to economy? What justice corresponds to it? What aesthetics?

Haneke's Politics of Horror

It is in light of these questions that I now want to consider Bouchareb's film – both its aesthetics and its politics – next to Michael Haneke's film *Caché*.

In *Caché*, a family of three (Georges, Anne, and their son Pierrot) receives two hour-long videotape recordings of their house. The tapes are wrapped in violent drawings: one shows a child with blood coming from its mouth; another shows a chicken with blood around its neck. The family also receives a tape that shows the farmhouse of Georges' parents, as well as a tape that leads to the door of an apartment in a cheap housing building on the outskirts of Paris. Georges suspects Majid, an Algerian boy whose parents used to work on the farm of Georges' parents, of having sent the tapes. When Majid's parents were killed in the 1961 massacre of Algerians in Paris that Rancière refers to, Georges' parents decide to adopt Majid. Six-year old Georges is annoyed that he has to share his room, his things, his life with Majid – his attitude reflects that of the French, who are annoyed at having to share their room, their stuff, their life with Algerian immigrants. He accuses Majid of coughing up blood in order to get him expelled from the house. He convinces Majid that his father has asked him to kill the farm cock: Majid chops off the cock's head and gets blood all over himself, angering Georges' father. Georges tells his parents Majid did it in order to scare him. Majid is sent to an orphanage. The drawings that accompany the videotapes refer to both these incidents.

When Georges goes to find out who is living behind the door of the apartment shown in one of the tapes, he finds Majid. Convinced that Majid is responsible for sending the tapes, Georges threatens him. Majid says he has nothing to do with the tapes. When Georges' son Pierrot disappears, Georges asks the police to search the house of Majid. Majid and his son spend a night in jail, but Pierrot remains missing. He will turn up the next morning after having spent the night at a friend's house. Shortly afterwards, Majid invites Georges to his apartment. He says, 'I had nothing to do with the tapes. I just wanted you to be present' – and slits his throat. The violent gesture tears open Haneke's clean, minimalist approach to the events and releases the tension that has been building up in the film. Majid's son shows up at Georges' office the day after. He claims to have nothing to do with the videotapes. The film ends without the viewer knowing who sent the tapes.

It is worth noting that there is a strong historical, and specifically generational, aspect to Haneke's film. Georges goes to see his mother to hear her out about Majid; the disappearance of Georges' son, Pierrot, is central to the film; Majid could have been Georges' brother, but was denied the right to a new family because of Georges' selfishness; there is also Majid's son, who spends a night in jail because of what happened between Georges

and his father in 1961. This generational aspect is inseparable from trauma: Georges is traumatized because of his history with Majid; Majid is traumatized because of what happened to his parents, and because he was sent to an orphanage; Majid's son is traumatized because he is thrown into jail for no reason and because his father commits suicide. These traumata can be traced back to 1961. They are thus more than the traumata of a generationally linked set of individuals: they are the psychic wounds of France itself, of the French nation-state and republic.

Due to his involvement in the expulsion of Majid from the family house, Georges seems to share the responsibility for French colonialism and the events of 1961. Although he emphasizes again and again that he is not going to feel guilty because of what he did to Majid, he seems to be haunted by a guilt that can be traced back to 1961. The problem of what came after 1961 is presented in the film as a problem of *adoption*: will France 'adopt' the children of those whom it massacred in '61? Will it adopt the children of its colonial history? Or will it act like a six-year old and expel them from the national family because it does not want to share its room, its things, its life with them? Moreover, if France decides to *adopt*, to what extent will it ask those whom it adopts to *adapt*, i.e. to *assimilate* to the French way of life? What degree of *adaptation* will be required in order for them to be able to take up their 'rightful place in French society'?

George's guilt is presented in the film through the videotapes, which mark the point of view of his trauma and his conscience. The suggestion seems to be that 'someone is watching' Georges and his family. At first, Georges thinks that this point of view is Majid's; when he goes to Majid's house, however, Majid denies that he has anything to do with it. Georges then receives a videotape of the conversation he had with Majid. This videotape shows Majid crying after Georges has left his house. As Anne points out when she sees the tape, it really seems as if Majid does not know that a camera is filming him. He seems to be genuinely unaware of the camera that is 'hidden' in his house. When Georges finds out Majid has a son, he thinks that the son sent the videotapes. But the son also denies having anything to do with the tapes. What Georges seems to have a hard time realizing is that the point of view that he is desperately trying to locate somewhere *outside* of himself, and tie to a foreign entity that can easily be construed as a scapegoat, this point of view is actually *inside* of him, and marks an internal perspective that requires a very different kind of searching and analysis. The camera is recording from the point of view of the super-ego.

Georges is evidently haunted by his guilt, by a demon from his past, and the 'eye' that is watching him and his family (his wife receives phone calls, his son receives postcards at school) is arguably the 'eye' from his past, the event from his childhood that is associated with an event in France's national history — i.e. his own eye. Haneke's *realist* film thus captures the *psychotic* reality of Georges' — and France's — psyche, of the French individual and collective psyche, and it is the clash of this psychosis with the film's otherwise realist aesthetic that produces its horror, the horror of the objectified, thing-like conscience that is watching Georges, Anne, and France at large. The *thing* is forcing all of these agents to remember.[20] The film thus tells a drama of the inside and the outside. What Georges perceives to be coming from outside is coming from inside. When the film reveals that the postcards Pierrot, Georges' son, receives at school have Georges as their 'sender', the viewer realizes that Georges is indeed the 'origin' of the videotapes, the drawings, the calls, and phone calls: they all come from him, from what is hidden *within him*. They offer us a 'view' onto what lies hidden within Georges — and France. Thus, even if, at first sight, *Caché* seems to show much less than Bouchareb's film, its aesthetic may ultimately be showing a lot more, due to the fact that it highlights precisely the hidden history that Bouchareb's film fails to show.

Interminable Cinema

Some may argue in this context that Haneke's film does not show enough; but those critics should consider what amount of showing could possibly do justice to the violent history that Haneke's film evokes. The response to Norindr's criticism of Bouchareb is *not* to ask Bouchareb to show more, or to be more historically precise in the showing, or even to choose documentary over narrative film — all of those responses would operate within the order of the terminable, suggesting there is a correct, final, and reconciliatory way of showing this history. As will be clear, I disagree with such a position: the showing that can be done in these situations, rather, is always interminable, and the question that the filmmaker confronts in this context is: How to show this without entering into the logic of the terminable, without giving in to the logic of a final solution? This is what Haneke pulls off and it is the mark of a great work of art.

How is Georges going to work through his guilt? Not by taking sleeping pills ('cachets', in French), closing the curtains of the bedroom, closing himself off from the world to escape his trauma. As the film suggests, even in sleep Georges is not safe from his past: he dreams about the day when Majid was taken away from his parents' house. This is of course obvious once one has understood that the POV that haunts Georges is that of his own conscience. To sleep will in fact evoke the past. The 'eye' of his past is everywhere; he cannot separate himself from this 'eye' that he is (the 'eye' that 'I' am). However, in the film this hidden 'eye' is not only presented as the source of Georges' terror; it is also an 'eye' that, through the film, invites a working through that is interminable. Thus, the 'cachet' that Georges is taking is not one but two: not only a sleeping pill ('cachet') to avoid the terror of the film of the super-ego, of the hidden ('caché') that the film remembers; but also Haneke's film *Caché* that invites another kind of response. The film's recording, the memory that it captures, thus has two faces in Haneke: on the one hand, its view offers a politics of horror; on the other, the film participates in the interminable analysis that would do justice to its memory.

I would like to thank Nathaniel Deines for his research assistance while I was preparing this article.

Notes

1   John Maxwell Coetzee, *Disgrace* (London: Vintage, 2000), p. 1.
2   Gayatri Chakravorty Spivak, 'Ethics and Politics in Tagore, Coetzee, and Certain Scenes of Teaching', in *Diacritics* 32, 3-4 (2002), p. 22.
3   Coetzee, ibid. p. 9.
4   I presumably do not need to point out that this decision will not be final either: there will be lapses, from joy to resentment and back. The sovereignty that my call for a decision might evoke is thus very much in question here.
5   Sigmund Freud, 'Analysis Terminable and Interminable'. In: James Strachey, (ed.) *The Standard Edition of the Complete Psychological Works of Sigmund Freud: Vol. XXIII,1937-1939,* (London: Hogarth Press, 1975), pp. 211-253.
6   De Boever, Arne, 'Scenes of Aesthetic Education: Rancière, Oedipus, and *Notre Musique*', in *Journal of Aesthetic Education* 46: 3 (2012), p. 76.
7   Freud, ibid., p. 215.
8   Ibid..
9   Alec Hargreaves, '*Indigènes*: A Sign of the Times', in *Research in African Literatures* 38: 4 (2007), pp. 204-216. I am not saying that *Les Indigènes de la République* did not share some of its ends with Bouchareb and Debouzze — indeed, the adjustment of the pension funds was high on their list as well. But they differ when it comes to the means.
10 The phrases in quotation marks are quoted from the Hargreaves article.
11 Note that the France's colonial occupation in Algeria and its reaction to Algerian resistance, famously referred to as 'the events', only came to be codified as 'war' due to demand of French soldiers that they be paid fairly — i.e. as in a situation of war — for putting their life on the line for France. Here too, politics remains within the limits of the finite. I would like to thank Olivia C. Harrison for pointing this out to me.
12 Panivong Norindr, 'Incorporating Indigenous Soldiers in the Space of the French Nation: Rachid Bouchareb's Indigènes', in *Yale French Studies* 115 (2009) p. 127. It is worth noting that while Norindr does not talk about the film, the special issue of YFS in which his article was published includes another article by Guy Austin about Haneke's *Caché*. Austin, in turn, never mentions *Indigènes*.
13 Ibid., p. 129.
14 Ibid., p. 136.
15 Ibid., p. 140.
16 Jacques Rancière, *Disagreement: Politics and Philosophy*, transl. by Julie Rose (Minneapolis MN: University of Minnesota Press, 1999), p. 28.
17 Ibid., pp. 29-30.
18 Ibid., p. 31.
19 Ibid., pp. 138-139.
20 It is worth noting that Georges is presented as a guardian of France's memory. His house is packed with books; he has a book show on TV. He is frequently shown in the film as sitting in front of rows and rows of books.

The Art of Teasing Out Change
Being Right, Wrong and Real

An Interview with Mat Fraser and Julie Atlas Muz

Tessa Overbeek

If you want to know how to make the most of your differences, ask Mat Fraser and Julie Atlas Muz. Presenting themselves as an odd couple seems to be their trademark. I first got to know them in 2012 as *The Freak and The Showgirl* in their cabaret show *Apocastrip Wow!!*. More recently, I saw them perform as Beauty and the Beast in their X-rated, socially engaged theatre version of the famous fairy tale. They met in 2006 in Coney Island, New York, where both were making their physical appearances work for them in their own unique, unexpected ways.

Fraser, born in the UK, was working there in a contemporary sideshow as Sealo the Sealboy, discovering what his life could have been like if he, like the performer whose stage name he borrowed and whose act he revived, had lived a century earlier as a 'natural born freak'. The name is also related to the condition that is the main reason why Fraser can perform in such a context: phocomelia is a term derived from the Greek words for 'seal' and 'limb'. Fraser's shortened arms and four-fingered hands are the result of his mother being prescribed Thalidomide to alleviate morning sickness while being pregnant with him, before it was discovered that the drug led to birth defects. As a result, thousands of babies were born with deformed limbs.

A son of two actors, who separated when he was nine after his father came out as being gay, Fraser has been near the stage from a very early age. Since there were no books on raising disabled children back then, Fraser's parents chose to treat their son like any other child, not giving him the impression that there were things he couldn't do and letting him try whatever he wanted instead.

That turned out to be quite a lot: after having discovered punk as a teenager and leaving college to pursue a career in music, Fraser spent fifteen years as a professional drummer in numerous bands. Always politically active, he participated in demonstrations for many different causes. When he encountered activists who were part of the disability rights movement, he said goodbye to his band mates and joined them. He later turned to acting for Graeae, Europe's main theatre company for disabled performers, as well as making angry, confrontational live art solo pieces. He created and performed in *Thalidomide!! A Musical*; recorded *Survival of the Shittest,* a rap album; made several short documentaries about disability; co-presented *Ouch!*, a monthly talk show for BBC's disability website with Liz Carr; won the Mr. Striptease 2007 title for an act involving prosthetic arms; was featured in several TV-series and plays; drummed with Coldplay during the 2012 Paralympics closing ceremony; and starred in *Unarmed but Dangerous,* supposedly the world's first 'cripsploitation movie', which showcases his various martial arts skills.

As the story goes, these particular skills were instrumental in stealing Julie Atlas Muz's heart, when they met at a neo-burlesque show that he hosted and she starred in. Backstage, Fraser showed Muz how to kill someone in one minute with a 'rear naked choke hold', leaving her deeply impressed. By then Fraser had already begun to fall for her, having just seen her perform her famous act *The Hand* in which she is hypnotized, fondled, undressed and eventually killed by a severed hand. He was seduced by the fact that she was prepared to be at once 'glamorous and ugly, sexy and frightening'.[1]

Her creative, political approach to neo-burlesque — which had made her famous in this relatively new strand of performance and won her the titles of Miss Exotic World and Miss Coney Island in 2006 — is in part the result of her own mercurial nature and development. While her parents, physicians who immigrated to the US from Ukraine, only saw professions like doctor or lawyer as suitable for their children, Muz opted for degrees in Dance and History instead, as she had been drawn to the stage ever since she saw *Cats.* Her parents' disapproval just fuelled her desire for a career as a performer, and she moved from Detroit to New York as soon as she could to pursue it.

After having performed as an experimental dancer, she soon discovered that this existence entailed many hours of rehearsals, but not enough opportunities to perform to her liking. She sated her hunger for the stage by diversifying, and complimented her activities by performing with theatre companies like Chashama, but also by accepting an offer to start developing and performing neo-burlesque acts at the Red Vixen Cabaret, where she got a chance to develop a very distinctive voice of her own in the genre. Like Fraser, Muz continued to accumulate activities in many different contexts, making playfully disturbing performances often involving exposing her body in one way or another, while at the same time working around the fact that looks can be deceiving, fond as she is of a good ruse to confound everyone's expectations.

Muz made a name for herself in the New York art scene by making bold performance art pieces like *I am the moon and you are the man on me,* where she plays the moon, in love with the men who try to colonize her. She also curated an exposition called *Womanizer,* which included a series of portraits of Mr. Pussy, probably the most unusual of her many alter egos, who appears when her vagina takes on a separate identity of its (or his) own, and then many different ones, as he likes to play dress-up. Muz also participated in several art biennials, choreographed and performed in dance pieces, including a somewhat dark take on Stravinsky's *The Rite of Spring,* inspired by the life and death of Jon Benét Ramsey, the American child beauty queen who was murdered at the age of six. She performed and created acts in the circus, and prepared Hollywood actresses for dance solos and swimming like a mermaid, another of her many specialities. More recently, she had a part in the French film *Tournée,* winner of several awards at the Cannes Film Festival, along with fellow artists from the Cabaret New Burlesque.

When Muz and Fraser met, both were already married and couldn't act on their mutual attraction. They did, however, start exploring the possibility of working together, and finding out where the combination of their very different backgrounds would take them. Since their perspectives differ from the dominant one - that of the white, middle-class, middle-aged, able-bodied man - they've always felt the need to represent alternative outlooks on what is commonly considered to be 'normal'. They see themselves as belonging to groups of outsiders who are either under- or misrepresented in mainstream media, which according to Fraser are the most important tools for changing social perception. For Fraser, the sheer lack of visibility of people with disabilities on such a large scale is a major cause for concern, if not outrage. He's been known to point out that disabled characters are often portrayed by non-disabled actors, often to great critical acclaim, while there are plenty of actually disabled actors waiting to be given a chance to take centre stage. This is one of the reasons why he has performed in so many different contexts himself, from Shakespeare plays to freak shows, showing that there are plenty of ways to influence people's perceptions.

Muz, an expert when it comes to playing with the gaze of the audience and mixing up categories like body and mind, high and low, glamour and violence and comedy and politics, has her own way of getting under people's skins and changing their views. The fascination with youth and beauty, the unequal treatment of women, race relationships and the 'luxury of freedom' are some recurrent themes in her work.

When Fraser and Muz collaborate, the fusion of their different backgrounds, skills and strategies leads to a potent performative cocktail that is impossible to categorize, plus being detrimental to expectations and, more importantly, prejudices. They continue to look for new ways to make people sit up, open their minds and change their conception of what it really means to be human, using all of the experiences that have shaped them over the years.

They made several cabaret shows together as *The Freak and The Showgirl*, the most recent one being *Apocastrip Wow!!*, with which they toured all over the world. At the beginning of this mind-boggling show, Fraser warns the audience: 'We are going to be nude during most of this performance, and you are allowed to look at us any way you want.' An intriguing, memorable sentence with impressive effects, which raised a lot of questions for me.

Fortunately, I got to interview them, after seeing them perform *Beauty and the Beast* in London. Very early on in their collaboration, Muz proposed a remake of this classic fairy tale, in which she would play the beautiful young girl, blossoming into womanhood and discovering her sexuality. Fraser would play the Beast, a role where he could use his arms and hands (which have no thumbs, making him lack two things that, in evolutionary theory, separate man from other animals, as he likes to point out) in new creative ways, which would allow him to work around the fact that deformity is often demonized.

They performed early versions of the show at several disability arts festivals, but decided to redevelop it into a theatre play in 2013, for which they sought support from the renowned director Phelim McDermott of Improbable Theatre. He helped them develop the show further by interweaving the original story with their own personal histories, adding puppeteers to the mix, and teaching them valuable lessons about improvisation, among other things. I saw it during a sold-out run at the Young Vic, one of London's more progressive theatres, but still 'the most mainstream place' where they have ever performed, according to Fraser.

More thematically coherent than *Apocastrip Wow!!,* less shocking (although still X-rated) and in a way traditionally romantic, *Beauty and the Beast* turned out to be politically revolutionary in a sneakier way, seducing the spectators into changing their perceptions by arousing their emotions, creating some cleverly crafted eroticism and conjuring up a world in which beastly can be beautiful and vulnerability can be bold.

Below, Muz and Fraser explain the roles they want to play in achieving social change and some of the strategies they employ to do so, and share lessons learned over the years, all the while emphasizing that the most important ingredient is love for the audience. If they sound like a married couple, that is because they are these days, and they complement each other, but also often disagree like one. Their work and words reveal that differences need to be overcome again and again, and highlight the importance of experiencing right and wrong to find something real.

Visibility and Perception

Tessa Overbeek — Out of all the different strategies that can be used to alter people's views and behaviours, you chose the artistic or showbiz one. Can you explain why you decided that this was the best way for you to contribute to your cause?

Mat Fraser — If you put me on the street in a demonstration, I am going to be aggressive. I like confrontation, so I'm not a good person to have at a demonstration. I'd want to charge the police. My skills are of a performing nature, or writing. So it's better for me to put my energy into the arts in this respect, because I believe that the number one problem is invisibility. There is a cultural apartheid of disabled people.

Julie Atlas Muz — But for the most part, the entertainment industry has been the most inclusive of any industry ever. That's because the most important thing is your talent. I mean, Sammy Davis Jr., a one-eyed, black Jew, was in the Rat Pack.

MF — He's a little bit like Black Pete for me. He gets to sit

at the top table if he doesn't say that the whole school
is racist.

JAM — But the key is, he was an icebreaker.

MF — Absolutely, and the icebreaker is important. I
see myself as an icebreaker in disability terms.

JAM — You can be living in the ghetto, or you can
support your icebreakers who help change the popular
perception of the world.

MF — Exactly, we needed him to be there at the time,
otherwise we wouldn't have ended up with... Sammy
Davis Jr., Sidney Poitier, Spike Lee. You have to have
those two people before you get to Spike Lee. My problem
is that we don't even have a Sidney fucking Poitier yet. So
I'm waiting for disability Spike Lee. I thought I was going
to be him when I was 28, but it doesn't look like that's
going to be the case.

TO — So what would need to happen for you to feel like
you are the disability Spike Lee?

MF — That somebody gives me a budget to make some
films. The power of the maker of the movie, and the
writer of the story, and the producer of the product far
exceeds that of the star of the vehicle. And without power
you can't change anything. And I want social change. I
also want a career and I want to be rich, but not at the
price of social change, in the interest of social change.
Sounds very lofty.

JAM — Yeah, you are very lofty today.

MF — I am as much of a prostitute as the next artist,
I really am. Otherwise I wouldn't work at The Box [a
variety theatre/nightclub in London, TO]. I adore working
there, but I'm only there to shock. I do the act with which
I won best striptease artist - I have my prosthetic arms on,
come out looking normal, strip out of my normality and

celebrate my beautiful freakishness. For me that's strong disability art. To other people, it's exploitation.

JAM – It's only exploitation if you don't get paid.

TO – If you made the act, is it still exploitation then?

JAM – You can exploit yourself.

TO – I wondered what you thought would be the most ideal way to contribute if you are a disabled artist, and what I conclude from your answer now is that you would want to be the director or the writer of work.

MF – I would like to be part of a project where the writing was informed, the direction was good, the producers were supportive and the product was about reality. A reality where disabled people are one in seven of the population, where they have jobs, relationships, and successes, like in reality. But in films, we don't get any of those things.

JAM – So you are asking for equality?

MF – No, I am asking for reality. Reality is not equal, but that's fine. I don't want to show equality, it doesn't exist. I want to show reality. I don't want to see disabled people used as the seven clichés of Hollywood. Because that's all they ever do.

JAM – How about an actor who gets an Oscar for playing a disabled person, actually being disabled?

MF – How about the actor who is disabled getting the Oscar for best actor, not for being disabled?Statistics show that the most guaranteed way to get an Oscar is to play a cripple.

JAM – The second best way is to play an ugly woman. Because that's so brave.

MF — It's easier for non-disabled people to watch other non-disabled people portray disability because they can suspend their disbelief and they don't have to worry about the actor actually having a disability. A hundred years ago they felt the same about black actors. So my thing is: visibility, visibility, visibility... If I could make films, they would be the kind of films that other people aren't making. With disabled people in them, being fully rounded human beings that live and breathe and think and love and fear just like everybody else. I am an advocate for disability rights, but in my chosen area, which is less about civic administration and more about entertainment, because I believe that the major defining attitude toward disability of the general public is shaped by the media's imaging of disabled people. And unless we control that imaging, it's going to be wrong. Because the mainstream still likes to show women as sex objects, men as powerful, and disabled people as recipients of charity. And of course we know that's not the case, we have to shake that up. So I've spent my life now trying to shake it up in various ways.

JAM — We have this terminology that is like a double-edged sword. You have people who understand the work, and who are changed by it. And there's another kind of person who is a do-gooder, someone who wants to do good for women or for disabled people, and is actually quite condescending. There's a level of ghettoizing: 'I am going to make myself feel better by doing something good for these kinds of people.' So already that's a separatist thing. It's a very subtle thing. It's the same with the children's charity drive...

MF — *Children in Need.*

JAM — It's a whole week in England where people get dressed up and ask money for disabled children. On the surface it seems like a very good, nice thing. But it also segregates in a profound way, and makes people feel good about themselves for raising money for these poor little children.

TO – Are you suggesting that, by participating in such an event, they can feel good about themselves, but don't actually have to change their perception?

JAM – I think you nailed it.

MF – Well yes, maybe, certainly the first bit, and maybe the second bit. There is nothing wrong with wanting to help people. It's an instinct that many of us humans have. We want to help somebody we think of as being weaker than us. And I don't think you could or should stop that.

JAM – No you shouldn't.

MF – It's a good part of human nature, I think. The other part wants to kill the thing it finds weaker. The hunter. And that's the bit we don't think is so good. But there are other people out there who build a career and feel good about themselves by helping other people. And they are not really helping those people. They are helping themselves, really, more. It's a fine line and it's an entire interview subject in itself. You have to talk about the charity model of disability, the social model of disability and the medical model of disability, which are all different prisms through which to understand disability.[2] We operate on the social model of disability, and not the medical or charity. Charity is a very very complicated thing. I want to help, of course I do. But the only poster ad we see is of the little disabled kid who needs the charity, please help him, otherwise his life is useless. No, it fucking isn't useless! If you only allowed him access to education and public transport, his life might be quite fulfilling. To present images of disabled people to ask for charity keeps disabled people as others, outsiders, and not equals. That is the inherent problem with using us as images for charity. But at the same time, because society doesn't provide for these people, sometimes others want to collect for them. It's very complicated.

JAM – It's not straightforward. It changes. Someone

can be just right on and really getting it, and then
sometimes it goes all wrong. And I, as a non-disabled
wife of a disabled man, get it wrong as well sometimes.

MF – I get it wrong! We all get it wrong! *Niet normaal* got
it wrong, an exhibition in the Beurs van Berlage that I was
part of. Thousands of Dutch kids and college students got
to think about disability in a slightly different way than
that which the television might tell them. And yet I think
ten per cent of the artists were disabled. And it's great,
but it could also have been a lot better. Ine Gevers, who
organized it, did an incredible thing and got a lot of Dutch
people to think about disability in a way that they would
not have before, and that's worth celebrating, rather than
criticizing her for getting some of it a bit wrong.

JAM – What I find lacking in the art world, or the
entertainment world that we live in, is the fact that
criticism and celebration are mutually exclusive. I think
being critical of something is actually being supportive
of it. Because you are furthering the dialogue.

MF – So before all of the other arguments, about 'is
it right what I am doing?', get out there and do it, and
then have a conversation about it. But you can't have
the conversation if no one is doing anything. So prolific
visibility is the most important thing for me. Everything
else can come after that. And yeah, other disability artists
critique me all the time.

Power and Love

TO – When you talk about freak shows, you sometimes
mention the choice to let oneself be objectified. Can you
say a bit more about what's so fascinating about that?

MF – Well, I'm stared at all the time. On the street I
don't have any power in the relationship of the starer
and the object of the staring. But on stage it shifts
immediately. I was interested in that. When I first did
the freak show, I went on stage to reduce the aspect of

the interest in me down to objectifying my arms. It's
extraordinarily powerful to be honest about the fact that
that's why people are there and allow them to objectify
me. Because I am interesting to look at; there are only
four thousand of us in the whole world. And it's OK to
look at me. This cuts into the essence of a freak show.
But for me, it's useless without having the power to
gently lead them down various trains of thought. When
talking, I can control the subject of discussion in the
room. So I simultaneously have all and none of the power.
I found that to be a delicious, confusing and intriguing
dichotomy. And then I thought: What I say becomes
more important now. Because I have five minutes to
colour the way you look at me and objectify me. I've
learned how to very quickly take the power and mould
the experience for people. And as an artist, I'm enjoying
the cultural considerations that the situation forces them
to make. While it's show business, and the business
relationship is that I will take some money from them on
the understanding that they get to see my body. But they
also understand that I am critiquing their experience, and
that they too can do that from their perspective. There is
no right or wrong here, because it is so complicated. It's
both and it's neither.

TO – Do you need words to take the power?

MF – No, you don't. I used to think you did until I met
Julie and I learned the power of dance.

TO – So Julie, how do you take the power, even though
you are in a position where you could also be objectified?

JAM – It's very simple. It's a quote from Patti Smith: 'You
have to have an evident love for the audience.' Then the
whole dynamic is changed.

MF – That's the key to everything. Sometimes I feel so
intimate with an audience, and comfortable talking to
them, much more so than in a normal social setting of a
conversation around a table.

TO — And is it just that you sincerely love the audience, and they automatically feel that, or is there something that you do to express that love?

JAM — There is form, and there is craft, and structure, and there are tricks. But if you have all of that, but not that very special love, then there is no point.

TO — What are the consequences of that love? To what degree do you feel inclined to give the audience what it wants/expects?

JAM — True love and friendship encourages growth and supports change. Love isn't about being static and not changing. That's something else. More like controlled obsession. I trust my audience to support me, even though I might make mistakes. I trust that they will see my intent. It doesn't work to second-guess your audience or yourself. As an artist, I think it's important to give your audience something that they want, but they don't know what they want yet. It's important to surprise them and the only way to surprise them is to surprise yourself. I try to use all methods to tell a good story, to take an audience along on a journey, and I try to use what is on the verge of being inappropriate but still appropriate. An audience always wants to be seduced to fall in love with the performer, even if the performer is playing someone evil. People are complex and want to be accessed on many different levels at the same time. You don't fall in love with someone just because they are beautiful. There are other elements that make you love them, aspects of them that you admire, that's the full package. One way that I deal with this tension of what others expect of me, what I expect of myself, and generally a weird relationship to my ego, is to create a different person. So far, in my mind I am and have been Julie Atlas Muz, Hard Candi, Julie the Mermaid, Mr Pussy and newly I am Juicy Hardcore. By creating different people, I can separate myself from my past ways of working and experience growth and change with my past work on the back burner of my brain. As

I get older, I feel a greater affinity to female artists such as Cindy Sherman who are constantly changing their image to the world. There is a great freedom in this that I am just beginning to realize overtly.

Freedom and Responsibility

TO — In the trailer for the documentary *Exposed* that you and Mat are part of, you say something like: 'I would like to be the kind of role model that takes people back to the time before the fruit of knowledge was eaten.' What do you mean by that?

JAM — I think that people have become too obsessed with how their bodies look as opposed to how they feel inside their body. The thrill of enjoying your body. Nudity on stage takes people off guard and they say to themselves: 'Oh I could never do that.' Being comfortable naked in public is something that I believe most of us are born with, but through social constructs such as 'appropriate behaviour' we are taught to cover ourselves up. Children are often very comfortable naked; it's a very childish thing to do, to be naked in public. Adults often find this very threatening, in part because deep in their bones they know that the shame of covering up your body is a nurture, not their true nature.

TO — Is it also related to the difference between right and wrong in a more general way?

JAM — I definitely think that it's about a lack of judgement. One of the hardest things that happens for an artist is that feeling of self-censorship, thinking: I can't do that because a) It's not good enough, or b) It's not appropriate. We've tried to eliminate those from the creative process. What's right or wrong depends on the context. Of course it's always wrong to murder somebody in life, but to pretend to murder somebody on stage can be very right. When you play with these kinds of things, sometimes people can't separate the artist from the art that they make. People can make really fucked up art work and still be a good person. But I think that you have to, in a way, be really responsible. There's an example that I can give you from my work that's very clear, and was very profound. I am a New Yorker, and 9/11 really struck a deep chord in my life. One way to process all of this is to make art work about it. For the tenth anniversary of 9/11 in New York City, I put together a big three-hour political cabaret [to raise money for the Uniformed Firefighters Association of NY Widow's and Children's Fund, TO]. For that cabaret, I wanted my alter ego Mr. Pussy to sing Bob Marley's *Redemption Song*.I wanted it to be about 9/11 and the mistreatment of the big disasters that have happened since, and for it to be very clear. I worked with a videographer, and when we came up with the first draft of the video, it was so powerful, and so moving, and so wrong. We had images of poor people, people running from the towers, the towers falling, and really bad images from hurricane Katrina and the mismanagement of that in New Orleans, and I couldn't take my eyes off of it. I was mesmerized and I knew I could not present that video to the public. I wasn't a responsible political artist, because I was highlighting and exploiting the pain of the victims as opposed to saying: Here is the pain of the victims and let's question how this pain came to be, and let's now highlight the people that are responsible.

Frank Herbert's *Dune* is basically my bible, and one of the issues in it is about the distinction between a human and an animal. An example they give is: if an animal is trapped, it will chew off its own leg to be free. But if a human is trapped, they will pretend to be dead until their trapper comes for them and then deal with that person. It takes a lot of discipline to do that. If I showed the first version of Mr. Pussy's *Redemption Song,* I would have been making art as a reactionary animal. It was a really big discovery that I made in my art-making process. I thought: I can't show that, I don't even want my alter ego to be associated with the feelings that are aroused.

TO – Because it was just too much?

JAM – It exploited victims. I don't think that's political. And then I was in Paris during *Nuit Blanche,* the night where all the museums and galleries are open. I went into a gallery and an artist was selling prints of photographs of people that were experiencing 9/11, as art work. Pictures of people with ice packs on their heads, covered in dust, and they were being sold for between seven and ten thousand euros. I thought: How fucking dare you? You think this is art? It's barely even journalism. It had a lot of justification about why it could be considered art, but in my interpretation it was animalistic greedy bullshit, and it was exploiting the people who suffered. Did those people get any of the seven thousand euros that someone bought that photograph for? It got me thinking and furious, but not in a way that propelled me forward; in a way that is destructive as opposed to creative.

Beauty and the Beast

TO – This new version of *Beauty and the Beast* is half fairy tale and half your real life story. And you play with this distinction, mixing comedy and theatre with real emotions and situations. Can you explain the advantages and disadvantages of this approach?

JAM – If you are telling the truth in an engaging way, you ride the edge of what's appropriate and you have to be very careful with how you show the audience what you are actually thinking and where the truth lies. In *Beauty and the Beast,* I have one laugh that I've just started getting, that I don't want. When I am talking about my mother, who said: 'Julie, why do you want to marry a cripple?' and then I defend my mother - because I was very proud of her for saying that: 'Most mother-in-laws in her position... She said what they only think.' And that gets a laugh, but that is about most mother-in-laws seeing their son-in-laws as cripples. And that's not the point.

MF – It's not funny, and it's not a laugh we want. So we

have to scientifically find a way of removing it by doing it
in a different way. We talk about it every night, about how
it should be.

JAM – It makes my mother seem like an asshole, and she
is not. Therein lies the conflict between being judged...
I don't mind you judging me for being an asshole, that's
fine, but don't you judge my mother. It's easy to flip it
the wrong side, and then you can go from loving your
audience to hating your audience, and then you have to
get the fuck out.

MF – We saw a program on TV last night about comedy,
where somebody made the observation about what's funny
and what isn't funny, and they said: 'It has to be true, it has
to be true to who you are and what you really believe.'

JAM – That was Roseanne Barr.

MF – And she said: 'It's so much more valuable when the
audience knows that something is true. It's much richer,
the comedy is better.' And then I thought: This is what
everyone says about *Beauty and the Beast*. That they find it
valuable because they know it's true. It's not a fiction, it's
a real story, made into a show. And they really respond to
it. I think that's one of the reasons this show is so popular.
I did not expect it to be this popular.

TO – You didn't?

MF – I thought we would get like, half success. It's
challenging shit, what we are doing! Pretending to have
sex on stage, all the nudity and deformity...

JAM – Wiping your butt...

MF – Washing my asshole in front of people, all of that
stuff. It's challenging shit. You don't see that on the stage
in mainstream theatre in this country. But the fact that
everyone has responded to it so well, it has to be because
it's a true story and it's real.

TO – When I was talking to you after the show, a guy came up and said: 'That was very erotic.'

MF – Funny. I don't see myself as eroticizing my body in that bath.

TO – But you did: (mime version of squeezing out sponge over chest)

MF – Julie told me to do that sponge squeeze. And that is a stripper move, I know. But I am not looking at the audience, I am in my own world. The director said: 'Just go with the physical sensation of having a bath for yourself. It's warm, it's comforting, and it feels nice.' The ass-washing is a political statement of mine. That's how I wash my ass. I want people to know that, to see it, and I don't want them to be able to turn away from that. It's an important political moment in my artistic career, the fact that I have gotten to a point where I can wash my fucking ass on stage... I don't want to make a whole show about ass-washing, but it was a nice little moment along the way. It's genuinely not meant to eroticize.

JAM – From my perspective it absolutely is. In this version of the show, it's a step towards physical intimacy. It unlocks the door and forces the audience to see you, first of all as a man on stage. A vulnerable man on stage. Eroticized. Enjoying or feeling your body, and then secondarily, and that's why it gets a laugh when you wash your ass, they remember that you are disabled. Because disability, like nudity, on stage, after three minutes, it's invisible. So you have to sometimes click their focus and say: 'Hey!' I am naked, and I am disabled.'

TO – I thought it was very interesting, the intimacy of the bathing scene. When you do the fruit stuff,[3] it's so outrageous that we can laugh it off. But when you are so vulnerable in the bath, there's more tension for us, and you feel more forced to think about what you are seeing.

MF – I think you are very correct and I think that the

director saw that very soon and understood that slightly before we did. Maybe it's all a little bit too much, watching all of that. So to have the fun with the fruit afterwards allows people to let off steam.

JAM – Phelim McDermott also says that in order to really get people to feel things, it's good to have them laugh for a second right before.

MF – We love it when people laugh and cry. Then it really stays with you. A big goal of mine is to... not manipulate the tears, because that's easy to do, but to let the tears come naturally, for people to be touched by the essence of what you are talking about. It's a beautiful thing.

TO – I never felt lectured, but felt like some categories still shifted in my mind.

MF – You can't tell the audience off for not being disabled. I've seen a lot of disability art. Far too much of it does that. I think with the sort of artists that we are, that are interested in some kind of change in the world, it's our job to be an *agent provocateur*. It is not our job to tell the audience what to think, but to make them question what they used to think beforehand, and then let them make their own mind up. If you only tell the audience what's wrong with a situation, and interrogate and analyze, dissect all the problems about it, and tell them that that's what they have got to stop doing, but you don't show them how to do it, that's no good. But if you just show them what could happen, it's much more powerful.

JAM – If one of the changes in reality that happen because of this show is that some chick who is a little bit attracted to a guy in a wheelchair actually gives him a chance and goes out with him on a romantic basis, that's massive social change. So if it's being able to see somebody who is disabled as a sexual being, great. If this show gets more people who are disabled laid, we've done our job.

TO — I wondered how you both incorporate your different backgrounds, perspectives and bodies when collaborating. Perhaps Beauty could have been foregrounded more? You refer to the role of a woman a few times, but it doesn't get that much attention in the play.

MF — The transformation of the Beauty character, inherent in the fairy tale, because ultimately the Beast just represents adult sexuality, isn't explored as heavily as the metaphor of disability meaning beastliness. You are right, and it's just the way it happened. It wasn't by design. I would've been interested to see a further development of that aspect of it as well myself.

JAM — When we were making it, I remember complaining: 'All my stories are about Mat. None of Mat's stories are about me!' It drove me crazy. A woman doesn't necessarily just judge her life through the lens of looking at a man. If we have to redo it, we'll maybe examine that a little bit. Sometimes there's just little twists that can make it. It's true, this production is disability-heavy. But I hope that the show will continue to evolve.

MF — And hey, our director is a heterosexual male. If that had been a lesbian, I think it might have been quite different. We didn't interrogate the sexual politics of it in the way that we interrogated everything else.

JAM — Although I will say... Fairy tales are coming-of-age stories, morality tales, sometimes for little boys, but primarily for little girls. There is never a mother figure. It's usually a girl leaving home, going to do something, transforming in some magical way to become the woman that she is. It's right at that precipice age of becoming a woman. And the fact that the final story that I tell is the story of my mother, made me realize: Ah, we are taking away the father, 'I want to be with my father, I miss my father' and saying who Julie's mother is, and how that woman is important. And I feel that

that story still needs to land. I don't understand that story yet.

TO – Maybe that's also why the laugh happens. Because you don't feel the importance of that particular part?

JAM – Or you feel the importance of it in a judgemental way. It's very complicated. I don't think *Beauty and the Beast* is overtly my most revolutionary work, but it is my most honest. I confide in the audience and reveal more of myself than in any other work that I've done. My speech about my mother at the end is something that took a lot of courage and trust to do. I have to trust myself to be clear in a very complicated emotional matter, my mother's acceptance of Mat's disability, and I had to trust the audience not to judge my mother, a woman who I love and respect very much. Therein lies that appropriateness in the relationship to the audience.

MF – Another thing I've learned along the way, after fifteen, twenty years of doing this, is that if you want a show to be about something, don't talk about that thing. Do something else. The audience will see it's about that anyway.

TO – Yet in *Apocastrip Wow!!* and *Beauty and the Beast,* you still explain about your arms.

MF – That's because I've worked in sideshow for so many years. I like to keep a little bit of that in the work. I think this is probably the last show where I explain my fucking bone system. I worked in the sideshow from 2000, and traditionally the natural born freak will come on stage, explain their medical condition and then do a feat of skill. There is something that really tickles me about that. I like bringing history back, even though nobody is aware that it's happening.

I am writing a play at the moment, a comedy about five people at an Elvis Presley convention. One guy is disabled, he's also gay. He's there because his lover was an Elvis fan and he died. He always thought it was embarrassing, but now that he's died, he wants to explore that part of his partner he never knew. Nothing to do with his disability, nothing at all. Other people, when he's not in the room, talk about his disability, a bit. But it's not really about that. Because I want to move on from that. For me, personally, *Beauty and the Beast* is the apex, the culmination of all that's come before for me, in imaging the body, referencing the body and presenting the body in that way. You meet me at a time in my life where I am ready to turn another corner. I turned a corner into burlesque, sideshow, short format, cabaret, nightclub, playing with the whole freaky thing, about fifteen years ago. And I can feel in the next year or two I am finished. I am going to move off into something else.

Mutual Vulnerability

TO – What do you think that something else will be about?

MF – The vulnerability, which I love to express and which is indeed a new part of the more mature aspect of my work, as I relax about everything because I am getting older, in some setting is what I want to do more of, because it's the human condition that we want to get people to understand is what we all share. And that's why we are all the same. The theatre, like in *Beauty and the Beast*, which has love, has a lot of vulnerability in it, that's a good place. But not on the sideshow stage. If you only see me for five minutes, you only really get the shock value of my body. That's why I don't accept roles in the theatre that are five minutes long. Because part of the reason I got into theatre was to make people feel more comfortable with disabled people on stage, by visibility. But if they only get the moment of shock, without connecting with the character's story, seeing their humanity, sharing their humanity, and caring about what happens, then there is no point in me being on stage.

TO – What do you enjoy about this step in a new direction?

MF – It's very joyful to be able to express vulnerability on stage and for it to be OK, for it to open up people's hearts. It's tough for me as a disabled person who will not portray the victim, because too often we've been portrayed that way, as the victim of mere circumstance. I reject that of course, so allowing myself to be a vulnerable victim of a situation in a dramatic scenario has taken me ten years to be able to do. Letting go of the worry that they'll think I am a victim because I've got short arms, and just thinking: No! It's up to them to decide why I am a victim in this situation. It's actually because of the love situation, not my disability, and allowing that to happen without needing to demonstrate that it isn't that. That's been one of the huge factors for me.

TO – That's interesting, because in so many situations you've been the tough guy who takes charge of everything, including the way you are being looked at.

MF – Maybe that's what I am going to be exploring in the next fifteen years: the deliciously difficult situation of portraying vulnerability as a disabled person without the vulnerability being because of the disability.

TO – Everybody is vulnerable, right?

MF – And my disability adds to my vulnerability, I understand that. And I am ready to say that that is a part of it. But the problem is that it feeds into the clichéd notion of disabled people and reaffirms a lot of the negative understanding of disability that keep us in bondage. So it's very difficult.

TO – You could say that there is also some sort of vulnerability for the onlookers in the way that they can become uncertain and uncomfortable by what they are confronted with and think: Oh no, am I looking or responding in the wrong way? It also reminds me of how you said that we could look at you and Julie however we wanted to in *Apocastrip Wow!!*

MF — When I was first hosting burlesque shows in New York, I'd throw in the old comment that basically says to the audience: it's OK, we can do jokes about my arms at some points during this show. This is burlesque, we have no politics. Of course we do have politics, but we need to make people think it's OK to be politically incorrect because this political correctness is a prison of behaviour that people are scared of. They think if it's disability, they are going to have to do political correctness and then they are worried about getting that wrong, so they choose to not do it at all. So it's very important, early on, in the comedy, freak, sex show, to go: no, we are not doing the politics tonight, you can just enjoy yourself. Because if they are worried about what they say or think about my arms for the whole show, they are never going to connect with the humanity and move along.

TO — This also makes me think about the mission statement[4] of your company OneOfUs, which ends with: 'We accept you', and everything you said about loving the audience. For me, it's like taking into account what they might be feeling, and saying: Whatever prejudice you are holding, it's OK.

MF — It is taken from the wedding scene in the film *Freaks*, when the non-disabled woman marries the short guy, Hans, she becomes accepted as 'one of us', an honorary outsider,[5] and we still mean it when we say it. It's the best way forward. We have to tell the audience that we love them, and the things that they think that we don't agree with: It's OK. We still love them, because if we put up a barrier, like: You can only like us if you believe in left wing socialist principles, then half the people won't make that journey. And the stuff about disability happens to everybody: fascists, liberals, everybody. Universal love, and the appreciation of the outsider body, and sexuality, and all these things that we have been conditioned to not like, you can't get people to reconsider them if you attack them for who they are. When we communicate that we love them, they can relax and decide whether they like us or not, and what they like about us. If they are too worried about being the wrong person, they are not going to get there.

TO — What does OneOfUs enable you to do that you couldn't or didn't do before?

MF — It focuses our work into a reason, it gives us a structure with which to go forward artistically, to house our productions within, and most of all lets others know who we are and what we do. Stuart Hall, the cultural commentator, points out in a new documentary that the place of your understanding of culture is never fixed. Every single time you input something new, your understanding of culture shifts imperceptibly. So you can't rest on your laurels, you have to keep working, and everything that comes along, you have to incorporate the consciousness of it into your work, to move through it and onwards, keeping your agenda. That's what we try to do, in an ever-changing way that reflects modern culture as much as we can. Sometimes that means we have to use different strategies for different shows. That's why OneOfUs isn't interested in only doing theatre. We want to do striptease, live art, theatre, cabaret, film... I am also doing a solo-show for museums, about historically reductive and dehumanizing aspects of representations of disabled people in exhibitions. That's a very different piece of work. It's because culture has so many different facets, that we are interested in working many of those.

Revelations

Thankfully, Muz and Fraser strongly believe in the importance of encouraging a critical dialogue around their work, because the conversation with these artists has led to interesting insights about how art and justice can reinforce each other and how to engage people in many different ways, while at the same time leaving them enough room to make up their own minds, allowing them to change their views in their own way.

They explained how freeing yourself from judgement is crucial to the creative process, and needs to come before being critical and responsible. The same rule may very well apply to the process of artistic interpretation. How can you examine your prejudices if you feel afraid to face them, or deny having them? Allowing the audience the opportunity, time, and freedom to feel that they can deal with the difference they are faced with might make responsible reactions come quite naturally.

Revealing your body holds a lot of power, that much is clear. The more we are told not to look at something because it is wrong, the more we might want to, while at the same time feeling an initial discomfort when we actually get the chance. Subjecting yourself to the possibly confused gazes of others, allowing yourself to be objectified, and dancing on the borders of the politically incorrect or the inappropriate seems like a very effective way of taking the pressure off, letting people adjust to what they see, and making them curious about what else they can discover beyond the boundaries of the body.

Fraser and Muz illustrated how as an artist striving for social change, the wisest thing to do can be to accept human nature, and to patiently deal with a situation, because embracing that which is can be essential to showing how it could be. To them, this means being the first to offer love and acceptance, without a guarantee of reciprocation, to sometimes control their indignation and longing for freedom and wait in their entrapment to deal with who is really responsible for causing it, but also to reveal their own uncertainty, vulnerability and imperfection in order to encourage others to let their guard down, which seems to be a prerequisite for any changes of mind, behaviour and society.

Art always involves the risk of venturing into the unknown, without which no real creative growth is possible. It is an area where breaking conventions is often accepted or expected, where reaction is provoked, but no immediate action is necessary, so the reaction itself can come into view. This makes it a perfect place to question the urge to be right and to face the fear of being wrong that so often keeps us apart, and makes us overlook the humanity that we share.

1   See him explain it here: www.youtube.
com/watch?v=d2aEZNDUTMQ.

2   The charity model presents the disabled
person as a 'poor unfortunate', or
admirable and brave, in order to evoke pity
and raise money but leaves little room for
the independence of disabled people; the
medical model focuses on the physical
impairment, its nature and severity and the
way it could be corrected, dehumanizing
disabled people and presenting them as
victims or problems for their families or
society at large. The social model of
disability disconnects the impairment
from the way disabled people are treated
because of it, and focuses on ways in which
they can be offered equal opportunities to
participate in society — both practically, by
providing physical access to for instance
buildings, and in terms of perception. This
is a short, simplified summary of the
discourse around these models. For more
information, see for instance: www.soas.
ac.uk/equalitydiversity/scheme/.

3   Fruit is eaten in some provocative ways in
this play, and later used to simulate sex by
the puppeteers, with surprisingly graphic
results.

4   'We are outsiders, with inclusivity at the
heart of what we do. Traversing the world
as radical artists looking for alternative
ways to be inside, the main thrust of our
work is to highlight, question and poke fun
at the absurdity of normality, using a
loving cup of artistic agitation. We accept
you, one of us.'

5   In this film from 1932, a group of sideshow
freaks is celebrating the wedding of their
friend Hans to the tall, blonde, athletic
trapeze artist Cleopatra, and they chant:
'We accept you, one of us.' This was also
the chant of the crowd when Fraser and
Muz got married themselves.

Part 3

Justice and its Geopolitics

The Aesthetics of Trauma
Aesthetic Justice and the Post-Soviet Condition

Viktor Misiano

The Transitional Period: the Justice of Injustice

If one were to agree that *justice comes after ethics and before utopia*[1] one would have to admit that in post-Soviet conditions this triad becomes extremely problematic. This is obvious, because the dismantlement of Soviet communism was carried out in the name of rejecting one of the components of this triad — the utopian perspective. So if the communist system appealed to the future, in which some better, yet non-existent order of things was to be realized, the new post-utopian, neo-capitalist perspective supposed a future realization of what had already been realized in Western countries and in pre-communist Russia. In other words, if communism was a reality aimed at the future, the future of post-communism became the present or the past.

At the same time, it is also apparent that to the extent that this (Western) present or (Russian) past was perceived as having bright prospects and as unquestionably superior to the reality of communism, its realization was seen as ethically justified. The method for carrying out these bright prospects was aptly and tellingly named 'shock therapy', so even at the semantic level it was accepted that constructing a post-communist order was extremely painful and that its ethical justification therefore sanctioned inevitable human suffering. Moreover, this new, more just order of things that was to succeed communism implied the rejection of the very idea of justice — social justice in particular, which started to be perceived as ideologized moralization. The just order of the future was to be unjust by definition — therapeutically unjust — as it was to replace social and economic equality under socialism with its opposite: a gap (often a glaring one) between social status and income. This, in fact, was carried out.

The period between the end of communism and the making of post-communism is usually referred to as *transitional*. What it in fact means is that, having left the disciplinary 'iron cage' of communism, reality has not yet assumed a new order. This phase calls into question yet another categorical triad — the dialectics of the private, the public and the common. With the start of the campaign of privatizing socialist property that was once held in common, the public sphere began to rapidly shrink and inexorably lose its inviolability, while the private sphere, though undergoing expansion, was not yet fully perceived as something complete and firmly rooted. Finally, it would be incorrect to consider that this amorphous and atomized 'transitional' reality could recognize itself in what could be called 'the common', because the social significance of what was taking place lay in the process of social disintegration and spontaneous, convulsive individuation that knew neither solidarity nor any other social bonds.

Hence, artistic experience recognizes itself not in *aesthetics,* based on a strict notional and doctrinal system, but in *aesthesis,* i.e., in the equation of art with the emotive and spontaneous experience of living. This experience was expressed most prominently and programmatically by the so-called 'Moscow actionism' of the 1990s, i.e, by the practice of transgressive, provocative action where the boundaries between the social, the media and art were erased. It is quite fair to discern in this geyser of creativity an 'opening up of many possible roads', which is, as Gielen claimed, one of the determining qualities of 'aesthetic justice'. However, this experience of spontaneous individuation in the transitional period had another side: subjectivity was deprived of any pre-established limits to such an extent that its boundless potentiality was experienced as a heavy burden. Hence, first of all, the actionist artists' unchecked focus on radicalism. Once they had taken the path of destroying unquestionable taboos, they apparently were not so much trying to break through to the zones of freedom that had once been off-limits, but were rather testing the durability of reality. Once an insurmountable obstacle was encountered, it became the new limit of the formation of subjectivity. Secondly, along with attempting to acquire external boundaries, the artists would try to define themselves from within, i.e., to equate their work and personality with a rigid identity: for instance, with that of the man-dog of Oleg Kulik, the orthodox Marxist of Dmitriy Gutov, the amateur artist of Avdey Ter-Oganyan, the fiery revolutionary of Anatoly Osmolovsky, etc. At the same time, in the context of the shapeless reality of the transitional time it was obvious that those identities were of a reduced and conventional nature. They were, in fact, role identities that were hiding a different kind of subjectivity that could not be reduced to strict determinants. However, that was not a trickster masquerade aiming to desacralize the foundations of the existing order. On the contrary, weary of any pre-established order, the artists were reaching for a mask, desperately hoping to be equal to it, while at same time realizing that this would be impossible.

The hardest and most problematic thing about this new disorderly world was that the very phenomenon of art turned out

to be systemically out of place there. Shapeless, transitional reality was determined, above all, by the logic of survival, whose temporality is the permanent *here and now*. Therefore it was impossible *to confront* such a reality. If one wants to survive, one should not model another world for oneself, but rather look for a place in the world that is available. Unpredictable and stripped of visible limits, this reality seemed beyond the power of imagination. It seemed a bigger *fiction* than the one that could be imparted to reality by an artist. Therefore, the resource of imagination, which art is, was not in demand during the transitional period. But it is due to this very fact that the task of vindication of art in a society that does not see its functional necessity — a vindication that assumed paradoxical shapes — became the ultimate objective of artists. Practicing aesthesis, artists appealed to aesthetics; the struggle to preserve the aesthetic was understood by them as ethically messianic, and the preservation of art as a social institution was seen as an act of justice.

In practice, it was a case of creating a new system of art capable of replacing the petered-out Soviet art infrastructure. In the survival mode, this could be carried out mostly in the sphere of the imagination and it materialized through strategies of individual and group conduct. In other words, the new order of art was carried out performatively and art itself became art's subject and content. Thus, artists were working *within the world or within society.* They were performatively devising and carrying out a better order of things while remaining in the sphere of 'the common'. Moreover, by means of such individual and group efforts they were, in fact, that very 'common'.

However, in the experience of transitional countries' artistic communities there is something that sets it apart from the Western communicational aesthetics, 'relational aesthetics', 'community-based practices', etc. that were emerging at the same time. Working *within the world or within society,* to post-soviet artists meant neither the *world* nor the *society,* but above all the institutional world of art. In the West, artists were abandoning art institutions, while in the post-Soviet world something opposite was happening: it was the institutions, paralyzed by crisis, that were abandoning the artists. That is why, working within the frame of the common and creating it, the art community did not realize its self-contained value. That sphere was understood by them as something transitional, defective and temporary. Art's true place was seen precisely in the sphere of the public, in the context of its power and economic interests. Therefore, performative practices served as ways for the common to imitate the public. Finally, the situation of working outside art's autonomy weighed heavily on the artists; their creative efforts were in fact directed at recreating that autonomy, even if only performatively, in order to circumscribe the boundaries of their professional sphere.

And yet the most peculiar trait of this period is how the common of the transitional epoch was constituted. In a situation where the public did not exist, the common was the only place where art could exist as an institution, i.e., the common was a replacement for the public. In practice, this meant that the common was formed through encounters of various individual projects of the public, and the more each of those projects was a continuation of its author's subjectivity, the less it allowed for the subjectivity of other authors, with their own projects of the public. To put it another way: the public and the collective bore the stamp of personal judgment, but the space of the common was the only condition and place of their existence. Therefore, the common, being a place of encounter of individual judgments that did not acknowledge one another, was constituting itself through conflict, i.e., through the denial of itself. This state of inevitable, permanent and often quite painful conflict is the condition that enables personal artistic statement, since only through group discussion of the public does an artistic statement assume contours and legitimize a work of art as a statement taking place in the territory of art.

Let us summarize the above points: the art system of 'transitional time' was created through performative interactions, it was an imitation of market infrastructure and it was inspired by relevant Western analogies and images of the Russian pre-communist past. Therefore, those early forms of critical stance and programmatic opposition that made themselves known in the transitional period also began appealing to the past, albeit to a past antipodal to the neoliberal present of the West and the capitalist past of Russia. The past hailed by non-conformist artists was the past of the Revolution and communism, i.e., it was the past that had a utopia, which is to say, had a future and knew not the 'the end of history'. However, there too the specificity of the transitional had made its adjustments. Transitional time is by definition a time of non-temporality; a time, it bears repeating, where the dimension of the *here and now* rules. Therefore, in the declarations and manifestos of the transitional period, the connection between the present and the past remained untraced. This is because the very 'transitionality' of the present did not set a clear demarcation between itself and the past and therefore did not allow for a possibility of its historicization. The past, held forth as a model, i.e., a kind of reverse utopia, that past would not be subject to analysis or articulated description. As a result, the connection between the past and the present remained unclear; it was impossible to construct a narrative continuity between the two. The past could be only pointed at with what was called at the time in Moscow's artistic circles 'gestures of relations'.

Stabilization: Corporate Arts System and Its Afflictions

In the 2000s, the establishment of the corporate state (where private and state interests intertwined) led to a formation of a network of institutions (with various degrees of public and private participation) in the art sphere. The art system was no longer a fact of group performativity: from an emphatic fiction it became a palpable reality, subjected to managerial *calculable* and *measurable* procedures, i.e., from the sphere of the common it moved to the sphere of the public. The common, meanwhile, was in fact reduced, since in the art community it was constituted by imitating the art system and therefore no longer had its raison d'être when that system had become real. The fact that the system was a new *iron cage* did not cause repulsion, since its alternative was the wearisome survival mode of the transitional period. The Soviet era did not know the experience of artists returning from the world of fiction to the world of reality that repulses them: 'the end of history' to them appeared as paradise come true.

The West continued to be the normative point of reference, but was demythologized by the procedures of *calculation* and *mensuration*. The West is now monetized and consumerized, reduced to the status of a showroom where Russia buys fashionable brands, including art products. The Russian past, meanwhile, is undergoing correction: now the points of reference are the examples of past stabilization, a continuity that is constructed by means of an articulated narrative. By the same token, the alternative to the official narrative can no longer be confined to 'gestures of relations', and is being constructed as another type of continuity and another narrative. In it, Soviet socialism appears not so much as it was, but as it could have been. The communist heritage is held forth as an example of another kind of modernization, as a resource of another globalization and universality.

In the art world, the task of creating an alternative historical narrative takes the form of interdisciplinary work wherein art practice overlaps with research and editorial practices that involve artists, philosophers, litterateurs, and sociologists. That, in fact, is tantamount to creating one's own alternative art system to the one created by the corporate state. Such was the case, for example, of the so-called work platform 'What is to be Done?' That is a case of a real, not a performative system, albeit incomparable with the dominating infrastructure in terms of capability. Thematizing and representing another narrative in its work, this alternative infrastructure is organized along the same principles as the dominant one, i.e., on the basis of the same procedures of *calculation* and *mensuration.* That is why artists insisted on the autonomy of their art product, but saw the organization of their work as pure management. It was just another corporation and not *their own spatial-temporal momentum.* The common is thus perceived by them as the public, created and controlled by themselves, and justice as a value alternative to the dominating one: clear, specific and unclouded by artistic metaphor.

The relations between the dominant and alternative art organizations were based on opposites. The 'moral majority' did not accept the thematization of the communist utopia by opposition intellectuals and artists. It was perceived as out of place in the 'end of history' era, in the context of a Russian-made, Western-based art system. That very interest in the national communist past, so alien to post-communist reality, was perceived as a business-dictated response to the Western demand for a leftist critical stance. Thus, an opposition organization was, paradoxically, accused of sabotaging post-communist pro-Western values at the bidding of the West. Attempts were made to exclude it from official art life, to banish it to where its patrons were — to the West.

The period of stabilization offered one more resistance strategy. It was based, for example in Anatoly Osmolovsky's

practice, on the fact that only then was resistance as such possible. It was because of the emergence of the corporate state and its infrastructure that the triad of the private, the common and the public had been finally restored and its inner dialectics started working. Precisely because of this, critically-minded artists and art activists were to treat carefully the art system that allowed them to criticize it. That is also why an alternative to such a system is impossible. It is only possible to exist critically within its limits. In other words, the common has to be rooted in the public, and utopia has to be acknowledged as practicable. In practice, all of the above was reduced to the production of a commodity product in which commodity fetishism was programmatically apparent. Basically, that means that justice has to be equated with public norms, and ethics is to be reduced to the ostensive demonstration of that equality. Art thus does not nourish itself with the resources of fiction that it introduces to reality, but is instead occupied with the analysis of its institutional reproduction, i.e. *concerns itself with measuring, quantifying, categorizing, systematizing and representing a reality.*

Finally, another alternative to the corporate art system emerged, seeking to establish itself in situations free from corporate communities, be they the dominant corporation or its antipodes. Thus, in the video work of Olga Chernysheva, we see characters who have dropped out of corporate and even social connections. They are migrants, people on the margins of society and outsiders. Works made on the basis of documentary footage show how these people have managed to create their own temporality in the day-to-day, to carve out a personal space and environment for themselves. Not pretending to be artists, they essentially have created *their own spatial-temporal momentum*, in which they are not bothered by their social deprivation, but on the contrary, come into their own in a situation of unrestrained freedom. However, they acquire this 'sustainable self' not so much *with regard to their social and natural environment* as in spite of it or, rather, by ignoring it. The personal narrative that is the foundation of their identity is not worked out at all, since the characters are uprooted from historical time and exist in the non-temporality, governed by unconscious rituals and repetitions. The freedom of these people is liminal; it knows no ethics because it is excluded from the collective; it knows no common because it is indifferent to the other; it does not appeal to justice because it does not want more than it already has.

Stabilization: 'Imitational Democracy' versus 'Imitational Criticality'

The political system that finally established itself under stabilization has been called 'imitational democracy'.[2] What it means is that post-Soviet society does have institutions of representative democracy, but civil society, remaining anaemic, does not tend to utilize them in appropriate ways. Moreover, the state and society establish an unspoken agreement: the former guarantees that the latter receives a part of oil and gas revenues in exchange for loyalty. In other words, by guaranteeing welfare in the private sphere, the state atrophies the common, thus keeping control over the public.

The tendency to maintain the appearance of a representative democracy confirms the fact that in the post-Soviet order there is no alternative to the neoliberal consensus. One can also suppose that, as time goes by and the traumas of the transitional period are overcome, civil society will start using democratic institutions correctly and the imitational nature of imitational democracy will slowly wane. Hence, one can also see why the criticism of the imitational nature of imitational democracy in post-communist societies is undertaken predominantly in keeping with liberal tradition. The state is called upon to observe civil rights spelled out by liberal democracy, and public opinion is called upon to consolidate and use available institutions appropriately. And it seems that these demands are far from utopian, as by keeping the neoliberal consensus, albeit superficially, post-Soviet society is gradually but inexorably rooting itself in it.

The above-mentioned process is corroborated by the emergence of the most advanced form of liberal criticism of imitational democracy that gained strength in post-communist societies towards the end of the second post-Soviet decade — the so-called 'criticality': critique of representational democracy as such. However, this critique of neoliberal ideology and its institutions is taking place in a society where representational democracy has not yet firmly established itself and exists mostly in imitational form. It is the international network of like-minded people rather than social movements in the post-Soviet world that is the point of reference for the advocates of direct democracy. Because of that,

not being rooted in the local context and having no narrative that might explain its mission in post-Soviet society, radical criticality itself becomes imitational. In other words, radical criticism can be mobilized by the ethical drive or may appeal to a fiction of another political order, but its idea of justice is not recognized by the public sphere and therefore has no prospect of becoming a fact of that domain in the foreseeable future.

This may explain why the left-wing critique of liberalism coming from young artists and intellectuals who took the stage in the middle of the second post-Soviet decade is becoming a form of negative group association, i.e., a way to make themselves stand out amidst an inhospitable context. Here again one sees 'gestures of relations', which, however, are not directed toward the examples from the past now, but toward the facts of contemporary global critical industry whose normative status is not yet accepted in the local context, although affiliation with that context becomes a sign of mutual identification for the members of the group. That group's fascination with contemporary radical Western thought is an example of what under current circumstances seems akin to the modernist fascination with the novelty of, in Gianni Vattimo's words, 'experiencing the value of the new as such'.[3] But it is precisely that which partly forces the post-Soviet political class to observe the rules of the neoliberal consensus: representational democracy is perceived as an attribute of globalized modernity that has become a prioritized consumption item. That leads one to suppose that the young intellectuals' choice of Western intellectual brands will not remain the prerogative of elite consumption for long and will find currency with local cultural industry as yet another manifestation of 'valuing the new as such'.

This rather ambivalent dialectics was, incidentally, described by that classic authority on Russian cultural theory, Yury Tynyanov.[4] From his point of view, the experience of parodying or imitating is ambivalent because it is inevitably wedged between the object of imitation and the context which (for now) does not accept this object. Hence, imitation always lays bare the conventionality of the imitated object since an imitated phenomenon has not yet become rooted in the context, has not dissolved in it, has not acquired a conventional terminology of designation and description in it. This is why the imitated is always perceived as, in the first place, a form, an intrinsically valued phenomenon that keeps its detached, external status. To put it another way, bringing imitational elements to bear on a foreign context underlines their unnatural, manufactured, theatrical nature, and therefore, in a way – their unrealness, insignificance and non-existence. At the same time, the use of imitational clichés presents the imitated behaviour itself as clichéd, over-used to the point of automatism, almost mechanical rather than human. In fact, these two types of rendering senseless and redefining together amount to a not always predictable social effect: the function of imitation leads to a drop in value of both the imitated object and the imitator. Hence, the existing condescending attitude to both imitational institutions of representational democracy and radical critiques of these institutions in the intellectual art milieu in post-Soviet societies.

At the same time, because of being wedged between the object of imitation and alien context, imitation always means violence. The reason is that it re-contextualizes its object in new circumstances. Imitation binds this foreign and new with its and imitation's own past. Laying bare the essential qualities of the imitated, it correlates them with certain qualities of the context where the imitation takes place. To put it another way, and at the risk of repetitiveness: there are grounds to suppose that imitational democracy and imitational criticality will find their place in post-Soviet reality, which in this case, however, will have stopped being post-Soviet.

This ambivalent picture of late stabilization needs one significant addition. At the end of 2011, the imitational mode of post-Soviet political life was disturbed by protest movements. Curiously, the protest movement itself was an obvious product of stabilization: people protest against that which is in fact stable, which has, it seems, established itself for the long haul. At the time, it seemed that the common had shaken itself loose from corporations and staked its own claim to the public. It seemed for a while that imitational democracy was turning into democracy proper. The protests were actually sparked by 'dishonest elections', i.e., the state's violation of institutions of representational democracy. However, as observers have demonstrated, 'the protesters who took to the streets attempted an experiment with projects of life-building, but within the bounds of a "normal life", examining these projects in the framework of personal commitment, family and career plans... These individuals, without yet knowing what unites them, responded to the call to take to the street... The main acquisition... for the participants, became

the subjectivity of independent individuals who had tested themselves... The boundary that separated the protesters from the world
of institutional politics... from the professional world of politics as
a place of the construction of public meanings, the maintenance
of which necessitates violence and bureaucracy — this boundary
was always felt,... was abidingly upheld... To the other side of this
boundary there always remained the private world, the world of a
civilized citizen who knows his or her possible and desirable future, who is partial to their privateness not being violated'.[5]

Thus, the common was understood by the protest movement of 2011-2012 as the sum total of private singularities that did
not form a collectivity. And if those singularities did envisage a
utopian horizon, it was seen as personal betterment or, to use the
nineteenth-century German term, as *Bildung*. Since utopia is a fact
of personal experience, it does not seek legitimization in big history: it needs neither a different social past nor a different common future. In the social context, the protesting subject exists in
the present, where it demands that the state honour existing social
contracts. Here justice is understood as formalized obligations and
rational procedures such as vote tallying based on 'calculable' and
'measurable' procedures. Finally, even in taking to the streets, the
protest movement did not lay claim to the public but continued to
consider it belonging to the corporate status quo — it merely did
not want it to invade its own enclosed private space.

Post-stabilization: 'The Aesthetics of Trauma'

Despite the fact that the protest movement did not encroach upon
the public, the state considered its tacit contract with society dissolved. It began appealing to a different type of social commonality: after the atomized crowd of the transitional period and the
corporations of the era of stabilization, the state turned to constituting the nation. That took the shape of the national leader addressing the citizens directly, bypassing the party system and political institutions. To put it another way, it was a process of nation-
alizing the common and subjecting the private and the public to it.
The 'calculable' and the 'measurable' could not be the constituting
mechanism here since their function is to impart, to diversify and
to delimit. A nation is a total commonality whose only diversification is its difference from another nation. Trauma turned out to be
the binding entity, bypassing rationality and political procedures.
For a start, trauma turns temporality in reverse, i.e., toward the

past. As has been demonstrated by experts, trauma is always a 'trauma of differentiation', a painful process of delimiting the past and the present.[6] Therefore, justice here begins to be understood as historical justice, and the resolution of trauma occurs as the past is making amends to the present or vice versa. Moreover, justice, to which trauma appeals, takes precedence over ethics and identifies itself as ethics.

The experience of trauma is also antipodal to *Bildung.* Shaping oneself originally supposes a cultural enjoyment, which it remains (albeit in somewhat risky forms) even in the case of self-assertion by means of protest. As for trauma, it is based on pain, on grief. While *Bildung* consolidates by bringing people who are experiencing similar though distinctly individual enjoyment closer together, trauma consolidates people by depriving them of the common enjoyment that is by definition the quintessence of the collective. A 'nation exists because its specific form of enjoyment can materialize by means of social practices and passed down to succeeding generations with the help of national myths that in fact constitute these practices... A national project is ultimately nothing other than a way in which members of a given ethnic group regulate their enjoyment by national myths'.[7] Hence, enjoyment is what trauma holds in store — that which the nation was deprived of by others, by its enemies. It is just that 'behind our attempts to ascribe to others the theft of our enjoyment we are hiding the traumatic fact that we never actually possessed that which has supposedly been stolen from us. The lack here... is primal'.[8] Thus, the other who is enjoying your enjoyment is none other than a reminder of your own fragmentariness, and therefore your wholeness is restored as if through proof by contradiction — by imagining the wholeness of the other. Thus, constituting a nation, the image of the other at the same time lays bare its inner emptiness. The utopian fiction therefore, instead of pointing out a possibility of a new and better world in a real future, presents itself as a fictional past loss. Except that the temporality of trauma is not limited by reversiveness: constituting the national common through the rhetoric of martyrdom and restoration of historical justice, the nation is restoring a linear teleological narrative. The nation becomes an imaginary community of people bound together by a common experience of pain in order to pass the evidence of their loss on to future generations. To put it another way, if, according to Freud, trauma is resolved when the patient admits

that it is a fact of the past, the consolidating effect of trauma works when the traumatic past returns in order to be relived as the present where the efforts to resolve the past are made, though they can never achieve the desired result.

Restoring the national common over the head of political institutions has exhausted the mission of imitational democracy without giving it a chance to become real. Imitational criticality also loses its raison d'être, having lost its chance of becoming something rooted and organic in the local context. As a result, the alternative to a nation consolidated by trauma can be found in another understanding of trauma: 'trauma as loss' is now juxtaposed with 'trauma as plot'.[9] That means that if a nation is consolidated by the idea of recovering the lost past — the past that was enjoyment — in the alternative case, trauma sets some general system of narrative coordinates. Specific situations of sacrifice assume the status of individual experience, and from that point of view the past and the present are then perceived. The past in this case does not replace the present and does not pretend to be continued and resolved in the future, but becomes the evidence of its own inviolability. It creates biographies and individual stories that are impossible outside the history of experienced trauma. In other words, the aesthetics of trauma, which artists have been creating lately, appealing to biography and personal narrative, attempts to actualize the politics of identity — concrete and specific identity that is an alternative to the totalizing construction of a nation. Programmatically admitting their fragmentariness and incompleteness, these artists avoid inner emptiness — something that distinguishes a nation aspiring to wholeness.

This identity acquired through trauma does in fact guarantee the individual a 'sustainable self', and that distinguishes it from the role of identity in the transitional period. At the same time, it is different from the subjectivity of *Bildung* — which is dynamic, open to various scenarios and therefore shunning any specific identification. What is symptomatic here is that the signalling colour chosen by the activists of protest movements was white, i.e., neutral, free from identity. Finally, in its apology of identity specificity, the poetics of trauma pits itself against the narratives of the stabilization era — both the state narrative and the alternative narrative that lays bare the all-encompassing, universal nature of the communist experience. The artists of trauma regard post-Soviet narratives as a continuation of Soviet totality and in polemics insist on identity as a right to complexity, particularity and difference.

Still, the identity of trauma poetics does not confine subjectivity to its personal 'iron cage'. Trauma, as Jeffry Alexander claimed, is inseparable from representation: it is directed outward.[10] The 'sustainable self' of the artists of trauma opens them up to the other. Understanding trauma as an experience that cannot be lived down, they experience it as essential to human nature and therefore capable of transcending singularity. Thus, Khaim Sokol, first among Russian artists began to thematize the defencelessness and hardships of economic migrants. His video works, created in a long-time collaboration with unskilled workers from Central Asia, unquestionably possess social meaning and appeal to solidarity and justice. However, these works were not born from party loyalty to political activism, but from a deeply personal and traumatic immigrant experience. And that is quite a contrast with the works of Chernysheva, where people on the margins of society, outcasts, do not experience their lot as a trauma and therefore remain enclosed in their self-sufficient singularity, incapable of solidarity with others.

By the same token, the sense of place comes to the poetics of trauma through the experience of one's own homelessness. Thus, Evgeniy Fiks, studying the question of his identity as a post-Soviet Jew, turns to the history of Birobidzhan, an administrative Jewish autonomy in the far east of the USSR. Although that Soviet social experiment, twenty years before the creation of Israel, turned out a failure, it is in Birobidzhan — and not in Moscow where the artist was born or in New York where he lives — where he is ready to feel the 'natural human desire to be someplace that one calls home' fulfilled.[11] Birobidzhan becomes a place and a nation precisely because it 'poses the provocative and unanswered (unanswerable) question of the relation between a people/commune and a place/territory, and problematizes the idea of (inter)nationalism and autonomy'.[12] In other words, Birobidzhan becomes a nation and a motherland because it has no place, which is to say, because it is a utopia. The aesthetics of trauma, though it insists on identity, which sets it apart from the aesthetics of justice, nonetheless understands identity *not as an act of being, but of becoming, between reality and utopia, between reality and imagination.*

Notes

1 The author frequently refers to the article
'The Matter of Aesthetic Justice' by Pascal
Gielen, also published in this volume.

2 Dmitriy Furman, *Dvizhenije po spirali.
Politicheskaya sistema Rossii v ryadu
drugih sistem* (Moscow: Ves'mir, 2010).

3 Gianni Vattimo, *The End of Modernity:
Nihilism and Hermeneutics in
Postmodern Culture* , transl. by Mira
Ginsburg (Boston: Eridanos Press, 1988),
p. 100.

4 See texts on parody by this classic
authority on the Russian formalist school,
for instance: Tinyanov U.N. *parodii* //
inyanov U.N. *Poetika. Istoriya literaturi.
Kino.* Moscow, 1977 pp. 284-310.

5 Alexander Bikbov, 'Self-trial Through
Protest' in *Moscow Art Magazine*, 'Digest.
2007-2014', Moscow, 2014, pp. 133-134.

6 Alan Bass, *Difference and Disavowal:
The Trauma of Eros* (Stanford CT:
Stanford University Press, 2000), p. 210.

7 Slavoj Žižek , *Tarrying with the Negative:
Kant, Hegel, and the Critique of Ideology*
(Durham: Duke University Press, 1993),
pp. 202-203.

8 Ibid., p. 203.

9 Sergei Ushakin, 'Nam etoj bolju dishat?'
in *ravma: punkti*, *Novoye Litearaturnoe
Obozreniye*, (Moscow: NLO, 2009), p. 9.

10 Jeffry C. Alexander, *The Meanings of
Social Life: A Cultural Sociology* (New
York: Oxford University Press, 2005),
pp. 85-108.

11 Evgeniy Fiks, 'Pejzazh Evrejskoj
avtonomnoj oblasti' in *Hudozhestvennij
zhurnal*, Moscow, 2014, p. 48.

12 Bikbov, 'Self-trial Through Protest' in
Moscow Art Magazine, 'Digest. 2007-
2014', Moscow, 2014, pp. 133-134.

The Aesthetic Impossibility of Justice
Collateral Damage

Hakan Topal

Social Justice and the Question of Artistic Research

A documentary that is research-based involves travel, observation, talking, listening, note-taking, sketching, photography, and the recording of audio and video. Today, many artists are realizing art projects that explicitly tackle global events of historical importance, such as the Arab Spring, war in Afghanistan, European colonialist histories, issues of social justice, neoliberal transformation, gentrification, racism, and immigration. All of these highly sensitive subject matters render a politically-charged contemporary art landscape that defies easy generalizations. Nevertheless, one can identify the crystallization of a tendency towards research-based art practices. Instead of simply taking these world events and social issues as input for their individual art works, artists are developing long-term engagements with the issues and producing interconnected projects. But how is this commitment to research in artistic production different from an ethnographic account by a social scientist who employs similar visual research tools? In what way do research-based art practices address urgent socio-political issues? What are the political agencies of these practices? In that regard, before discussing my own research project, I will highlight the premise of artistic research and raise some questions in relationship to the idea of aesthetic justice. A reference to research usually implies a specific social [or natural] scientific methodology or combination of tools and techniques that are employed to identify certain patterns in natural or social worlds. When we use the terms 'research' and 'artistic' in conjunction, it immediately creates a difficulty, as it refers to a systematic and somewhat verifiable approach mixed with personal expression and gestures. In contrast to any scientific model that aims to either explain or interpret social or natural phenomena, the outcome of artistic research can be best measured by its ability to engage with seemingly unrelated matters, things, and concepts. An art project creates its own space of engagement, and therefore its own set of rules. Art is a hybrid way of knowing the perceivable world and expanding its limits. The tangible aspect of artistic research and production is the basis for new forms of intelligible affects, emotions and sentiments beyond instructive explanations or interpretations.

What is an artistic method? When an artist enters into a social realm to conduct a research project, her/his intuition generates in-situ knowledge. Intuition is a practical method and fundamental aspect of artistic knowledge production, implemented in the here and now. In this regard, in artistic research, perhaps more so than any other scientific examination, intuition is utilized as a method to identify a wide range of new productive modalities. As explained by Henri Bergson[1] — and later expanded by Gilles Deleuze[2] — intuition differs from material knowledge (something already known), but it is never the transcendental (pure) idea. Intuitional tools eliminate the assumed split between the material reality (realism) and the conceptual realm (idealism). The idea of divine inspiration is no longer required to express the moment when the artistic idea occurs. Instead, an 'eruption of intuition' occurs within the material site of the mind, at the very membrane of the brain. According to Elizabeth Grosz, 'intuition is the method by which unique and original concepts are created and developed for objects, qualities and durations that are themselves unique and specific'.[3] There is no complete picture of the world; our experience within the world is always durational and partial. Therefore, intuition pulls us toward the possibility of action, toward an experience, and allows us to 'enter into the things' rather than 'circumvent' them:

> Intuition is a mode of 'sympathy' by which every
> characteristic of an object (process, quality etc.) is
> brought together, none is left out, in a simple and
> immediate resonance of life's inner duration and
> the absolute specificity of its objects. It is an attuned
> empiricism that does not reduce its components and
> parts but expands them to connect this object to the
> very universe itself.[4]

For instance, a painter, poet or sculptor knows what to do next, often without actually rationally calculating his/her movements. Intuition activates a possibility; it breaks the usual processes. In other words, intuition allows a slight creative opening by interrupting an ordered flow. It is a durational moment where new types of knowledge can emerge. For that matter, one can argue that artistic research aims to create systematic possibilities where intuitional production can take place; a synthesis of the new experience of artists and the intellectual operations they engage. We need to think of artistic research as an immersive experience, a different, but legitimate way ofunderstanding social phenomena, objects, things, and concepts.

Artistic work is never accidental — even random encounters are carefully crafted. Intuition provides the basis for the systematic exploration of aggregated content and its combined affects. Certainly, practitioners of other fields utilize intuition to further expand their field; however, for art, a sensible engagement with the social realm defines an artistic output that can be only evaluated within the framework of the experience, both as the producer and the viewer within the expanded space of art work. Accumulated documents, images, and recordings serve as a personal archive. Later on, these documents can be utilized to realize different work. For projects that have artistic research at their core, the formal outcome may appear secondary to the research; however, we need to remind ourselves that documents have very specific formal qualities. While artistic research brings our attention to the importance of the site and to a moment of personal engagement, the outcome is not taken for granted; the final result has to be carefully executed in consideration of aesthetic qualities.

Roboski: Justice Yet to Come

On 28 December 2011, unmanned air vehicles (UAV) spotted a group of individuals crossing the Iraq-Turkey border near the village of Roboski — also known by its Turkish name, Ortasu, located under the jurisdiction of Uludere district, fifty kilometres from the closest city of Sirnak. During the night of 28 December, an intelligence report about a possible guerrilla group passed to the Turkish military's high command, and consequently the military ordered an air strike with limited information received through the aerial footage transmitted by UAV. Two F16 jet fighters launched an attack on 'suspected terrorists' by trespassing Iraqi airspace — an international military action that would require the government's direct approval. Very soon, it became apparent that the individuals crossing the border were villagers from Roboski, who were routinely smuggling gas, cigarettes, and tea from northern Iraq — a trade that is well-known by both local authorities and military outposts. In fact, the day before the incident, the local governor was playing football with some teenage boys from the same village; some of the kids left the game early and when he asked where they were going, they smiled and opened their arms, gesturing that he already knew they were on their way to Iraq. He agreeably smiled and returned back to the game. Smuggling is the only viable income for residents of these border villages.

Thirty-four out of the thirty-five villagers in the group were killed — nineteen of them were under eighteen, still in school — and most of them were from the Encü family, the largest family in the village. The next morning their relatives went to an adjacent mountain where they found some of the group still alive; however, the local military outpost refused to fly helicopters to bring the injured to the hospital.

I consider my research project about Roboski not as an autobiographical undertaking or a social scientific field survey, but rather as an extension to my long-term artistic commitment situated in the Anatolian and Mesopotamian landscape. Over the years, I have tried to systematically understand the unique conditions in which social, political, and cultural events unfold there. In preparation for my journey, I diligently looked at the press images taken in and around Roboski. I felt that something was absent in all those editorial images and television coverage — all of which reduced the scene to predefined media clichés. In fact, any scandal on TV is covered with the same formal televisual sequences. Even thoughtfully produced documentaries about Roboski utilized the same mass-media aesthetic, with an excessively sentimental depiction of the victims' lives and their families. Despite this overflow of sappy emotionalism, there was a void of justice, which I thought could not be simply represented within predefined media templates.

As opposed to forming a specific personal documentary narrative like a reporter, I wanted to use video as a durational device replacing photographic stills. I decided to take long shots of portraits of people and landscapes as a silent monument without sound. I did not record any of my conversations, ensuring the immediacy of my personal encounters. After all, there have been a lot of interviews conducted by other cultural producers. Looking at the vast amount of material online, I felt that everything that needed to be said had somehow been said and recorded before. Therefore, I considered silent video portraits, which depict subtle movements, delicate gestures, and motions, breathing, and sighing as forms of intimate utterances. Looking at these images, it is sometimes hard to know that the video is still running. Time is momentarily suspended.

In video portraits, as opposed to photographic portraiture, I identify three interlocking durational layers in my work on

Roboski: first, the time when the video is taken within the actual site and the context. Second, the time when the viewer encounters the mother who is holding a photograph of her son in silence. Looking for a while, a delicate void appears, and the viewer recognizes that something is missing, which cannot be simply articulated with any other utterances. Third, the photograph of her son, the picture frame within the video. All of these durations unfold concurrently within silence. Silence in fact is never silent; there is always noise, there is the sound of the fan, streets, and household appliances while you are watching the video. Yet, silence points out that something is missing. A justice yet to come. I personally choose video as a durational tool to record the portrait of the families, as I think a narrative framework would override the interwoven time structure.

Condolence: A Larger Political Context of Injustice
During the course of the forty-year-long war between the Kurdish guerrilla group PKK and the Turkish military, there have been mass killings, torture and systematic human rights abuses. However, this unprecedented incident was different than all the previous ones. Thanks to social media and independent journalists, the public was much better informed and people quickly mobilized around the issue. The massacre generated outrage and resentment amongst the public. A wide-range of political parties and NGOs demanded justice in its very basic form — to find and punish the responsible persons who ordered the attacks on unarmed Turkish civilians.

Turkish Prime Minister Tayyip Recep Erdogan undermined and diluted the significance of the issue by side-tracking the matter through various discursive tactics. In April 2012, Erdogan, rather shamelessly, likened the incident to abortion, saying that women who have abortions are killing babies and people should concentrate on that, not Uludere — an analogy that created steadfast backlash from women's organizations and human rights activists. In fact, abortion has been a right for woman in Turkey since 1983, and so this was another attack by the neoliberal Islamist government on civil liberties. Nevertheless, the prime minister's comments side-tracked the issue and changed the agenda. Although the Erdogan government openly took responsibility for their 'fatal error', they refused to provide an official apology and blocked the process of justice to persecute the responsible parties within the state.

Similar to crimes committed by armies around the globe, the Turkish state provides an invisible shield around their soldiers in order to protect them and block further scrutiny. To eliminate social backlash, it offers a set amount of payment to victims' families to cover up the state crimes. Like numerous cases in Iraq and Afghanistan, the Turkish government offered a small sum of 23,150 Turkish liras (around $10,000) per body, as condolence fees to the Roboski families. Erdogan later increased this figure to 123,500 Turkish liras in a public parade of 'sympathy', only to draw further criticism of his ignorance about the families' demands. The Roboski families refused to take the offer until they found the murderers. Since then, the families have staged various public demonstrations and gatherings in order to keep the issue alive.

As one travels toward the east, the concept of hospitality takes on new meaning, which makes you wonder about the use of the word in Western cultures – including Western Turkey. There is an inherent generosity in the lands of Mesopotamia, and its people shares this bigheartedness, they give and provide whatever they can.

I drove all the way to Cizre, stopping in a few spots; interestingly, there were not many checkpoints along the roads. All the previously occupied military posts were empty. I stopped at Cizre for an hour before heading to Sirnak. I walked down the main street. Cizre's streets were busy. All signs were written in Kurdish, Turkish, as well as in Arabic. The colours of the PKK, red, green, yellow, were dominantly seen everywhere, as if being a silent protest declaring independence. In the 90s, paranoid policemen used to change the traffic lights, thinking that they were subtle PKK propaganda!

Eventually I left Cizre and headed to Sirnak. When I arrived, you could see the mountains circling the city. Cudi Mountain, probably the most infamous one among all, is a monument in itself, and a reminder of the deadliest fights and thousands of young people lost in the region. Zeynep, an executive secretary at the Sirnak municipality, told me that her father disappeared in the 1990s shortly after the military police had jailed him. Years later, she received a phone call from him. He said that after having been tortured for days, he managed to flee the jail with other prisoners and they moved to a PKK camp in Northern Iraq; he had not called his family for a long time in order to protect them. Zeynep revealed that seeing her father for the first time was like meeting a stranger. She could only recognize his eyes because they were exactly the same as her brother's, who is in prison now for being a member of PKK.

The grim reality in the region is intertwined with intimate relationships with the guerrilla group and the ongoing conflict with the Turkish state. Almost all the people I met had some sort of personal connection to PKK, albeit they might not directly support it. For a long time, the state and the majority of the Turkish population were unable to see this connection between Kurdish resistance movements and the people. The Turkish state did not face its recent and past histories (including the Armenian genocide), therefore it is impossible to argue that peace can be sustained on a foundation that is defined by cultural and ethnic discrimination, inequality and injustice, specifically in Southeast Turkey. Precisely for this reason, I believe that the killing of thirty-four villagers from Roboski represents a critical reference case for the democratization of Turkey and an open discussion of the crimes of the state.

However, the issue of collateral damage and the question of peace are not limited to Turkey. Western democratic societies, specifically the United States, likewise utilize military tactics, namely drone attacks on alleged terrorists. The killing of civilians raises many ethical issues and questions of legitimacy of (Western) democracies.

Within the milieu of continuous international and local conflicts, ongoing ethnic struggles, and national and civil wars, more and more civilians are being killed as a result of so-called 'collateral damage'. For instance, in Afghanistan, Pakistan, Palestine, and Turkey a war is being raged against an ambiguous enemy that is determined not to give up no matter what the consequences. It is a war defined by honour and morality, and not by the economic, calculative rational of modernist states. An organized military power on the one side and dispersed guerrilla groups on the other side characterize an 'asymmetrical' conflict, with unsolidified political camps composed of peace organizations, political parties and NGOs. It is not possible to 'win' these wars. There is no surrender; there is no end to a conflict; rather, continuous high alert conditions are normalized through various localized wars, which produce their own leaders and political actors, all of which rely on the continuity of the conflict itself — global war is a perpetual motion machine. Unlike in a traditional battle where societies agree that one side has lost the war and they need to surrender to the enemy, the ongoing conflict does not have any ethical resolution, which leaves the whole population in a constant state of shock. Global wars are not to be won, but are staged more like reality TV. Both the military and politicians recognize the fact that it is impossible to achieve any of their operational goals within vast territories where guerrilla groups have the full support of a local population, especially after the horrible crimes that the state has committed without any retribution. But they cannot stop. Heavy arms, artillery and ammunition are used to intensify the possibility of civilian death and inflict terror as a means to control and contain the conflict, while military checkpoints and outposts define the borders of conflict, both as the metaphorical and literal site of terror.

The war machine employed by the state does not have any social capacity to separate civilians from guerrilla forces; instead, it aims to immobilize a large segment of the population, delay public services such as education, the development of civic infrastructure or business improvements. The conditions generated by the wars effectively deepen the social, economic, and cultural gaps between neighbouring societies.

For instance, apartheid in Palestine should not be understood simply in tactical terms, as a way of maintaining the borders and controlling the flow of bodies; rather, it is employed to suffocate any possible constructive efforts within Palestinian society itself. Apartheid is imposed to effectively delay civic, economic, educational, and cultural services, which stalls Palestinian society, creates a further gap between the modern, powerful state of Israel and poor urban ethnic clusters in Gaza and Ramallah. Even if tentative peace is reached after long negotiations, a destroyed social, civic, and economic infrastructure takes years to rebuild.

At the same time, the ongoing large military deployment in crisis zones is used as an ideological tool to indoctrinate young soldiers and their families. While war is used to keep the working classes under control, war industries benefit the most from these ongoing conflicts. Unchecked expenditures create infinite business opportunities within the war economy. The very continuity of this industry depends on the commitment of both politicians and the military to seek out so-called military solutions for social problems.

The state not only utilizes military means to crush resistance; it also engages law as an apparatus to eliminate opponents in the public sphere.[5] When state violence spills over into an urban domain, more and more civilians are subjected to the brutal consequences of actual clashes. No matter what they do, the military's special forces, anti-terror units, UAVs or intelligent bombs cannot properly distinguish the enemy from the civilian population. When a strike causes civilian deaths, the military is already authorized to pay a condolence fee, which is calculated by certain rationalized economic principles. For instance, the United States Army in Afghanistan utilizes a clear pay scale, which defines the amount of money paid in the case of any death, loss of limbs, killing of domestic animals or damage to vehicles.[6] While the destruction of a vehicle or the death of a person would cost American taxpayers $2,500, an arm or a leg would amount to only around $500. Unlike the United States' diligent statistics on American deaths and injuries, there are no reliable records to determine how many civilians are killed during wars; in fact when it comes to civilian deaths in Iraq or Afghanistan, the numbers are rounded off in digits, tens, hundreds, or thousands to delineate the number of killings.

Condolence payments made by states imply a disturbing question: How can a life be valued according to institutional principals? How can compassion and support in the face of death be translated into monetary terms and stripped from any so-called humane relationship, creating a fundamental contradiction in the face of death?

One of the most difficult but illuminating conversations in Roboski that I had was about the condolence payments offered by the state. My question was frank: Obviously, the money would not bring back their loved ones but if there were an official apology from the government, wouldn't the condolence payments help to ease the pain? Ferhat Encü, a young university student from Roboski who had become the spokesperson for the families, paused a moment and responded that they would consider negotiating the payments once the government had found the murderers who were responsible and brought them to justice. In order to come to a peaceful resolution with the State, they needed to sit down with representatives, discuss and come up with a figure that is appropriate for the scale of the event.

Ferhat further explained that when there are local killings, in order to eliminate bloody 'honour killing' wars and to mitigate tension between families, villagers were usually encouraged to sit down and face each other with the help of local brokers. Through condolence payments, they would seek to resolve a conflict, which can potentially last decades. Yet, there are some procedures involved, which are meant to delicately and ethically navigate the complex nature of death and pay proper respect to the bodies of the dead. First and foremost, any kind of negotiation happens after the fortieth day of passing – the day that mark the end of the period of grieving. Depending on the financial ability of the 'accountable' person or family, the group decides upon a fee through a careful process of concession. This process usually requires a tense but necessary moment of facing each other. Ferhat cited that after a recent incident, when one of the villagers was killed in a local fight, the family agreed to receive around 250,000 Turkish lira from the murderer's family – a much higher figure that Turkish state offered. Ferhat explained that after the Roboski killings, the state did not show any of these moral considerations. First and foremost, the government's offer to villagers was taken as an insult because it was announced right away and they were pressured to immediately accept it. Furthermore, Erdogan's public effort to give additional money was particularly disrespectful and showed that he had no consideration regarding local traditions and values – even though the Prime Minister claims to be a compassionate religious man. Therefore, the government's offer was seen more like bribing to keep the villagers quiet, rather than a considered effort to support them during very hard times.

Ferhat asked his brother Veli to accompany me in the village. I visited many homes and talked with the families. Older women generally do not speak Turkish, so our conversation included long pauses with them hugging the picture frames to show how much they missed their sons. Short translations by men usually included their own commentary. I visited a family. Their son was studying to be a technical drafter; his father said he asked him not to go to Iraq, because they did not need the money, but he insisted, went anyway, and as a young person it was adventurous crossing borders, smuggling goods, helping his family, and he wanted to prove his manhood. His mother came to meet with me with their son's photo album, composed of hundreds of photographs, mostly taken at the school with his friends. Going through the album, she cried, showing me his pictures one by one.

As highlighted by many writers, including Roland Barthes, and Susan Sontag, there is an intimate connection between photography and death. A photographic image signifies the absence of the subject while presenting it at the same time. Photographic reality oscillates between the exact moment a photograph was taken and the moment that it was presented to a viewer. In that regard, the photograph is more than a simple historical record. It is a physical object that is hung on walls, placed in vitrines, hugged and kissed — a warm object and constant reminder of an intimate connection to lost loved ones. Photography is the reminder of the void left by the state.

For an artist, the question is: How do you translate this loss through an artistic research project? Is it possible to depict injustice? Loss is a void; it is impossibility. Listening in silence allows this void to take shape. When I went to Roboski, I did not have a pre-defined agenda, other than thinking about the question of justice. The ultimate purpose of this research project is to eventually create a video monument. It is important to establish a bodily relationship between the images and the viewer. A temporary monument that expands the framework of the technical limitations of the video medium, and creates a spatial relationship with the immediate area around it. In other words, an installation that calls our attention to the context of the presentation while presenting the work itself.

When I visited the Roboski families, I clearly explained my intention of realizing a temporary monumental art installation to them. I told that I wanted to create an art work where audiences can look into the video portraits and contemplate the question of justice — that was the only way to face the prolonged injustice. As I write this article, it is now over 800 days since the government blocked a civilian investigation.

Condolence and Compensation

Condolence, support and sympathy require an intimate relationship, a direct humane connection; one has to be able to appreciate someone's grief and recognize the impossibility of death. The void, the emptiness of a missing person pulls one person to another. However, the state does not have the ability to recognize this form of intimacy. While there are specialized units in the military to deal with the death of soldiers and their families, there is no specialized institutional body which deals with its own terror.

When an incident occurs, the Turkish state has a procedure for calculating condolence payments to civilians: forty times the salary of an officer of a certain rank. The condolence payments given to the families of soldiers are much higher — recently the Turkish government increased the payment to families of dead soldiers to 400,000 Turkish liras. In other words, when the state is involved in violence and inflicts terror on a population, the situation presents itself as impossible; the state, which is required to guarantee the conditions of justice, becomes a liability to society as it does not allow itself to be scrutinized. The State is the state of exceptions; with its secrets and hidden in-situ operational mechanisms in order to protect its military and police from any outside scrutiny, it provides a protective shield against any personal wrongdoing, specifically within the boundary of high alert zones.

This imprudence of the armed forces presents a dilemma with regard to the notion of individual accountability. For example, when a doctor commits an error in the operation room or an engineer makes a mistake in his building design, he/she is personally responsible for their actions, however when the military or the police commit crimes, the state provides a safeguard as an initial protection from juridical scrutiny. For instance, how many American drone operators are punished, while killing hundreds of civilians? The answer is 'zero'.

In this regard, military operational logic contradicts the juridical notion of individual responsibility. Within a top to bottom hierarchy, individuals have to obey the exact rules and orders given to them. This collective nature of military action diffuses the actual liability of the personnel. In order to find the responsible actor for any crimes, one needs to follow the chain of command. Therefore, according to the law, the government bears the ultimate responsibility for the wrongdoings of its military in the Roboski Massacre.

Deliberating the recent events in Palestine and Kurdistan, it is impossible not to identify an uncanny similarity between the tactics and methods employed by the Turkish and Israeli states. Although the neoliberal Islamist Turkish government has been a prominent critic of Israeli actions in Palestine in recent years, its own actions in Turkish and Iraqi territory were very similar to those of the Israelis until the 2013 peace process with the PKK.

The Erdogan government's contradictory (and hypocritical) approach becomes visible when we look at its declarations about Palestine and Syria. For instance, when the Israeli army raided the humanitarian ship Mavi Marmara on international waters and killed nine Turkish activists, the Turkish government steadfastly demanded an apology and justice for the actions that had been committed in international waters. Israel rejected the claims on similar grounds to those used by the Turkish government in rejecting justice in Roboski. Both countries claimed that the killings were an unexpected outcome of a military raid, and should be considered collateral damage. Both Israel and Turkey persistently reject any possible investigation of their commanders and soldiers involved in these incidents.

Finally, the idea of justice cannot be sustained through simple monetary compensation but through a proper recognition of the mistakes of the state. It is about establishing official visibility. However, by systematically ignoring the facts on the ground, the state distorts reality.

The Gezi Uprising shifted many power dynamics and crystalized political fault lines. The 'Axis of Power' comprised of the Islamist front, the Hizmet Movement (a global religious movement led by Pennsylvania-based Fethullah Gülen), and Erdogan's AK Party, once allies, became enemies. Since 17 December 2013, there has been an ongoing investigation into corruption, which involves many ministers, including Erdogan's son, with police recordings of corruption leaked to the media.

Allegedly, policemen and attorney generals close to the Hizmet/Gülen Movement disclosed the documents and audio recordings of corruption and launched an unprecedented attack that will have much larger consequences. However, these leaks also betrayed something more deeply dishonest and corrupt than a simple bribery case. They showed an absolute dissolution of the separation of powers through high-level government involvement in non-governmental institutions. Among these leaked recordings, a phone conversation between the editor of a major newspaper, *Fatih Saraç*, and the Prime Minister's close associate, Taner Yıldız, who is also the Minister of Energy and Natural Resources, is rather noteworthy. In short, the conversation entails a journalist reporting to the Minister the following: 'Thanks to Allah, we saw the event (referring to the Roboski memorial day) neither on TV nor in the newspaper.' The politician approvingly responds: 'Exactly, exactly.'

This short dialogue exposes how a media conglomerate decided not to cover a major news story. Ignoring newsworthy events may not be surprising; however, this short conversation is maliciously intertwined with Islamist religious morality. It is astounding to thank Allah for the fact that journalists did not 'see' the mothers who lost their loved ones holding pictures of their sons or that families and tens of thousands of justice-seeking supporters were overlooked or that justice will never come as long as the people are not seen.

Regarding regimes of visibility, every time I see the same Roboski mothers in the media at various demonstrations, I can recognize them holding the same pictures in their hands, showing them to the public and making sure that we all see them together with their lost sons. Again, photography is intrinsically tied to the idea of the impossibility of death. Seeing is not simply seeing, it is also appreciating the void. When the government censored the news of the mothers holding their sons' pictures, perhaps it was not political agency that terrified them but their own inability to see and appreciate this very void.

Epilogue

Justice requires a steadfast ethical stance against the horrors of the state, while condolence, support, and compassion necessitate personal commitment beyond the monetary valuation of life according to rationalized calculative logic. In that regard, the Roboski project's goal was not to make the event visible — it already had extensive media coverage both in Turkey and internationally — but instead, to create a specific and intimate truth about the incident, made known to the viewer through bare images. Documents, video portraits and landscape pictures are not data to be instrumentalized for a specific outcome; rather, they contain agency that directly communicates with other objects, documents and subjects in an expanded context. In other words, artistic documents can be treated as particular art works, which are both part of a personal experience and the productive activity of research that has a transformative capacity for both the artist and the viewer.

Research that undertakes affects and emotions can move beyond social science. On a personal level, recording moving images as still as possible is a way to acquire first-hand knowledge about a specific context without adding additional structure

through editing. I use videography just like still photography, except that I explore duration as artistic substance. Although video is a highly technical procedure that can be verified in an objective manner, the geographical site cannot be depicted through its representative device. In a way, images are always generic, and a conceptual process is required to further manifest a location, the context. In other words, the accumulation of all my images of Roboski is not about representing a particular case study, or lifting a veil over the Roboski massacre in a manner similar to a criminal investigator. After all, the terror of the state has been exposed by other actors, including human rights organizations and the villagers themselves. The Roboski project has been about active engagement with the political agency of the victims and their families. I believe that the duty of an artist is first and foremost an ethical one, and to recognize any utterances of subjects who speak truth, even the most silent ones in certain cases. I am responsible through my work, its integrity, and the ways I develop my artistic approach; in return, research outlines my relationship to the larger social political context. Aesthetics is the end result that actively produces intimate knowledge and contributes to the possibility of justice.

Notes

1   Henri Bergson (1946), *The Creative Mind: An Introduction to Metaphysics* (New York: Dover Publications, 2010.)
2   Gilles Deleuze, *Bergsonism.*, transl. by Hugh Tomlinson and Barbara Habberjam (New York: Zone Books, 1991).
3   Elizabeth Grosz, 'Bergson, Deleuze and the Becoming of Unbecoming', in *Parallax* , 2005, vol. 11, no. 2, pp. 4-13. Here p. 7.
4   Grosz, idem., p. 8.
5   Eyal Weizman's work on 'lawfare' is a great study of how the state instrumentalizcs both local and international law to inflict violence on the Palestinian population. See: 'Lawfare in Gaza: Legislative Attack' www.opendemocracy.net/article/legislative-attack.
6   'The Department of Defense's Use of Solatia and Condolence Payments in Iraq and Afghanistan', United States Accountability Office, 2007. (Retrieved from http://goo.gl/J15q5Q).

The Aesthetic Impossibility of Justice

245

Six Acts
Or an Experimental Approach to Justice

Niels Van Tomme
in Conversation
with Carlos Motta

Niels Van Tomme *Six Acts: An Experiment in Narrative Justice* started off as a series of readings of historical speeches by moderate liberals and left-wing political leaders, which were staged in public space in the period leading up to the 2010 presidential elections in Bogotá, Colombia. I was wondering if you could elaborate on the specific political context that prompted the piece, and why it was important to organize the performances around the time of the elections?

Carlos Motta 2010 was a critical year in Colombian politics because it marked the end of Álvaro Uribe Vélez' 12-year mandate, an extreme right-wing government characterized for its militaristic, neoliberal and pro-U.S. policies. The 2010 elections thus represented an opportunity to change directions, to implement new political, economic and social agendas and to hastily reclaim the country's immediate future. Unfortunately, 2010 also reassured the imminent and ongoing crisis of the Colombian Left. No strong candidates of the Liberal Party or independent parties could realistically contend against Juan Manuel Santos, Uribe's former Minister of Defence and endorsed candidate, who ultimately won the elections.

Moderate liberal and leftist ideologies have been historically threatened and actively exterminated in Colombia. In its modern history, six liberal and leftist presidential candidates have been assassinated: Rafael Uribe in 1903, Jorge Eliécer Gaitán in 1949, Jaime Pardo Leal in 1986, Luis Carlos Galán and Carlos Pizarro in 1989 and Bernardo Jaramillo in 1990. Although each one of these leaders had unique ideas for the country, some of them moderate and others radical, they were all aware that the roots of Colombia's violent conflict lie within its profound social and economic inequality. They proposed projects of government that defied and denounced hegemonic power in its many forms: militaristic, elitist, insurgent, etc. Colombia's civil war has been a particularly bloody one, and there are many factors that need to be exposed in order to understand it in depth. Any attempt to summarize it here would be incomplete; but in broad terms, there have been a few main actors including government and military forces, paramilitary groups, drug traffickers, and radical leftist guerrillas at war to seize power and to protect their political and economic interests.

Six Acts was strategically set at the time of the 2010 elections to respond to the crisis of the left, using the form of political speech to re-insert the fallen leaders' radical ideas of social transformation into the public sphere at a time, in my opinion, when they were greatly needed. The speech-'acts' were an attempt to honour threatened ideas, and the men that died voicing them, but also to use narrative aesthetics to rethink the concept of *justice*. If justice isn't served by judicial means, can we think of experimental approaches to justice? Could aesthetics represent a break from failing normative institutional forms of *reparation*? Could aesthetics come to terms with the pervasive social effects of political violence?

NVT — How exactly should we understand the term 'narrative justice', as mentioned in the title of the piece? Where did it originate from and how can it be applied in an artistic context?

CM — The concept of 'narrative justice' refers to a notion of justice detached from the judicial field and focused on narrative and communication as pillars of a possible reconciliation. I borrow this term from Columbia University Psychology Professor Jack Saul, who has developed performative workshops with victims of trauma using narration as a means of conflict resolution. From another perspective, it could be argued that violence, inequality and oppression, as well as politics at large, social justice, and activism manifest in the form of narrative constructions, and as such, I am interested in intervening that representational system to question, challenge, and understand its terms. This enables me to make use of fiction, forms of documentary, and performance strategies to try to construct spaces for social and political interaction based on the memory of violent and traumatic events.

NVT — By staging these re-enactments in public space, you choose to confront bystanders in their everyday life. How did you reconcile the historicity of the subject matter to the contemporary settings used in your work?

CM — I consider that Colombia is a country that tends to seek refuge in amnesia, perhaps due to a survival or self-protection drive. In spite of the State's recent initiatives to render the victims visible, in Colombia it is common to forget the past, no matter how many times these images may be repeated before our eyes; to forget those who have been assassinated or forced to disappear is habitual. That is why Colombia has historically tended to be an unfair country that has been indebted to its victims.

The 'acts' constituted interventions in the framework of everyday life, aimed at repeating, emphasizing, and recalling the same words of denouncement that cost these political leaders their lives. And they sought, through performance and fiction, to go back to important historical moments of the conflict with the wish of generating encounters among the passers-by, which might make it possible to reconsider the value of those ideas that were chastised. Through this work, I was interested in approaching history from the perspective of 'documentary fiction'. In this case, fiction enables me to forge a space for memory mediated by artistic strategies.

NVT — There's a particularly interesting encounter in one of the videos documenting the *Six Acts*, where one of the 'acts' clashes with the real world intrusions of bystanders, unaware of the staged aspect. To me, this unfolding scene, in which people believe the re-enacted speech to be real and demand of its performer to respond to their problems and help with their struggle, highlights some of the limits of socially and politically engaged artistic practices, especially in directly addressing an emancipatory struggle for justice. Why did you decide to interfere, and to expose your interference to the audience?

CM — Let me recount what happened. After 'ACT IV', the act where actress Atala Bernal performed a 1989 speech

by liberal leader Luis Carlos Galán, she had indeed an
interaction with the public that had observed her reading
on the square. A group of elderly protestors obviously
'believed' the actress's words, despite the fact that they
had originally been spoken in 1989. The group was
protesting in front at the main square of Soacha in front
of the City Hall — the place where Galán was assassinated
— against the delay in the payment of elderly bonds,
their main source of income. The merging of Atala's
reading performance and the micro context of the elderly
protestors made these words resonate as immediate and
urgent for them. They approached Atala, desperately
asking her for help. At that moment we had to 'break' the
space of fiction and tell them that ours was a fictional and
symbolic project and that unfortunately we had no access
to the authorities other than sharing the material we had
been filming.

This was challenging and certainly anti-climactic
for the public. In fact, the interaction was incredibly
challenging for all of us on many levels: What happens
when the space of artistic representation is viscerally
confronted to everyday politics, when fiction and truth
collide? What ethical problems are triggered by this
public intervention? How are class relations made
evident by this interaction? What constitutes the event
as a democratic platform: the performance itself or its
documentation? How does this happening exercise reflect
the 'political efficacy' of art?

What was conceived by us as a symbolic gesture
was read as literal and as factual. Our attempt to question
the potential to symbolically produce a democratic
exchange became a democratic exchange in itself beyond
our expectations. But we could not 'deliver' what the
speech promised, and the elderly protesters could not
help but be disappointed by our 'deceit'. But did we really
'trick' them? Did this artistic platform 'fail' or did it indeed
succeed in creating a conversation about the limits of
power? How does this act represent all subjects involved?

On an ethical level, this episode made evident
the socio-political relations that are at work in Colombia
on a daily basis: class relations of access and privilege.

The production of art and intellectual discourse are a luxury in a context where basic needs — such as food or shelter — are people's immediate necessities and priorities. We — artists, actors — have made ourselves belong to a class with access to abstract reasoning, even if we may intend to use this privilege to produce counter-knowledge, or to question power. But how implicated are we in reproducing oppression and exclusion with our initiatives? I believe as producers of culture we must be very careful not to reproduce forms of alienation and exclusion based on what our intellectual or liberal agendas might dictate as politically correct or artistically progressive. Perhaps our task as cultural makers is to recognize the complexities at work in the tactical juxtaposition of social realities and artistic gestures in order to not lose our critical perspectives.

NVT — That sounds like a huge responsibility that not many by-definition-privileged cultural workers would be willing to take...

CM — It is difficult to see past one's privilege, but that shouldn't justify not trying.

NVT — I was wondering how the piece functions differently from the staged events, the 'acts' so to speak, when it gets exhibited in a gallery setting, with its video documentation displayed simultaneously on different channels? How should viewers engage with such an abundance of materials?

CM — The 'acts' were conceived as a series of site-and-context specific performative interventions that were time-sensitive and ephemeral. They were also primarily directed towards a live public that encountered them by chance. The experience of the piece on the streets back in 2010 was charged with urgency: the desire to *rupture* everyday life during the electoral period with symbolic representations based on historical speeches. Those moments were documented and are the basis of the video installation I produced, but the

videos are yet another form of representation that,
in my opinion, can't reproduce the immediacy of the
moment in all its complexity. The videos however aren't
only documentation. They were carefully directed and
edited to generate a singular experience of the events,
consciously aware of the language of documentary and
video. The installation is designed to amplify the script
of each act in order to intellectually reveal the
particularities of the context that prompted them. In a
sense, *Six Acts* is two works, the then and the now, the
experiment and the review, and in a figurative way, the
event and its document.

NVT — You mentioned earlier that you're interested in
approaching history from the perspective of 'documentary
fiction'. The way I understand it, 'documentary fiction',
as a relatively recent genre, asks of the viewer to handle
primary sources, to unlock meaning and interpret
information, opening up a new mode of narrative in
which the viewer is asked to analyze, contextualize,
and draw conclusions from documents. How exactly
should we, according to you, understand this apparent
contradiction of terms? What kind of effects are you
trying to achieve with it?

CM — Back in 2010, the idea of 'documentary fiction'
wasn't discussed as much as it is today. In fact, I started
using the term in response to my experience working
on *Six Acts* unaware that there was an already-forming
discourse around the subject. For me, the fictionalizing
of these historical speeches through their interpretation
and performance seemed like a useful artistic strategy,
to *estrange* or distance them, from their source, place,
and time of deliverance. An eerie dislocation of time
and place occurred when hearing Jorge Eliécer Gaitán's
speech from 1948, where he poignantly demands
President Mariano Ospina Pérez to stop the violence and
reminds the president that our 'flag is mourning'. Gaitán's
words, re-spoken in 2010 in front of the presidential
palace, were strikingly contemporary; they spoke directly
to Uribe's abuse of power.

The locus of criticality in *Six Acts: An Experiment in Narrative Justice* is not the performer's body but the shift in the narrative from documentary to fiction and from referential to symbolic. In order to enable this shift to take place, the actors and I decided to restrain the 'theatricality' and formal performance of politics simply to the act of reading in public space. We decided not to use the exaggerated physical gestures typical of Colombian politicians, their voice levels and affectation, etc. I asked the actors and actresses to interpret the speeches rather than traditionally perform them, to interiorize their meaning as it affects them today rather than to try to represent the leaders that originally delivered them. I was hoping that this decision would focus the audience's attention on the words themselves and not on the performances as such.

Regarding the 'apparent contradiction of terms' you refer to in your question: I actually don't see this tension as a contradiction. In fact, documentary practices are narrative constructions that often refer to real-life events, yet as constructions, they are always at play with strategies of representation, namely devices of description, naming, and narration that are implicitly perceived as 'real'. The 'experiment' aspect mentioned in my project's title was meant to point to the normative ways we've come to believe and understand the very processes of historization and representation as 'objective' and 'true,' as well as institutional processes such as judicial justice as the primary — if not only — way to come to terms with oppression. Research shows that people impacted by death, loss, and trauma caused by violence, for example, often find ways to deal with these experiences subjectively, to move on, in ways that can't be systematized and that remain at the margin of formal institutions.

In terms of the desired effects of this experiment, I wasn't looking for tangible effects necessarily, as in proving the effectivity of political art in producing social change, for example, or any other grand ambitions of the sort, but rather in pointing to the vulnerability and yet oppressive nature inherent to the process of constructing narratives of ideology and power, as well as resistance and liberation. In retrospect, I have come to think of *Six Acts* as a self-referential methodological inquiry that tackled big political questions and proposed bold ideas in order to analyze the ways we have come to *make* meaning.

NVT — In general, there seems to be an unresolved tension between the political intention of your work and the artistic sphere in which it is performed and shown. How do the political gestures of your artistic practice go beyond being merely performative in nature, and can they be applied to a broader societal realm?

CM — They *don't*. I believe the political aspect of my work lies in its attempt to question forms of representation and to critically engage the field of art —even if its subject matter is political in a referential way. I have chosen to communicate my ideas through the language and strategies of art, and the political effect of the work can only be measured from within that field. But that doesn't mean that the work would be ineffective. In fact, art's potential of social transformation, in my opinion, can only depart from the ability to transform itself and its vehicles of communication.

I'm often bothered by what is referred to as the *inefficacy* of political art, or its inability to change people's social realities directly. Critics often underestimate the actual political potential of an *encounter*. The efficacy of some of the 'acts' in *Six Acts*, for example, whether or not it was intended, laid precisely on the activation of a site of conflict and in colliding a symbolic gesture with the so-called social needs of the public, thus potentially creating a democratic platform of exchange.

NVT — I was wondering if you could share something about your background: Where did you grow up and how has that initial milieu influenced your work? How did you become invested in the struggle for solidarity and justice?

CM — I grew in up in Bogotá in the 1980s, perhaps one of the most violent decades in Colombia's recent history. My generation – throughout the social spectrum – grew up in fear. In cities, we were constantly afraid of explosives and bombs; and in certain rural areas, people feared massacres and the wide-reaching effects of war. There's a common saying that suggests that no one in Colombia, despite class or wealth, has been exempted from experiencing violence – even if for some folks violence has undoubtedly marked their lives in ways I can't even begin to understand. Everyone has had a death, a kidnapping, or some other form of aggression in or close to his or her family.

However, I'm a very privileged Colombian from a pretty liberal background and with great access to education – things that enabled me to form critical positions about politics early on and to grasp the complexities of the Colombian context regarding social inequality and war. As a sensitive person, I resisted getting used to these inequalities even if I was reproducing them merely by *being* me. I also rejected the idea of getting used to violence, so I looked for ways to digest it and transform it. I trust these instincts led me to become an artist, perhaps with the ambition to find a structure to speak up and act up against forms of exclusion and oppression.

I'm also a gay man who dealt with constant bullying throughout my adolescence. This particular experience of social exclusion triggered my interest in processes of solidarity: How did my experience as a gay upper class white Colombian relate to that of a mestizo woman in the countryside unable to find work? Can one even start to compare them when our life experiences are so obviously different on every level? Is it presumptuous to even think of struggles of class and sexual orientation as similar? These are questions that I have looked to embrace in my work as an artist and a citizen. Hegemonic power manifests itself in perverse ways and, without losing perspective, I believe building positions and projects of solidarity within seemingly different struggles is an important task.

NVT – Have you further explored the concept of 'narrative justice' in different contexts?

CM – Back in 2005, I began a cycle of works which were eventually grouped under the title *Democracy Cycle*. These works approach the concept of democracy from different perspectives: U.S. foreign policy and intervention in Latin America in *La buenavida/The Good Life*; political exile and cultural assimilation in Scandinavian societies in *The Immigrant Files: Democracy Is Not Dead; It Just Smells Funny*; ideological genocide in Colombia in *Six Acts: An Experiment in Narrative Justice*; religious faith as a form of social liberation in *Deus Pobre: Modern Sermons of Communal Lament*; and the systematic discrimination of diverse sexual and gender expressions internationally in *We Who Feel Differently*.

Through these projects, I have been primarily investigating three ideas: How do democracy's promises reflect the perspective of marginal groups that exist outside the reach of normative representative legislation? How can Art be used as a way to question the structure of power, to think about artistic platforms that engage democracy as a subject matter and to propose alternative sites for democratic exchange? And, what is democracy?

The idea of 'narrative justice', understood as a critical intervention into narrative constructions of ideologies and histories, is central to these questions. Aesthetic justice inherently rejects normative understandings of justice – especially when they have proven to fail – it questions them and provides experiential and alternative approaches to institutional processes.

NVT – This seems key to a new understanding of justice. How, then, would you describe the difference between aesthetic justice and 'ethics', and how can it be an alternative to a normative approach?

CM – 'Aesthetic justice' derives from the need to rectify processes of institutional injustice that result in forms of social oppression, exclusion, and oblivion. Not unlike legislative justice, an aesthetic approach should be procedural, determined, and considered, but unlike the legislative approach, it must be flexible, responsive, plural, unorthodox, heterogeneous...

‘Aesthetic justice’ differs from ‘ethics’ in that ethics are principles of knowledge that don’t necessarily imply action. ‘Aesthetic justice’ should thus be an ethical practice; and note the *operative* word here is ‘practice’. Legislative justice often fails in its inability to perform, in its passivity. But could a person or community in need of reparation benefit from this approach? An aesthetic process may simply shift the terms of expectation from power toward some other form of reparative process, perhaps simply symbolic.

The Days of the Commune
Notes and Reflections

Zoe Beloff

In 2011, I began work on *The Days of the Commune*, a staging of Bertolt Brecht's play in public spaces around New York City. It was inspired by real life events and performed in solidarity with Occupy Wall Street. It grew into a multi-platform project, website, film and installation. Today I am writing these notes with the hope that they might be a useful starting point for other artists. I will begin by outlining the inspiration behind this work, describe what we did on a practical level and end by considering some of the questions that the project raises.

A couple of years earlier, in the depths of the financial crisis, I came upon *Saint Joan of the Stockyards*, a play that Brecht wrote during the Depression. It shows simply and clearly how captains of industry and speculators on Wall Street use the stock market to work against the people. I started to think that my next project should engage with Brecht's writing to try an illuminate what is happening today. Just as I began to read more about his life and work, the Occupy encampment sprang to life not far from where I live. I decided to put down my books and find out what was going on.

Was I part of Occupy? I'd call myself a fellow traveller, or a friendly witness. I didn't do any organizing. I did not camp out. Initially, my participation consisted of bringing a sketchbook. I make no claim that my rough documentary drawing was in any way a political act. But it did give me time to observe and to think. When you draw, you become part of something, perhaps because you can't draw everything in front of you. Like writing, rather than recording, you effect a transformation that does not say' this is what happened', but rather 'this is my experience at this particular moment'. Drawing directly from life is an odd idea in the twenty-first century, but it is a way to pay attention over time in a very different way than people do with their iPhone cameras or DSLRs.

I called this series of images 'Drawings of Modern Life', a first inkling that I was thinking about Paris in the nineteenth century, when documentary drawing was important. I started to study the work of Manet and Courbet. It was their images of the end of the Paris Commune of 1871 and people dying on the barricades that initially let me to start thinking about connections between the Commune and Occupy.

History Lessons, or An Eruption of Past into the Present
During the months of the Occupation, at the forefront of my mind

was the question of what I as an artist/filmmaker could or should contribute. It is not an easy question. It is one everyone must answer in his or her own way. If I had to describe what I do best, I would say: creating a dialog with the past. So I felt that that was where I should begin.

I should make it clear that I am not interested in a nostalgic escape from the present but rather in thinking about how we can re-imagine events in the past as an inspiration for the future. The philosopher Slavoj Žižek explores history in a similar way. In his book *In Defense of Lost Causes*, he explains that that the new can only emerge through repetition. The past is not simply what happened. Rather, one must grasp the radical 'openness of the past itself' – which he says 'contains hidden, non-realized potentials.'[1]

My task came to me all at once. Reading a biography of Brecht, I discovered that in 1949 he wrote a play, *The Days of the Commune*. I knew that I had to stage it. The Paris Commune was the first great occupation in modern history where workers took control of their city and attempted to create a progressive, secular social democracy. They were for internationalism and against militarism and imperialism. This included separation of church and state, universal suffrage, and the people's right to have a roof over their heads. They believed that higher education and technical training should be free and open to all. Women spoke up and formed their own union. They demanded equal wages for equal work. Artists also spoke up. Courbet became one of the leading figures of the Commune. The *Manifesto of the Federation of Artists* proposed that art institutions should be run by artists, free of commercial considerations. In the end, the people were massacred in the streets by the French army, arrested, imprisoned, and deported.

One hundred and forty years later, we live in a very different world. However, what remains is, I believe, the force of their inspiration. In the face of impossible odds, they decided to take their future into their own hands. And their ideas about how to live together with equality and sharing, with reason and not force, their belief that together we ordinary citizens can change our world, are just as alive and urgent today as they were then.

Brecht's play shows us both the point of view of the working people of Paris and the perspective of the men in power, Adolphe Thiers and Otto von Bismarck. It asks us to think about how political and economic forces shape lived experience and to

imagine what would happen if a new kind of people's democracy
took over a city right now. How could they survive against the
forces of global capital? Should the people occupy the banks?
How should they respond to armed attacks? Brecht doesn't provide answers. Instead, he invites each of us to think for ourselves.

For me, one of the most important scenes in the play is
a short exchange between Genevieve, the delegate in charge of
education who has always stood for peace, and Pierre Langevin,
a worker delegate to the Commune. The end is very close now.
They are working late at City Hall. They can hear the enemy's
guns. They look at the banner proclaiming the principles of
the Commune. In 1871, these freedoms were radical; now we
take them for granted. But then Brecht has Langevin ask some
hard questions:

> Freedom of the Individual: Does that include the
> freedom to make business deals against the public
> interest; to live off the people; to conspire against the
> people and to deal with their enemies?
>
> Freedom of Conscience: But what exactly is dictated to
> them by their consciences? I'll tell you. Whatever their
> rulers want to be dictated. From the moment a child can
> walk.
>
> The Right of Assembly: Does this mean that the financial
> wolves, the parasites of the press, the military hyenas
> and all the lesser bloodsuckers are free to reassemble the
> Versailles and use the freedom of Freedom of Speech
> to publicize opinions of all kinds against us? Is there a
> guaranteed freedom to spread lies?

In America, we are taught that we live in a free country.
But what does that really mean?

A Stage in the Street

From the beginning, it was clear to me we would perform the
play in public spaces around the city. Had I had access to a theatre, I would not have used it. The Communards took over their
city and defended it in the street. All the contemporary protest
movements have stood their ground in the streets, from The Plaza

del Sol to Tahir Square. I was inspired by the Occupy encampment in Zuccotti Park as an extraordinary theatre of the people. It wasn't simply a place where people lived. The activists choose the most visible location to live in public and enact together a new egalitarian community. Rather than simply protest, they did something much powerful; they attempted to show quite concretely that another world was possible. They improvised on the spot a participatory democracy, where people shared their resources. It was never meant to be a real city over the long term. It was a proposal for a city yet to be.

The activists and everyone who took part in the General Assembly meetings each night were trying to do two things at once: to run a city in miniature on one square block, and to change the world. I would come home from these events elated. I know it sounds crazy, but I felt like even if I hadn't been in Petrograd in October 1917, at least I was here now.

A Work in Progress

Since we had no space in which to rehearse, we would rehearse in public. The play itself would be a rehearsal on both a practical and a conceptual level. My idea was that we would work on Saturdays and Sundays. Each day we went out, we would work on one scene. Thus over a period of three months from March through May, the months that the Paris Commune actually existed, we would rehearse the play, scene by scene from beginning to end. This would be our task. The work that actually goes into making a performance would be visible. I thought of it as a rehearsal for a commune yet to come. Indeed the concept of the 'incomplete', that freedom itself is always a work in progress, is there in the play itself.

> **Langevin** – I drink to the incomplete.
>
> **Genevieve** – Why the incomplete, Monsieur Langevin?
>
> **Langevin** – It's on the way to Freedom.
>
> **Genevieve** – And Freedom now, is it an illusion?
>
> **Langevin** – (laughing) In politics, yes.

I think it is important that this is a work over time. You see the seasons change: at first, everyone is blue with cold; and at the end, it is summer. You can see how we all learned on the job, and the performances at the end are a far cry from those first days. Building a social movement takes time and work. The project makes this visible. In a certain sense, it is a document of a certain time in New York in the year 2012.

I had been thinking a lot about the film *History Lessons* by Jean-Marie Straub and Danielle Huillet. It is based on Brecht's story *The Business Affairs of Mr. Julius Caesar*. The actors wear togas, but they are clearly situated in contemporary Rome, with cars driving past. Again, Brecht wanted to demythologize Caesar, to explore the idea that history did not have to turn out as it did. By taking *The Days of the Commune* out of the theatre, we would literally wrench it out of its historical context and place it in present-day New York.

Indeed, when constructing the final film version of the project, I made a conscious choice not to include any archival photographs, although the Communards, well aware that they were making history, thoroughly documented their actions. For me, historical photographs give us the illusion that we somehow have unmediated access to the past, as though history were a fixed entity, like a movie with a single storyline. In fact, I wanted to show just the opposite, that we invent the past as we speak of it. The past is just a picture that we ourselves create, and this picture it is as much about us as it is about those long dead. In one of his last essays, 'On the Concepts of History,' Walter Benjamin writes about this idea that the past can be modified by the present: 'Articulating the past historically does not mean recognizing the past "the way it really was". It means appropriating a memory as it flashes up in a moment of danger.' He passionately declares that the '"eternal" past of the historicist' is just sentimental rubbish. The task of the historical materialist is to blast a specific event or work out of time in order to see and use it anew.[2]

So I began my film of *The Days of the Commune* as a picture story, the occupation of Zuccotti park segueing into the 1870 siege of Paris. At times, scenes revert from live action to a sequence of pictures where the actors turn into comic book figures — suggesting a storyboard for events yet to come rather than a replica of events past. I was inspired by series of very simple watercolours by Diego Rivera of a boy and his father going to a demonstration that he made while visiting Moscow in the 1920s. They are like a little film on notepaper.

Preparing for the Production

December 2011: My first tasks were to paint a poster and to register the domain name 'thedaysofthecommune.com'. Both were essential to getting the word out. The poster became one side of a broadsheet that we handed out at all our performances. It explained briefly the history of the Paris Commune, something about Brecht, and what we were doing. It also provided a link to the website. Thus, even people who could only spare a minute or two could have something to take away with them. Just as every protest today exists both on the street and online, I knew from the beginning that each scene should be filmed and then almost immediately uploaded to the website so anyone anywhere could follow our progress. Today, everything needs to be visible in the real world and in the virtual one, local and international.

I painted sketches of the principle characters for the costume designer Erika Munro. In keeping with the spirit of the production, nineteenth-century Paris would be literally overlaid over contemporary New York. Besides, it was cold when we began in March 2012. Performers wore skirts over jeans, army caps over woolly hats. Erika made some costumes and found many of them in a thrift warehouse in New Jersey. She sewed new trim on old army coats and Catholic school berets became sailor hats for the tough Communard women.

I created all the props and scenery myself out of corrugated cardboard. The choice of cardboard was obvious. I was inspired by the use of cardboard signs at the Occupy encampment and, of course, banners carried on marches. Cardboard is the medium of protest. Having never done this before, I had to find a new visual vocabulary. How to paint a cardboard cannon or a dead rat? How big should they be for an audience to read them clearly? The most difficult objects to deal with were the rifles. They are important in the story: Phillipe Faure and his brother Francois have an armed standoff; the National Guardsmen carry rifles. I made some out of cardboard and I realized that from a distance, they looked quite realistic. In New York is it illegal to carry fake firearms. We had enough problems at Zuccotti Park without getting arrested for fake guns. Then suddenly the day before we were to do the performance, I had an idea, I would bolt the guns to blue backing

cardboard so that they would be pictures of guns, not fake guns. And the police accepted this semiotic distinction. You can see them checking us out in scene three but they didn't say anything and the actors just kept going.

The Participants

It was important that our commune reflect the diversity of New York today. I put out a casting call on the Occupy Listservs and on bulletin boards in downtown theatres calling for a band of performers of all ages, sizes, and gender orientations, no experience necessary. Actors, activists, and enthusiasts answered my call. At the beginning, there were thirteen. But, like any movement, it grew and changed. I was constantly rounding up new people. There were about thirty cast members in all. Some joined us for a weekend or two, others for the whole three-month period. Every performer played multiple roles: one character was often played by several actors, since not everyone was available at the same time. For example, Papa was played on Saturdays by Michael Paul Britto and on Sundays by Pietro Gonzales. Sometimes women played men. This was one reason performers wore the name of their character around their neck. Actors who played actual historical figures wore pictures of them drawn on cardboard and tied to their heads. The crew was very small, a production manager, a soundman, and my partner Eric Muzzy, who was the cinematographer. Because I believe that everyone should get paid for work, I made a decision to give everyone something, $20 each session, enough for travel and a hot lunch.

Brecht wrote his plays for everyone. He wanted them to be both entertaining and inspire people to think. He said even a donkey should understand them and he kept a little wooden donkey on his desk to remind him. So it was very important to me that the production was colourful and lively, that it grab people's attention. *The Days of the Commune* is really a great pageant. It is also a musical with songs by the radical composer Hanns Eisler. Each day we went out to perform, we began with a song accompanied by an accordion player. Even the police guarding Zuccotti Park enjoyed them.

Taking Action

When we began performances in March 2012, I had no idea what to expect. I wondered if the performers would stay through the production, week after week. I set out simple ground rules. We would work on location from 11:00 to 1:30 PM. We would not go over time. But the very real possibility of rain and the fact that someone always seemed to get sick on Fridays made scheduling tough. Inevitably, in the last minute, someone would find themselves playing a part they were not expecting.

I did not know if we would get kicked out of Zuccotti Park on day one. We did not ask for permits. I couldn't afford to, and I felt that in the spirit of the Commune we should take the stand that public spaces should be free and open to all. My position was that if we were thrown out, we would just decamp to a nearby space and keep going. As a matter of principle, we wouldn't let the authorities stop us. Amazingly, it worked.

We spent the first month in Zuccotti Park, then moved on to other locations that resonated with the play. The Commune encompassed all of the city of Paris and I wanted us to share our ideas with New Yorkers in many different places. One of the performers, Joanie Zozike, suggested the community garden at East 6th Street and Avenue B. This became the location for the working people of the Rue Pigalle. Community gardens or allotments are an important part of working class life, where people who can't afford fancy homes can have their own green space. They are very much in the spirit of the Commune. The big meetings of the delegates to the Commune were held outside the main branch of the New York Public Library, on 42nd Street, in front of the great Beaux Arts building with the stone lions. The Commune believed that education should be free and open to all, and I believe that the library embodies this idea. At times, there was a direct connection between the scene in the play and the location. For example, there is a scene outside the Department of Education that we staged outside New York City's Department of Education, the Tweed Courthouse on Chambers Street. I decided to stage the scene with Bismarck and Jules Favre at the Opera outside the Met at Lincoln Center. It was a moment of comedy, albeit one in which in which the leaders of the 'free world' discuss the imminent slaughter of the Communards 'mit fire und brimstone,' while the opera blared from a boom box. We definitely took passers-by by surprise.

In the final scene, the bourgeoisie watch the destruction of the Commune from the ramparts of Versailles. I would have liked to stage it in the boardroom of the JPMorgan Chase bank, but unfortunately I did not have access. So I decided on Governors Island, which is off the tip of Manhattan and affords a great panoramic view of the city. It also has an old fort with cannons dating back to the civil war. When we all went out on the ferry, there weren't just twenty-two Communards in full costume, but also a whole crowd of civil war re-enactors. I had to tell everyone not to get mixed up and end up in the wrong conflict. You can hear shots from the re-enactors' rifles on our soundtrack while helicopters circled overheard.

Directing and Performing

Brecht was an enormously demanding director. He insisted on six months of rehearsal. He believed that actors should not disappear inside their characters. He did not want them to create an illusion. Instead, he wanted the actors to show us the character as clearly and precisely as possible, almost as though reporting on them. The actors he liked most in America came from the tradition of vaudeville because they communicated and entertained simultaneously, without swindling the audience into a state of belief.

I sometimes wonder what Brecht might have thought of our rag-tag production. I decided from the beginning that I had to take a new approach to directing. I knew I would be confronted by a great collage of different performance styles, from highly theatrical to naturalistic to bare line readings. Rather than try and shape them into a unified whole, I decided I would simply embrace them all and allow them to co-exist. I told the actors, 'occupy your characters' and they did.

I learned from the facilitators of the general assemblies at the Occupy encampment. My job was to give a basic structure to the scenes. I decided on the locations. I decided how much of the play we would cover on a particular day, who would play which parts and I outlined the basic blocking so that the performers knew where to stand and move. I sketched the groupings out in advance and went over them each morning with the cinematographer. From there we went to work.

In a lot of ways, I think of the performers more as re-enactors than actors in the conventional sense. Re-enactment is a very popular and indeed very American activity, whether it is of the War of Independence or the Civil War — anyone can participate and play whomever they choose. One can say that the casting is radically non-mimetic. For example, a young woman can be a

Yankee soldier. It is a really democratic reinvention of history that everyone understands. And this idea that the performer can be simultaneously themselves and their character, side by side as it were, I find liberating and inspiring.

I only corrected an actor if I thought they were not speaking loud enough to be heard or if there was something in the script that they did not understand. If they mangled a French word horribly, who cared? In our Commune, people were free to pronounce things any way they wanted. After all, this was New York in 2012, not Paris in 1871. I believed it was more important that they represent themselves as New Yorkers than that they realistically portrayed the Communards.

What was interesting was that the performances changed and grew over time. At the beginning I asked the actors to familiarize themselves with their lines. I felt that requiring them to learn lines by heart was too much to expect for the little money I could give them. But gradually some actors started to do this anyway, and the others were impressed. They watched the scenes online and were inspired to memorize their scripts. Some started to rehearse with each other between performances so that the scenes at the end are far stronger than those at the beginning. I think this was the project's most tangible success. Even if it was only amongst ourselves, we, as a group, learned a lot.

Learning Together

I believe that politics and indeed art are not about teaching but about learning, and one must begin with oneself and those around one. Brecht wrote '*Lehrstücke*', learning plays. *The Days of the Commune* was a structure to think with and through. At the end, as the working people are dying on the barricades, Genevieve Gericault says that they have made mistakes, but they are learning, to which Jean Cabet responds: 'What is the use when you will soon be six feet under?' And Gericault replies: 'There is more to the world than just us.'

Though the Paris Commune grew out of historical circumstances very different from our own and only lasted three months, I do not think it was a failure. Those working people of Paris lead us by their example, precisely because they did something for themselves that seemed impossible. They were not afraid. They created a potential. Writing about revolution, Žižek quotes Samuel Beckett: 'Try again. Fail again. Fail better.'[3] Only half-jokingly,

I say that this could have been our motto as we all struggled to work together to create better performances. There is no line between rehearsing and performing. It is all a rehearsal, a work in progress.

Looking Back

In retrospect, it is clear the project raises questions. Politically, could my time and money have been put to better use than in this quixotic venture? I am often asked about the audience response. How many people saw this? In reality, the live audience was very small. In the barren windswept plaza that is Zuccotti Park in March, we were, at best, a magnet for cell phone cameras. The other Occupy groups, holding meetings there, paid us scant attention. Only in the community garden did we have anything that resembled a sustained audience and that was perhaps because the community garden organizers publicized the event and it was a really nice place to sit and spend time. On a practical level, if I were to do this kind of work again, I would aim to hire someone to do outreach.

Brecht wanted to entertain and educate. He expected the working class to rise to the occasion. I am aware that *The Days of the Commune* is not an easy play. It demands a serious level of thought, time, and commitment. The fact that we took three months to perform the play made it especially difficult. Today, who has the time, while scrambling to make a living, to care what Parisians thought so long ago? After all, New York is hardly likely to be invaded by the Prussians any time soon.

The production could not have been more different to the short street performances produced by the Occupy Performance Guild that focused on contemporary events. They were agitprop. We were not. We were not effective in this sense. One might say we were not successful. But should art be measured in these terms?

The concept of 'aesthetic justice' stresses the importance of shining a light on the interdependence in our society, focusing on those who are most vulnerable. In this regard, I think we can learn a lot from Brecht. Through his plays, he wanted to show how the power relations within society work objectively, to lay them bare. He asked his audience to think, rather than simply identify with suffering or heroism in the tradition of bourgeois theatre. He believed that art did have a part to play in changing the world. And to change the world, one must forge a new kind of art. Sometimes I think this seems a more radical idea now than when Brecht was writing. Today, too often, form is thought of as nothing but a vehicle for rapidly and painlessly transmitting a message. But at the same time I think we respect Brecht most if we don't call him 'master', but take his advice to think for ourselves as artists, boldly, but being ready to use whatever we can lay our hands on right now.

I can only speak for myself, and then only provisionally. I believe that art should never be 'at the service of'. Once art is instrumental, a tool for doing something, it becomes an advertisement, even if what it promotes is an idea. This might be useful but it is not art. Art's strength is its autonomy, its freedom. It does not have to ingratiate itself or to charm. It is a party of one. Art, and I use this word in the broadest sense, invites you to come to it, but it does not seduce. It lives its own life. It is very independent.

I think Brecht understood this. Undoubtedly, Marxism was key to his understanding of the world. He believed in Communism because he always sided with the underdog. But he was not a member of the Communist party. He wrote *The Days of the Commune* in East Berlin but it was banned in East Germany during his lifetime, apparently for being to 'defeatist', and was not performed by the Berliner Ensemble until 1956. He himself wrote in a journal entry dated 1952: 'By nature I am a difficult person to control. Authority that does not command my respect I reject out of hand, and I can view laws only as provisional suggestions for regulating community living that are constantly in need of change.' His friend Hans Viertel described him thus: 'Bertolt Brecht was a one-man political party in close coalition with the Communists.'[4]

I believe that art is not about teaching, but about learning, struggling to understand the world in all its complexity. That is why for me, being a teacher (my day job) and being an artist (the work of my spare time) are fundamentally different. Teaching is instrumental. Teaching implies that there are answers. Learning implies that there are questions. *The Days of the Commune* is written in this dialectical spirit. It is all about asking questions that have no easy answers, ever. There is a telling exchange in the play, when the French army is on the verge of overrunning Paris and the Communards are still arguing about what to do.

Art Does Not Want a Regime

I believe that art should be generous and open its doors to everyone. After all, Brecht wrote musicals and was inspired by gangster films. But that doesn't make it easy. Sometimes we do have to work to rise to the occasion. For most people, the world of the 'fine arts' is a foreign country that they know little or nothing about. But popular art-making activities are everywhere, on Youtube and on the street and all around us. Here are some thoughts I have about art.

> Art sides with the underdog
> Art is a question
> Art is proposal
> Art cannot be predetermined
> Art is entertainment and thinking
> Art is a gift
> Art does what it can with what it has at hand
> Art does not fit in
> Art won't be dumbed down

But there is no necessity to call our *Days of the Commune* 'art'. I can just call it an activity undertaken together.

Notes

1   Slavoj Žižek, *In Defense of Lost Causes* (Brooklyn and London: Verso Books, 2008), p. 141.
2   Walter Benjamin, *Selected Writings, Volume 4, 1938-1940* (Cambridge MA: Belknap Press Harvard, 2006), pp. 391, 396.
3   Žižek, op. cit., p. 210.
4   James K. Lyon, *Bertolt Brecht in America* (Princeton NJ: Princeton University Press, 1980), p. 302.

No Show
Refusal as Critique

Nat Muller

Out with Resistance – In with Refusal

'Resistance' has become an over-used buzzword within contemporary art practices. Not only does it offer a tinge of combative bravado, but it also adds political currency and momentum to a scene that has been accused, by some,[1] of operating with little accountability when making politicised or emancipatory claims. Within the arts, 'resistance' as a means of opposition too often becomes something that is malleable and negotiable, or to use an *en vogue* term, it becomes reduced to the discursive. Any activist will tell you that a porous or pliable mode of resistance is not very effective. I am making a blatant generalization for the sake of argument, but the 'resistance' found in contemporary artistic practices is more often than not armed to the teeth with noble intentions, and copious amounts of critical theory and terminology borrowed from political philosophy. However, when push comes to shove, the effectiveness of these types of 'resistance', not only as a mode of critique but as an ideological position and strategy for change, is debatable.

A first question to be asked is whether – and why – the arts in the first place would want to compete on a level playing field with political and social activism. Should art not be doing something else on the level of affect, perception, symbolism and power? And does art's power to effectuate change of some sort, however minor, not lie elsewhere? Obviously, there are many grey zones, but pushing artistic practices in a strait jacket of socio-political functionalism, as we have seen happen over the past decade or so encouraged by policy makers, funders and artists themselves, cannot be right either. I am not discussing commitment or intent here, but questioning the reach of art to further palpable and material political and social change, especially from within the institutions of art such as museums, gallery spaces and biennials. Can artists really be actors with actual agency within these institutionalised art contexts, or do their interventions of resistance remain on a low-risk and cosmetic discursive level, a preaching to the converted that never even reaches the danger zone, or a trickles down into the real world? Should art want to do this at all?

There is a difference between producing work that critiques, pushes boundaries, is abrasive, makes us think and see things anew, and work that claims, naively or self-righteously, to be able to solve the problems of the world just because it simply resists something. What would the intervention of Pussy Riot have meant had they remained in the white cube instead of crashing Mass at church? What would the work have meant as a critique, had the video not gone viral, and had its members not been arrested? I am absolutely not calling for artists to get themselves arrested, but rather making a point that a claim to radical engagement will always require radical measures. War cannot be waged from the safe confines of the white cube. Here again, I have nothing against the white cube (I actually like the white cube!), nor do I feel that artists should be up in arms and on the barricades. The point I'm making is that there is often a severe disconnect between the radical and lofty claims made for resistance and revolution, and the actual actions. There is also a difference between artists who have demonstrated a long-term, often very personal, investment in social and political issues, and those who pick and mix because revolution happens to be sexy, and apparently has market value. Twenty-five years ago, queer activist Pat (now Patrick) Califia put it very succinctly: 'We can't fuck our way to freedom.'[2] For art practitioners who are — rightly — concerned with the ways of the world, there is a useful lesson to be learnt here. Bluntly: the woes of the world will most likely not be solved by an art project.

At a recent talk[3] at Witte de With Centre for Contemporary Art in Rotterdam, curator and critic Tirdad Zolghadr, who moved to Palestine recently, lamented that whenever there is a political articulation in contemporary art, it usually is overly ambitious and fraught with impossible demands. He characterised the modus operandi of contemporary art as indeterminate, open-ended, ambivalent, and postponing meaning. I would argue that meaning is not necessarily postponed, but rather that it is located elsewhere, and that the beauty of art lies precisely in this ambiguity. Perhaps the mistake contemporary art has made too often over the last two decades is that it has been too pre-occupied with migrating the many meanings inherent to it to a limited realm of interpretation, namely that of political and social commentary. This has the effect that other factors, such as poetics, aesthetics, and affect as powerful instruments of critique, are neglected. The result is that art can only do part of its job, namely the production of meaning. The insistence of specific contemporary practices to engage with the complexities of the real world in a hyper-functionalised/problem-solving way may result in the locking out of fantasy and the imaginary. These are particularly (and traditionally) the realms where art and cinema create spaces of criticality and of possibility. If we lose that, then what have we got in return, if anything?

What if the current notion of 'resistance' were to be refused, especially by artists working in challenging political environments or with inflammatory content? Could 'refusal' be thought of in a productive and critical way? The issue with resistance is that it always has to acknowledge that which it opposes. This creates an interdependency that has to be continuously reinforced between the act of resistance and what it resists. With refusal the rejection is singular, and then things – ideally – move on. Refusal is not a novel strategy in contemporary art. For example, the conceptual art of the 1960s is marked by a refusal of the object. Likewise, time-based practices like live art refuse to be ossified within a specific temporal moment. These – often ephemeral – performances develop and change over time and with every iteration. The concerns of refusal here can be said to be conceptual and aesthetic foremost. Though these refusals are artistic as well as political gestures, they do occur primarily within the realm of art. If larger political and societal concerns are at stake and call for a refusal, then how would that be channelled into an aesthetics of refusal? How does refusal operate in contexts where security, freedom of expression and of political association are under pressure, such as in the Middle East, particularly since the 2011 uprisings? How do the politics of imagery and of representation come into play here, and which strategies of refusal do artists use when many outside the professionalised sphere of artistic production – broadcasters, citizens, activists, propagandists – engage with the image as a means of resistance, or of quiescence?

A Refusal of the Image

Academic Lina Khatib writes in the introduction to her book *Image Politics in the Middle East: The Role of the Visual in Political Struggle* that:

> Politics in the Middle East is now seen. The image has claimed a central place in the processes through which political dynamics are communicated and experienced in the region. States, non-state actors, oppositional groups and ordinary people are engaging in political struggle

through the image, and the media, especially the visual media, are not only mediators in this context, they are also political actors, deliberately using images to exert political influence. The image is at the heart of political struggle, which has become an endless process of image battling, reversing, erasing and replacing other images... Political struggle, then, is an inherently visual productive process. It is also itself visual to a large degree: It is a struggle over presence, over visibility.[4]

A refusal of the image, or of a particular set of images, would then result in an undoing of presence and visibility, or at least problematize visual representation. Many practices of by now internationally established Lebanese artists such as Rabih Mroué, Joana Hadjithomas and Khalil Joreige, Walid Raad, Lamia Joreige, Walid Sadek and Akram Zaatari, often grouped together as the post-civil war generation, have used (visual) absence and disappearance as conceptual and aesthetic tropes. This generation came of age during Lebanon s civil war (1975-1990) and for more than fifteen years has focused its work on dealing with the aftermath of the civil war. This is exemplified in plays by Rabih Mroué, such as *Looking for a Missing Employee* (2003), where the artist presents the unsolved case of a disappeared civil servant from Lebanon's Ministry of Finance through a variety of documents and newspaper clippings; Hadjithomas and Joreige's notion of latent images in their acclaimed work *Wonder Beirut* (1997 − 2006), where the film rolls of photographer Abdallah Farah, active during the war, remain undeveloped; and Walid Raad's Atlas Group's acclaimed video *Operator #17* (2000), where allegedly a Lebanese security agent trained his camera on the seaside Corniche, only to film sunsets instead of keeping an eye on the comings and goings of political pundits, spies, and double agents. Or in Walid Sadek's project *Love is Blind* (2006), where imagery is denied altogether and only wall labels referring to paintings by Lebanon's best-known modernist painter, Mustafa Farroukh, make up the exhibition.

The Lebanese political arena is to this day mired in the power play of sectarian loyalties. The absence of political accountability for the atrocities perpetrated during the civil war, the fate of the many disappeared, and an amnesia erasing recent and contemporary political history still very much define the

Lebanese condition. It is therefore no surprise that absence and disappearance feature heavily, on a structural level, in the work of Lebanese artists. Absence and disappearance mark the desire to retrieve something that was lost, or to critique the persistence of this self-imposed void in the Lebanese psyche.

However, there is another issue at stake too. 'There is,' as Suzanne Cotter writes in her introduction of Modern Art Oxford's 2006 Lebanese group show *Out of Beirut*, 'a deep mistrust of the image as a reliable document of history.'[5] This engaged withdrawal from imagery, and from visual representation, within the Lebanese art context has most famously been theorised by the Iraqi artist and theorist, and former resident of Beirut, Jalal Toufic. T.J. Demos summarises his position aptly as follows: 'not only [have] images literally been destroyed, but... like memory in post-war Lebanon, [they] have somehow become unavailable to the senses, following what [Toufic] calls the 'radical closure' of a 'surpassing disaster.'[6] These practices have mostly been described as manoeuvres of withdrawal, and disengagement, from the charged imagery of conflict and ruin. It is an effort, in an era with 24-hour news cycles, to preserve the specificity of the experiences of war that can never be fully captured or conveyed by an image. Except for Sadek's project that shirks from the image completely, traces, clues, and remnants of the visual have always been important material elements in these works, whether this is found footage or a latent image on a film roll. Lately, though, the gestures of refusal have become more radical.

The most remarkable example comes from Akram Zaatari, an artist who for the most part of his career has concentrated his oeuvre around interrogating and unveiling what lies behind and beyond the image, rather than refusing it. Zaatari is one of the co-founders of Beirut's Arab Image Foundation, a unique organization established in 1997 dedicated to the collection, preservation, and study of photographs from the Middle East, North Africa, and the Arab diaspora. As such, his role as an artist intertwines with that of a curator, collector, and researcher. Zaatari's fieldwork of 'digging' into the visual history of the region uncovers narratives that have been forgotten or glossed over. All the more surprising then that his project *Time Capsule* (2012) for dOCUMENTA (13) has been based on an inverse logic. Here, the artist entombs painted objects, inspired by different photographic devices and film formats and imagined to be the work

of a photographer losing his sight, underground on the bank of
the river Fulda in a concrete foundation block. It resembles the
radical preservation tactic of Beirut's National Museum during
the civil war, casting their archaeological objects in concrete to
protect them from the violence. Whereas previously Zaatari has
brought objects and documents of the past into the world and into
the present moment, here he is sealing them, freezing them in
time and space, and removing them from public view, though they
are buried in public space.

Following the suspension of his membership of the Arab
Image Foundation and his resignation from its board in 2011, it is
as if Zaatari is waiting for a different time, when these images can
unfurl their meaning again in a different way, perhaps untainted
by certain institutional and other ideologies. The project itself is
– though visually understated – conceptually striking and bold in
its critique. In a recent interview with Anthony Downey, Zaatari
commented: 'I've come to realize that it's only possible to talk
about conflicts once they cool down, once conflicts aren't conflicts anymore'.[7] As the prospect of sectarian strife can flare up
in Lebanon at any moment, the conflict is, in fact, far from over.
Zaatari seems very much to suggest that at certain times, images
should be removed from sight, however temporarily.

A Refusal to See

Artists and filmmakers Joana Hadjithomas and Khalil Joreige
have in their practice predominantly been concerned with history, memory, time and the politics of visual representation. Their
work has pondered, amongst others, the retrieval of lost images or
ghostlike images. For example in *Lasting Images* (2003), they restore an 8mm film that belonged to the archive of Joreige's uncle
who had disappeared during the civil war. Severely damaged, the
film reveals traces of people, like spectres that refuse to disappear.
It is as its title indicates, an image that has not fully come into being, but that lasts, an image that stubbornly refuses to disappear
and forever is latent.

However, the 33-day Israeli July war on Lebanon in 2006
produced a cut in their practice. It was partly brought on by a
photo editor at *The Guardian* newspaper who had used an image of their *Wonder Beirut* series to illustrate the July war, instead
of using an actual photo-journalistic image of the bombarded
Southern suburbs of Beirut and the hard-hit Shia villages in

the South of Lebanon. Here an imaginary image from an art project was taken to illustrate a war that was still in full swing. The artists found the appropriation and DE contextualization of their image so disturbing that it prompted a re-assessment of their practice. They decided not to bring latent images into being anymore, but either produce new images or refuse them altogether.

Their feature film *Je Veux Voir* (2008) is a case in point. It was made in the aftermath of the July War and stars French cinema icon Catherine Deneuve and Lebanese playwright and visual artist Rabih Mroué. Filmed as a road movie, Mroué chauffeurs Deneuve to Bint Jbeil, his heavily bombarded family town in the South of Lebanon. Deneuve insists on seeing for herself the devastation wrought by the war. Mroué, on the other hand, is apprehensive about seeing the destruction. When asked by Deneuve why, he replies: 'I don't like to be a tourist in my own country... But now, with you it'll be different'. The film (*Je Veux Voir*) will make it interesting. Little is shown of the destruction en route, and Mroué's refusal 'to see' the debris of the war is telling. He has experienced the war himself, so what could the viewing of more images possibly add? It is this very tension between Deneuve's desire to see in order to understand, and Mroué's understanding that images in and by themselves will not explain anything, that propels the film. *Je Veux Voir* probes the degree to which we can learn or know anything through images in the wake of violence and destruction, and examines the promise of cinema and art to open up avenues of understanding, otherwise closed to us. Cinema is after all as much about seeing as it is about suspending disbelief and allowing oneself to be immersed in a story or plot. Deneuve betrays the suspension of disbelief in the scenario by demanding to see everything. The filmmakers, though, do not give in and show very little, re-affirming their conviction that the meaning of cinema and art is to be found as much in the realm of the imaginary as it is in reality.

The Performative Refusal of Presence

Absence takes on a different shape in the latest piece of playwright and artist couple Rabih Mroué and Lina Saneh. In *33 Rounds and a Few Seconds* (2012) they counter the online disembodied hyper-presence of social media with the ultimate form of absence, namely death. Throughout the play, absence is consciously performed as a refusal of presence, a refusal 'to be' in the world, in 'real life' (offline) or 'on screen' (online), and hence to be co-opted by those worlds. The play focuses on the suicide of a young activist and artist appropriately named Diyaa Yamout, Arabic for 'light dies'. Rumour has it that the story of Yamout is based on the actual suicide of Nour Merheb, a young Lebanese secular activist who, like Diyaa Yamout, took his life and sent a suicide note to friends and family expressing the desire to be cremated, which is forbidden in Lebanon.

33 Rounds and a Few Seconds is completely devoid of human actors, and human presence is mediated through the tools and devices of modern communication technology. The stage is designed to resemble a domestic workspace or living room: phones ring, printers spit forth paper, a record plays on a turntable, the TV shows a 24-hour news cycle and half-drunk cups of coffee sit on the desk. The technological artefacts are not exactly props; rather, in the absence of human presence they take on a subjectivity that supports, and at times breaks, the unfolding of the play's narrative, which mainly unrolls on a large projection screen displaying Diyaa Yamout's Facebook page. On this Facebook page, comments of Yamout's friends come up incessantly. First the comments express dismay and disbelief at his death, yet as the play progresses the online discussion turns more violent. Yamout's absent body becomes the battleground for airing ideological differences.

Moreover, there is a double absence at work here. Yamout's Facebook page lacks a profile picture, meaning that there is an absence of the photographic representation of his physical body in addition to the absence of his physical body from this world. A closer look reveals that no picture of Diyaa Yamout can be spotted on his Facebook page at all. The only images that remain on Yamout's profile page are those that show up in his photo stream. They show the 'Arab Spring', demonstrations across Egypt, Syria, Tunisia, Libya, and Bahrain, and images of self-immolation. Lebanon, a country that did not join in the uprising, is as conspicuously absent as Diyaa Yamout. Not only does this serve as a reminder of the geo-political context Yamout found himself in, a region in disarray and turmoil, but it also stresses that Lebanon, with its dysfunctional sectarian political system, remains mired in stasis and therefore is unworthy of an image.

Yamout does not exist as an image in the whole play; we only get to know him by proxy. This begs the question whether in the performative realm of social media, and by extension the theatre, he actually exists at all as an agent. Paradoxically, Yamout is only defined by his absences. In addition to Yamout's sending of his suicide note, he allegedly also filmed his own death, but no one can trace the tape. There is, characteristic of Lebanese contemporary art practices, a paucity of images in this piece. However, the withdrawal from visuality is pushed to an extreme and becomes awithdrawal of bodily and mediated presence altogether. Yamout has not only denied himself a profile picture or any type of visual referent in the virtual sphere, but his desire to be cremated — that is, to deny himself a body after death in the physical world — emphasizes he wants to undo himself of any kind of presence.

In the end, this play is as much about ownership (the fate of your physical and data body after your death) as it is about ontology (how can you be in this world) and teleology (the most definite end, death, seems not so finite anymore in the digital era). Even though Yamout, in his desperate suicidal act, has vowed to completely retreat from the physical world and by corollary from the virtual world by taking his own life, the world itself seems to reject his refusal.

A Refusal to Show

Up to this point, I have discussed the practices of Lebanese artists. Akram Zaatari makes an important point when he notes that a discussion about conflict is only possible *a posteriori*. The practice of Joana Hadjithomas and Khalil Joreige suggests that a similar approach may well be true for the image. A few years before Syria's uprisings against the regime of Bashar al-Assad turned into a bloody and protracted civil war, Syrian photographer Hrair Sarkissian conceived his acclaimed project *Execution Squares* (2008). Viewing these images now, it is as if the past has come to haunt the present and continues to bode ill for the future. In this series of photographs, Sarkissian photographed at dawn what at first glance seem unassuming deserted squares in Syria's three principal cities: Damascus, Lattakia, and Aleppo. Now, these cities conjure up the imagery of war and devastation but this was not the case in 2008. The city squares Sarkissian has shot seem pretty generic, without too many identifying traits. Some bear posters or statues of former president Hafez al-Assad, others are populated

with palm trees or advertising billboards. However, the photo
captions betray that these squares are actually execution grounds
where public hangings take place.

Once we learn this information it is impossible to view
these sites, and these images, in scenic terms only. They become
highly politicised. Sarkissian's refusal to show us anything *a
posteriori* in terms of evidence, except for the empty 'crime
scenes', leaves the images open to speculation and to the imaginary. This gap of information operates in a far more evocative
manner than showing the executions or the corpses. It is as if he
were performing forensics in the negative, where as little evidence
as possible is shown. In fact, it suggests that in Syria, under this
regime, any city square is a potential execution ground and could
have borne witness to gruesome deeds. At the moment of writing, and as the bloodshed in Syria rages on, this project becomes
eerily current. Moreover, the seriality and the typological quality
of the photographs not only reinforce the idea that a repetition of
violence is likely to take place or is eminent, but the calm visual
compositions, careful studies of site and urban landscape, also
monumentalize these sites. Paradoxically, it is only in Sarkissian's
photographic documents, combined with their captions, that the
squares can take on a commemorative role. In and by themselves
the sites, as physical locales, refuse to divulge anything.

A Just Refusal

The practices that I have sketched are particularly poignant in a
time when we are always expected to say yes, to be engaged, and
to show and share everything every minute of the day through social media in our professional and in our private lives. The refusal
to cater to these pressures and the spectacle of representation,
especially in challenging political circumstances, is refreshing.
Moreover, it counterbalances the desires of an increasingly globalised art world, always hungry for new and engaged imagery. In
this sense refusal is, of course, a resistance of sorts. However, it is
a just and aesthetic refusal that on the one hand protects material
too sensitive to be frivolously tampered with or instrumentalized,
and on the other hand allows for speculation in an increasingly
self-righteous contemporary art world where speculation as a critical and artistic strategy is steadily frowned upon. What aesthetics, and by corollary what art, do we imagine without speculation, without blunt refusals, indeed without risks? Speaking of his

dOCUMENTA (13) project, Akram Zaatari said that the strategy he used is in fact a script for 'a gesture of radical preservation — of documents and artefacts in times of risk.'[8] Now is most definitely a time of risk and of preserving ideals to safeguard freedoms. If anything, the gestures of refusal cited by artists like Zaatari, Mroué, Sarkissian, Hadjithomas, and Joreige remind us of the essence of 'aesthetic justice'. Namely, aesthetic justice is exactly that, when risk is placed in the hands of the subject, of the viewer: to take position — or to refuse consciously and willingly to do so.

Notes

1   See for example David McNeill, 'Putting Sincerity to Work', in *The Rhetoric of Sincerity*, Ernst van Alphen, Mieke Bal and Carel Smith (eds.) (Redwood City CA: Stanford University Press, 2009), pp. 157-173.

2   Pat Califia, *Macho Sluts: Erotic Fiction* (Boston: Alyson Books, 1988), p. 15.

3   Tirdad Zolghadr's talk at Witte de With in Rotterdam was held on February 3, 2014.

4   Lina Khatib, 'Introduction: The Visual in Political Struggle', in *Image Politics in the Middle East: The Role of the Visual in Political Struggle* (London: I.B. Tauris, 2013), p. 1.

5   Suzanne Cotter, 'Beirut Unbound', in *Out of Beirut*, Suzanne Cotter (ed.) (Oxford: Modern Art Oxford, 2006), p. 30.

6   T.J. Demos, 'Out of Beirut: Mobile Histories and the Politics of Fiction', in *The Migrant Image: The Art and Politics of Documentary during Global Crisis* (Durham: Duke University Press, 2013), p. 186.

7   Anthony Downey, 'Photography as Apparatus: Akram Zaatari in Conversation with Anthony Downey'. www.ibraaz.org/interviews/113 ,last accessed February 9, 2014.

8   Yves Aupetitallot, 'Interview with Akram Zaatari', in *Akram Zaatari. Time Capsule, Kassel. 24/25.05.2012* (Naples: Mousse Publishing, 2013), p. 36.

Contributors

Zoe Beloff grew up in Scotland. She studied art at Edinburgh University and in 1980 moved to New York to study film at Columbia University. Beloff works with a wide range of media including film, projection, performance, installation, and drawing. She considers herself a medium, an interface between the living and the dead, the real and the imaginary. Each project aims to connect the present to past so that it might illuminate the future in new ways. She is currently working on the IFIF (Institute for Incipient Film), a project to promote films that were dreamed up, sketched out but derailed before they could be realized. Through speculative films, images, and texts, the project explores both original ideas and their relevance to society today. She is currently focusing on Eisenstein and Brecht in Hollywood, and films they might have made. Beloff's projects have been featured in international exhibitions and screenings; venues include the Whitney Museum of American Art, the M HKA museum in Antwerp, the Pompidou Centre in Paris and Freud's Dream Museum in St. Petersburg. Beloff's publications include *The Coney Island Amateur Psychoanalytic Society and Its Circle* (2009) *Adventures of a Dreamer* (2010) and *The Somnambulists: A Compendium of Source Material* (2008). She has been awarded fellowships from the Guggenheim Foundation, the Foundation for Contemporary Arts, the Radcliffe Institute at Harvard and the New York Foundation for the Arts. She is a Professor in the Departments of Media Studies and Art at Queens College CUNY.

Arne De Boever teaches American Studies in the School of Critical Studies at the California Institute of the Arts, where he also directs the MA Aesthetics and Politics programme. He is the author of *States of Exception in the Contemporary Novel* (2012) and *Narrative Care* (2013) and editor of *Gilbert Simondon: Being and Technology* (2012) and *The Psychopathologies of Cognitive Capitalism: Vol. 1* (2013). He also edits *Parrhesia: A Journal of Critical Philosophy* and the critical theory/ philosophy section of the *Los Angeles Review of Books.*

Mark Fisher is the author of *Capitalist Realism* (2009) and *Ghosts of My Life: Writings on Depression, Hauntology and Lost Futures* (2014).

His writing has appeared in many publications, including *The Wire*, *Frieze*, *The Guardian*, and *New Humanist*. He is Programme Leader of the MA in Aural and Visual Cultures at Goldsmiths, University of London. He has also produced two acclaimed audio-essays in collaboration with Justin Barton: *londonunderlondon* (2005) and *On Vanishing Land* (2013).

Mat Fraser is one of the U.K's best-known disabled performers, and is a multi-disciplinary performing artist, actor, writer, and musician. Always interested in the relationship between disability and entertainment, his wit, subversive lack of political correctness, sideshow style and playful sexuality combine to make work that is new, challenging, and funny. He also hosted the opening ceremony for the 2012 Paralympics, drummed with Coldplay in the closing ceremony, and is a regular performer at The Box. Recent credits include *American Horror Story: Freak Show*; *The Fades*; *Cast Offs*; and *Holby City*; documentaries such as *Born Freak & Happy Birthday Thalidomide*; as well as his award-winning plays such as *Sealboy:*

Freak, and *Thalidomide!! A Musical*, and the controversial 'cripsloitation' action film *Unarmed But Dangerous*. He is the titleholder of the Erotic Award (U.K.) for Best Male Striptease artist 2007.

Pascal Gielen (1970) is director of the Arts in Society research centre at Groningen University, where he is Associate Professor of the Sociology of Art. Gielen is also editor-in-chief of the book series 'Arts in Society' (Fontys School of Fine and Performing Arts, Tilburg & Groningen University). He has written several books on contemporary art, cultural heritage and cultural politics. His publications include *Being an Artist in Post-Fordist Times* (2009, NAi Publishers), *The Murmuring of the Artistic Multitude* (2009, 2010 and 2015, Valiz), *Teaching Art in the Neoliberal Realm* (2013, Valiz), *Creativity and other Fundamentalisms* (Mondriaan Fund, 2013), *Institutional Attitudes* (2013, Valiz) and *The Ethics of Art* (2014, Valiz). Gielen's research focuses on cultural politics and the institutional contexts of the arts. His books have been translated in English, Korean, Russian, Spanish and Turkish.

Kerry James Marshall
uses painting, sculptural
installations, collage, video,
and photography to comment
on the history of black identity,
both in the United States and
in Western art. He is well
known for paintings that focus
on subjects that historically
have been excluded from
the artistic canon, and has
explored issues of race and
history through imagery
ranging from abstraction to
figuration to comics. Marshall
said in a 2012 interview
with *Art + Auction* that, 'it is
possible to transcend what is
perceived to be the limitations
of a race-conscious kind of
work. It is a limitation only
if you accept someone else's
foreclosure from the outside. If
you plumb the depths yourself,
you can exercise a good deal
of creative flexibility. You are
limited only by your ability to
imagine possibilities.'

From 2013 to 2014, the
Museum of Contemporary
Art Antwerp (M HKA),
Belgium, organized 'Kerry
James Marshall: Painting
and Other Stuff', a European
survey of his work, which
travelled to the Kunsthal
Charlottenborg in Denmark
the Antoni Tapies Foundation
in Barcelona and the Museo
Nacional Centro de Arte
Reina Sofia in Madrid. Other
recent exhibitions include
'Kerry James Marshall: In the
Tower' at the National Gallery
of Art in Washington, DC
in 2013, and 'Kerry James
Marshall: Who's Afraid of
Red, Black and Green' at the
Vienna Secession in 2012. In
2016, a major United States
retrospective will open at the
Museum of Contemporary Art
in Chicago, and travel to the
Metropolitan Museum of Art
in New York, and the Museum
of Contemporary Art in
Los Angeles.

Marshall has work in
numerous public collections,
including the Museum of
Modern Art, New York;
the Whitney Museum of
American Art, New York; The
Studio Museum in Harlem,
New York; the Metropolitan
Museum of Art, New York;
the Walker Art Center,
Minneapolis; the National
Gallery of Art, Washington,
DC; Los Angeles County
Museum of Art; Birmingham
Museum of Art; San Francisco
Museum of Modern Art; Art
Institute of Chicago; Museum
of Contemporary Art Chicago;
and the Museum of Fine Arts,
Boston. Marshall was born
in Alabama in 1955, and grew
up in Watts, Los Angeles. He
is a 1978 graduate of the Otis
College of Art and Design and
currently lives and works in

Chicago. He is the recipient of several awards, grants and fellowships, including the MacArthur 'Genius Grant' in 1997.

Viktor Misiano was born in Moscow in 1957. From 1980 until 1990, he was a curator of contemporary art at the Pushkin National Museum of Fine Arts in Moscow. From 1992 to 1997, he was the director of the Centre for Contemporary Art (CAC) in Moscow. He curated the Russian participation in the Istanbul Biennale (1992), the Venice Biennale (1995, 2003), the São Paulo Biennale (2002, 2004), and the Valencia Biennale (2001). He was on the curatorial team for the Manifesta I in Rotterdam in 1996. In 1993, he was a founder of the *Moscow Art Magazine* (Moscow) and has been its editor-in-chief ever since; in 2003, he was a founder of the *Manifesta Journal: Journal of Contemporary Curatorship* (Amsterdam) and has been an editor there since 2011. In 2005, he curated the first Central Asia Pavilion at the Venice Biennale. In 2007, he realized the large-scale exhibition project 'Progressive Nostalgia: Art from the Former USSR' at the Centro per l'arte contemporanea, Prato (Italy) as well as at the Benaki Museum, Athens; KUMU, Tallinn; and KIASMA, Helsinki. His latest exhibition project is 'Impossible Community', realized in 2011 in the Moscow Museum for Modern Art. Since October 2010, he is Chairman of the International Foundation Manifesta. Misiano is a docent at the Nuova Academia Belle Arti (NABA), Milano and has an honorary doctorate from the Helsinki University for Art and Design. In 2014, his book *Five Lectures of Curatorship* was released by Ad Marginem Publishing, Moscow. He lives in Moscow (Russia) and Ceglie Messapica (Italy).

Carlos Motta is a multi-disciplinary artist whose work draws upon political history in an attempt to create counter-narratives that recognize suppressed histories, communities, and identities. Motta's work has been presented internationally in venues such as Tate Modern, London; The New Museum, The Guggenheim Museum and the MoMA/PS1 Contemporary Art Center, New York; Institute of Contemporary Art, Philadelphia; Museo de Arte del Banco de la República, Bogotá; Museu Serralves, Porto; Museu d'Art Contemporani de Barcelona; National Museum of Contemporary Art, Athens; Castello di Rivoli, Turin; CCS Bard Hessel Museum of Art, Annandale-on-Hudson; San Francisco Art Institute; Hebbel am Ufer, Berlin; Witte de With, Rotterdam; Sala de Arte Público Siqueiros, Mexico City; and many other public, private and independent spaces throughout the world.

Carlos Motta's work was recently included in 2014 in 'Under the Sun: Art from Latin America Today' at the Guggenheim Museum, New York; '19 Bienal de Arte Paiz', Guatemala; and 'X Gwangju Biennale', South Korea. His *Nefandus Trilogy*, three new short films on pre-Hispanic and colonial sexuality, had its World Premiere at the International Film Festival Rotterdam, and was on view at 'The First International Biennial of Contemporary Art of Cartagena', Colombia; Jeu de Paume, Paris; Marres: House for Contemporary Culture, Maastricht; and Museo de Arte Contemporáneo de Castilla y León in 2014. Also in 2014, Motta was announced as a finalist for the Future Generation Art Prize of the Pinchuk Art Centre in Kiev and delivered a keynote presentation during SF MoMA's Visual Activism symposium in San Francisco. Together with AA Bronson, Motta convened in November 2013 the event 'ritual of queer rituals' at Witte de With in Rotterdam. Motta guest-edited the e-flux journal April 2013 issue, *(im)practical (im) possibilities on contemporary queer art and culture.*

Motta is a graduate of the Whitney Independent Study Programme (2006), was named a Guggenheim Foundation Fellow (2008), and has received grants from Art Matters (2008), NYSCA (2010), Creative Capital Foundation and the Kindle Project (2012). He is part of the faculty at Parsons The New School for Design and The School of Visual Arts.

Nat Muller is an independent curator and critic based in Rotterdam. Her main interests include the intersections of aesthetics, media and politics; media art and contemporary art in and from the Middle East. She has held staff positions at V2_Institute for Unstable Media in Rotterdam and De Balie, Center for Culture and Politics, Amsterdam. She is a regular contributor to *Springerin* and *MetropolisM*. Her writings have been published in *Bidoun, ArtAsiaPacific, Art Papers, Canvas, X-tra, The Majalla*, the MIT journal *Art Margins* and *Harper's Bazaar Art Arabia*. She has also written numerous book chapters, catalogue pieces and monographic essays. With Alessandro Ludovico, she edited the *Mag. net Reader2: Between Paper and Pixel* (2007), and *Mag.net Reader 3: Processual Publishing, Actual Gestures* (2009), based on a series of debates organised at Documenta XII.

Muller has taught at universities and academies in the Netherlands and the Middle East, and has curated video and film screenings for projects and festivals internationally, including for Rotterdam's International Film Festival, the Norwegian Short Film Festival and Video D.U.M.B.O in New York. She is a board member of the IMPAKT Media Festival (Utrecht), and sits on the advisory board of Artterritories (Ramallah), the arts organization TENT (Rotterdam), and is a member of the selection committee of the Fund for Creative Industries and e-Culture (NL).

She was an external advisor to the Dutch Ministry of Culture on e-culture in 2009 and a member of the Mondriaan Fund advisory committee (NL). In 2012, she curated 'Spectral Imprints' for the Abraaj Group Capital Art Prize 2012 in Dubai and in 2013, Iraqi media artist Adel Abidin's highly anticipated solo exhibition 'I love to love...' at Forum Box in Helsinki. Nat Muller is editorial correspondent for *Ibraaz*, a member of the editorial board of *Broadsheet* Magazine (Adelaide) and most recently was a speaker on BBC World's award-winning programme 'The Doha Debates'.

Her projects in 2014 include 'Memory Material' at Akinci Gallery (Amsterdam), 'Customs Made: Quotidian Practices & Everyday Rituals' at Maraya Art Centre in Sharjah (UAE), This is the Time. This is the Record of the Time at the Stedelijk Museum Bureau (Amsterdam) and the American University of Beirut Gallery, and 'Disquiet' at Pi Art works/Zilberman Galeri (Istanbul). For TENT (Rotterdam), she conceived the debate series 'Breaking the Bank: Art, Value and the Global Economy'. In 2015, she will be curator-in-residence at the Delfina Foundation's

Politics of Food Programme, 'Sex, Diet and Disaster', and will curate Dutch-Iraqi artist Sadik Kwaish Alfraji's solo show at Ayyam Gallery in Dubai.

Julie Atlas Muz, a former Miss Exotic World and Miss Coney Island, is one of the most acclaimed and prolific conceptual performers and choreographers anywhere. Most famous for her legendary status in neo-burlesque, Muz has been named a Franklin Furnace Artist, Lambent Fellow, Valencia Biennial Artist, Whitney Biennial Artist, and Artist-in-Residence by Chashama, Joyce Soho, Dixon Place and Movement Research. Since 2010, she has been touring large-scale theatres in France with the Cabaret New Burlesque as well as creating and starring in radical dances in Spiegeltents and nightclubs around the globe. Julie has created and toured *Beauty and the Beast* and *The Freak and the Showgirl* and *Apocastrip Wow??* with her husband Mat Fraser. Both shows have garnered extreme critical acclaim. She has begun to licence some of her signature solos in places such as Las Vegas and Dubai, with her new cloned dance group of dancing beauties,

The A-Muzes. Muz proudly champions the tradition of naked ladies in public spaces as acts of political resistance initiated in the eleventh century by Lady Godiva.

Tessa Overbeek (1982) studied Arts, Culture and Media (BA) and Literary and Cultural Studies (MA) at the University of Groningen, the Netherlands, where she also taught courses in the Sociology of Art and Academic Writing. She currently works as a freelance writer, editor and researcher and has published articles in various books and magazines, as well as online.

Gerald Raunig is a philosopher; works at the ZHdK in Zurich and at the eipcp; co-edits the multilingual web journal *transversal* and the journal *Kamion*. His books have been translated into Serbian, Spanish, Slovenian, Russian, Italian, Turkish, and English. Forthcoming: *DIVIDUUM. Machinic Capitalism and Molecular Revolution, Volume 1.*

Dieter Roelstraete is currently Manilow Senior Curator at the Museum of Contemporary Art Chicago, where he recently organized 'The Way of the Shovel: Art as Archaeology' (2013), and 'Simon Starling: Metamorphology' (2014). He is also a member of the curatorial team convened by artistic director Adam Szymczyk to organize Documenta 14, which will take place in Kassel and Athens simultaneously in the spring/ summer of 2017. From 2003 until 2011, he was a curator at the Antwerp Museum of Contemporary Art (M HKA), where he organized large-scale group exhibitions as well as monographic shows, including 'Emotion Pictures' (2005); 'Intertidal', a survey show of contemporary art from Vancouver (2005); 'The Order of Things' (2008); 'Liam Gillick and Lawrence Weiner—A Syntax of Dependency' (2011); 'A Rua: The Spirit of Rio de Janeiro' (2011); 'Chantal Akerman: Too Close, Too Far' (2012); and the collaborative projects 'Academy: Learning from Art' (2006), 'The Projection Project' (2006), and 'Kerry James Marshall: Paintings and Other Stuff' (2013). A former editor of *Afterall* and cofounder of the journal *FR David*, Roelstraete has published extensively on contemporary art and related philosophical issues in numerous catalogues and journals, including *Artforum*, *e-flux journal*, *frieze*, *Metropolis M*, *Monopol*, *Mousse Magazine*, and *Texte zur Kunst*.

Hito Steyerl (born in Munich, 1966; lives in Berlin) works as a filmmaker and author in the area of essayist documentary film/video, media art and video installation. Her works are on the interface between cinema and fine arts, and between theory and practice. They centre on the question of media within globalization and the migration of sounds and images. She is currently a professor at the UdK Berlin and is a guest tutor at Goldsmiths College, Malmö Art Academy, and Bard, among other teaching positions. She also has written a book about documentary in the field of art and edited several others. Her work has been shown at numerous international film festivals, the biennials of Venice, Istanbul, Gwanju, Taipeh, Sjanghai and Berlin, and at Manifesta 5 and Documenta 12. Her installations have been presented in numerous group shows and recently in solo exhibitions at the Art Institute of Chicago and the Van Abbemuseum in Eindhoven. Her work and essays are widely published in (monographic) catalogues as well as online. Recently, two publications were published: *Too Much World* and *The Wretched of the Screen* (both by Sternberg Press).

Julia Svetlichnaja is a political theorist and writer educated at the universities of Saint-Petersburg, Leysin and London. Dr Julia Svetlichnaja is currently working on the book *Art and the Political: Pluralising Hegemonies* for Routledge, New York, which identifies social and political emancipation as the core matter of aesthetics. Julia's PhD thesis (under the supervision of Professor Chantal Mouffe, the Centre for the Study of Democracy, London) has suggested that the particular role of contemporary artistic practices in today's emancipatory project lies within constructing 'shimmering identities' which resist processes of totalization. Apart from her passion for the subject of art and politics, Svetlichnaja's research interests also include the 'subject/object society', the construction of democratic spaces and the development of democratic theory in the era of Post-Fordism and the decline of political subjectivity.

Hakan Topal is an artist living and working in Brooklyn, New York. He is an Assistant Professor of New Media and Art + Design at Purchase College, SUNY and a graduate faculty member in the School of Visual Arts' MFA Programme. Trained as a civil engineer (BS), he continued his studies in gender and women's studies (MS) and sociology (MA). He received a PhD in sociology from the New School for Social Research with a concentration in urban sociology and sociology of arts. His dissertation was titled *Negotiating Urban Space: Contemporary Art Biennials, The Case of New Orleans*. He was the co-founder of the international art collective 'xurban_collective' (2000-12) and has exhibited his collective and individual art works and research projects extensively in institutions such as the Eighth and Ninth Istanbul Biennials; apexart, New York; Thyssen-Bornemisza Art Contemporary (TBA21), Vienna; Kunst-Werke, Berlin; ZKM Center for Art and Media, Karlsruhe; MoMA PS1; Platform, Istanbul and the Ninth Gwangju Biennial. Topal represented Turkey in various international exhibitions including the

Forty-Ninth Venice Biennial Turkish Pavilion. His texts and projects have been featured in various international journals, books and catalogues. He is co-editor of the book *The Sea-Image: Visual Manifestations of Port Cities and Global Waters*, which is the outcome of visual research and an international symposium for the Istanbul European Capital of Culture 2010.

Niels Van Tomme (BE, 1977) is a New York-based curator, researcher, and critic working on the intersections of contemporary culture, politics, and aesthetics. Currently associated with the Center for Art, Design and Visual Culture at UMBC in Baltimore, he merges academic research with accessible and often confrontational exhibition-making. He is the appointed curator of the Seventh Bucharest Biennale, set for 26 May — 17 July 2016. His exhibitions and public programmes are shown at venues such as The Kitchen (New York), Värmlands Museum (Karlstad), National Gallery of Art (Washington, DC), Contemporary Arts Center (New Orleans), Gallery 400 (Chicago), and Akademie der Künste (Berlin). His most recent exhibition project,

'Visibility Machines: Harun Farocki and Trevor Paglen', opened at the Center for Art, Design and Visual Culture in late 2013 and is currently touring internationally.

His curatorial endeavours have received grant awards from The Andy Warhol Foundation for the Visual Arts, The Elizabeth Firestone Graham Foundation, Lambent Foundation, and The Nathan Cummings Foundation, as well as critical acclaim in publications such as *Afterall, Artforum, Art in America, Afterimage*, and *The Wall Street Journal.*

Van Tomme is a Contributing Editor at *Art Papers* magazine, while his writings in a wide variety of publications explore contemporary art, literature, and music in relationship to broader societal and cultural developments. His books include *Where Do We Migrate To?* (2011), *Visibility Machines: Harun Farocki and Trevor Paglen* (2014).

Samuel Vriezen (1973) is a composer and writer working and living in Amsterdam. In addition to some seventy compositions for various instrumentations, Vriezen has published poetry and essays in a variety of Dutch

and international literary
and scholarly reviews, as well
as being active as a poetry
translator and as a pianist. In
2008, his first poetry collection,
4 Zinnen, was published by
Wereldbibliotheek; in 2013, his
first solo CD, of original music
and work by Tom Johnson,
was published by Edition
Wandelweiser Records. A book
of essays on a variety of artistic,
political, and theoretical
subjects, *Netwerk in eclips*, is
forthcoming.

Christian Wolff (1934) is
a composer and scholar of
classical literature, the son of
literary publishers Helen and
Kurt Wolff. At age sixteen,
he met John Cage, who
encouraged his development
in experimental music; Cage
would later claim that Wolff
could not be considered his
pupil, since he learned more
from Wolff than the other
way around. Deciding that
composition was not a way to
make a living, Wolff pursued
an academic career in classic
literature, teaching at Harvard
until 1970, then at Dartmouth
in the departments of Classics,
Comparative Literature, and
Music until 1999.

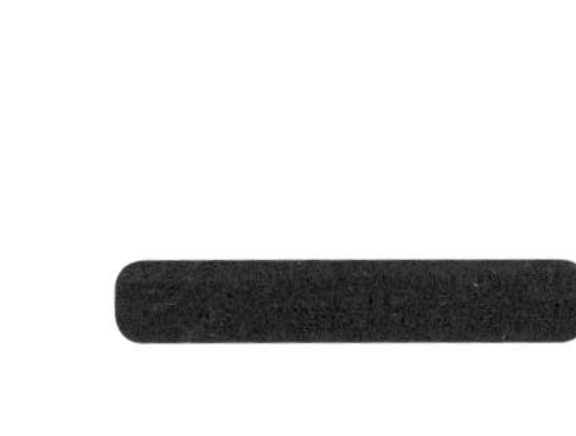

Index

Colophon

Colophon

Aesthetic Justice
*Intersecting Artistic and Moral
Perspectives*

Editors
Pascal Gielen
Niels Van Tomme

Authors
Zoe Beloff, Arne De Boever, Mark
Fisher, Mat Fraser, Pascal Gielen,
Kerry James Marshall, Viktor
Misiano, Carlos Motta, Nat Muller,
Julie Atlas Muz, Tessa Overbeek,
Gerald Raunig, Dieter Roelstraete,
Hito Steyerl, Julia Svetlichnaja,
Hakan Topal, Niels Van Tomme,
Samuel Vriezen, Christian Wolff

Antennae Series n° 14
by Valiz, Amsterdam

Part of the Fontys Series
'Arts *in* Society'

Translation
Jane Bemont & Leo Reijnen (Pascal
Gielen & Niels Van Tomme), Aileen
Derieg (Gerald Raunig), Vitaliy
Eyber (Viktor Misiano)

Copy editing
Jane Bemont

Index and proof check
Elke Stevens

Production
Pia Pol

Design
Metahaven

Paper inside
Munken Print 100 gr 1.5,

Paper cover
Bioset 240 gr

Printing and binding
Ten Brink, Meppel

Publisher
Valiz, Amsterdam, 2015
www.valiz.nl

ISBN 978-90-78088-86-8

This publication was made possible
through the generous support of

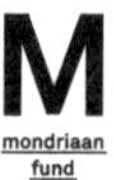

Mondriaan Fund, Amsterdam

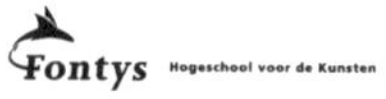

Fontys School of Fine and Performing
Arts, Tilburg

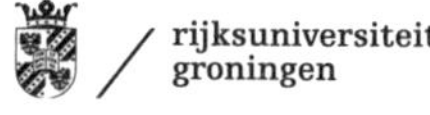

Groningen University, Groningen

The authors and the publisher have made every effort to secure permission to reproduce the listed material, illustrations and photographs. We apologise for any inadvert errors or omissions. Parties who nevertheless believe they can claim specific legal rights are invited to contact the publisher.

Distribution:
USA /CAN/LA: D.A.P.,
www.artbook.com
GB/IE: Anagram Books,
www.anagrambooks.com
NL/BE/LU: Coen Sligting,
www.coensligtingbookimport.nl
Europe/Asia/Australia: Idea Books,
www.ideabooks.nl
ISBN 978-90-78088-86-8
NUR 651

Printed and bound in the Netherlands

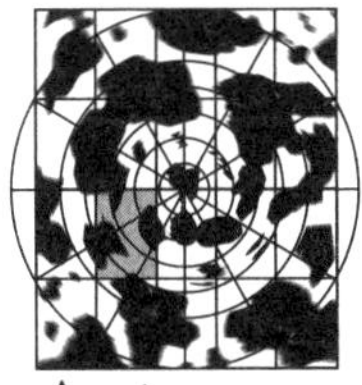

Antennae

Antennae Series

Antennae N° 1
The Fall of the Studio
Artists at Work
edited by Wouter Davidts
& Kim Paice
Amsterdam: Valiz, 2009
(2nd ed.: 2010),
ISBN 978-90-78088-29-5

Antennae N° 2
Take Place
*Photography and Place
from Multiple Perspectives*
edited by Helen Westgeest
Amsterdam: Valiz, 2009,
ISBN 978-90-78088-35-6

Antennae N° 3
**The Murmuring of the
Artistic Multitude**
*Global Art, Memory and
Post-Fordism*
Pascal Gielen (author)
Arts *in* Society
Amsterdam: Valiz, 2009
(2nd ed.: 2011),
ISBN 978-90-78088-34-9

Antennae N° 4
Locating the Producers
Durational Approaches to Public Art
edited by Paul O'Neill
& Claire Doherty
Amsterdam: Valiz, 2011,
ISBN 978-90-78088-51-6

Antennae N° 5
Community Art
The Politics of Trespassing
edited by Paul De Bruyne,
Pascal Gielen
Arts *in* Society
Amsterdam:
Valiz, 2011 (2nd ed.: 2013),
ISBN 978-90-78088-50-9

Antennae N° 6
See it Again, Say it Again
The Artist as Researcher
edited by Janneke Wesseling
Amsterdam: Valiz, 2011,
ISBN 978-90-78088-53-0

Antennae N° 7
Teaching Art in the Neoliberal Realm
Realism versus Cynicism
edited by Pascal Gielen,
Paul De Bruyne
Arts *in* Society
Amsterdam: Valiz, 2012
(2nd ed.: 2013),
ISBN 978-90-78088-57-8

Antennae N° 8
Institutional Attitudes
Instituting Art in a Flat World
edited by Pascal Gielen
Arts *in* Society
Amsterdam: Valiz, 2013,
ISBN 978-90-78088-68-4

Antennae N° 9
Dread
The Dizziness of Freedom
edited by Juha van 't Zelfde
Amsterdam: Valiz, 2013,
ISBN 978-90-78088-81-3

Antennae N° 10
Participation Is Risky
*Approaches to Joint
Creative Processes*
edited by Liesbeth Huybrechts
Amsterdam: Valiz, 2014,
ISBN 978-90-78088-77-6

Antennae N° 11
The Ethics of Art
*Ecological Turns in the
Performing Arts*
edited by Guy Cools & Pascal Gielen
Amsterdam: Valiz, 2014,
ISBN 978-90-78088-87-5

Antennae N° 12
Alternative Mainstream
Making Choices in Pop Music
Gert Keunen (author)
Amsterdam: Valiz, 2014,
ISBN 978-90-78088-95-0

Antennae N° 13
**The Murmuring of the Artistic
Multitude**
*Global Art, Politics and Post-
Fordism*
Pascal Gielen (author)
Completely revised and enlarged
edition of Antennae N° 3
Amsterdam: Valiz, 2015,
ISBN 978-94-92095-04-6